ELECTORAL REFORMS IN INDIA

About the Editor

Anjoo Sharan Upadhyaya is Professor in Political Science, Faculty of Social Sciences, Banaras Hindu University, Varanasi. She holds a Ph.D. from Banaras Hindu University, in International Studies and Masters' from Allahabad University. She has done post-doctoral research at London, UK and Uppasala University, Sweden.

She has been serving on the faculty of Department of Political Science, Faculty of Social Sciences, Banaras Hindu University for the past 28 years. Apart from teaching, she has served as Dean, Faculty of Social Sciences (1st January 1998 to 1st January 2001); Director, Integrated Rural Development Programme, Banaras Hindu University (1st January 1998 to 1st January 2000); Head, Department of Political Science (August 1998 to June 2001) and recently as Research Director, Institute of Conflict Resolution and Ethnicity (INCORE), The United Nations University, Northern Ireland.

In recognition of her work, Prof. Upadhyaya has been selected for various national and international awards. Starting from Swedish International Co-operation Fellowship to undertake an international training programme at Uppsala University; Academic Visitor at the Department of International Relations, London School of Economics and Politics (LSE); Member, International Planning Study Team, United Nations University, Ulster University (UK) to conduct a feasibility study to create a UNU Centre for Ethnicity and Conflict Resolution; prestigious Woodrow Wilson Guest Scholar Award at the Woodrow Wilson Centre for International Scholars, Washington DC; Member, Academic Council of the United Nations System (ACUNS); Awarded ACUNS Fellowship to participate in the ACUNS/ASIL Workshop at Brown University; Member, Commission on International Conflict Resolution at the Council of the International Peace Research Association (IPRA), Kyoto (Japan); invited by the Ministry for Nationalities and External Relations, Republic of Daghestan (Russian Federation) as a subject expert in Problem Solving Seminar on Ethnic Disaffection and Local Self-Governance; and Visiting Fellow, Henry L. Stimson Centre, Washington DC.

Professor Upadhyaya has published extensively both Nationally and Internationally on themes related to issues of Self-determination, ethnicity, conflict, federalism, gender and Development.

ELECTORAL REFORMS IN INDIA

Edited by

ANJOO SHARAN UPADHYAYA

CONCEPT PUBLISHING COMPANY, NEW DELHI-110059

Cataloging in Publication Data—DK
Courtesy: D.K. Agencies (P) Ltd. <docinfo@dkagencies.com>

Electoral reforms in India/ edited by Anjoo Sharan Upadhyaya.
p. cm.
Papers presented at an international seminar held at Varanasi in January 2000.
Includes bibliographical references.
Includes index.
ISBN 8180691705

1. Elections—India—Congresses. 2. India—Politics and government—Congresses. I. Upadhyaya, Anjoo Sharan.

324.0954 21

ISBN : 81-8069-170-5

First Published 2005

Published and Printed by
Ashok Kumar Mittal
Concept Publishing Company
A/15-16, Commercial Block, Mohan Garden
NEW DELHI - 110059 (India)

Phones : 25351460, 25351794
Fax : 091-11-25357103
Email : publishing@conceptpub.com

DEDICATED

TO

THE MEMORY OF MY FATHER

LATE SHRI MAN MOHAN SHARAN

Preface

India can be justifiably proud of its achievements as the largest democracy in the world, having a functioning electoral system since 1947. Over a period of time, the Indian electoral system has evolved unrivalled capability to ascertain the political will of a vast electorate, comprising extremely diverse ethnic groups with varied levels of awareness and aptitude.

Notwithstanding the usually high voter participation (up to 67% in many regions), the electoral system has not been without tensions and problems, which have become glaringly manifest in recent years. There is an overwhelming concern as how to diminish the malpractice, corruption, influence of caste and ethnic allegiances, the control exercised by patrons and the fluidity of party loyalty among successful candidates. The frequent episodes of violence coinciding with the elections are yet another symptom of electoral malaise. Naturally there is a premonition among all those concerned with the fate of democracy, that if the diminishing effectiveness of the electoral system is not rectified in time, these may stultify the entire electoral exercise in the context of the growing democratic expectations and assertions of the people.

Though there have been frequent election surveys and forecasts in recent decades, not much has been done to examine the malaise impinging on the electoral system from a problem solving approach. The present volume emphasises this very approach to reflect on the problematic of electoral reforms. The aim is to offer recommendations and prescriptions to ensure that the electoral system stands less burdened and also to look at options offering a better monitored, cost effective, and more efficient system that could respond truly to the democratic aspirations of the cultural and other plural identities of the country.

Indian democracy is now mature enough to withstand a serious review of the very process through which elections are conducted and to improvise ways and means to respond to the changing socio-economic and political strivings of the masses; to diminish the trend of disproportionate representation leading either to over or under representation of the regions and identities. Thus it is time to look for the instructive examples from other democratic experiences where such exercises have been undertaken and implemented at times with the help of national and international expertise to reform and consolidate the electoral system.

Of varied segments deserving critical review of the electoral process, three of them warrant special attention: voter awareness, voter education and election procedures. A variety of suggestions have been mooted by the concerned agencies such as the Election Commission, Law Commission, Non-governmental Organisations and political parties. This may include the imperative to cleanse the poll arena and for that a candid exchange amongst all the stakeholders *i.e.* the politicians, the administrators, the academics and the common citizens is needed. There are pressing issues about the use of money and muscle power in elections, booth capturing, criminalisation, defection, delimitation of constituencies, state funding of elections and powers and rights of the Election Commission etc.

There are also suggestions to install 'neutral governments' two or three months before the Assembly elections in States. In Bangladesh and Greece a neutral administration takes over before the elections. To begin with, we can leave the Centre aside and start with the States. The Supreme Court has already shown the way in chalking out the method for selection of the Central Vigilance Commissioner (CVC). Similarly, the work of delimitation of constituencies and implementation of anti-defection laws could be handed over to the Election Commission. They can lay down some guidelines and parameters and start working on the delimitation because delineation of boundaries and balancing of electorate must be done cautiously. Some significant steps have already been taken. There is no dearth of innovative suggestions. Fresh perspectives may come from anywhere as they transcend geographical boundaries. These and related themes were dealt with in an International Seminar at B.H.U. in January 2000 from which arose the present volume. The objective of the Seminar and the present volume has been to stir a nation-wide debate on the prospects of electoral reforms in India.

The first paper in this volume, "Deliberations on Electoral Reforms" is a report of the seminar. The subsequent papers are in part presentations at the seminar and in part papers, which were submitted by experts who could not attend. One or two papers are updated versions of papers, which have been previously published but are included here because of the important contribution that they make to the debate. To reflect the different perspectives in the current debate, some of the papers deal with similar issues but from different perspectives and with different conclusions.

The book opens with a paper by Jayaprakash Narayan "Distorted Verdicts." Jayaprakash Narayan examines one of the basic flaws of the Indian electoral system: voter registration and polling irregularities. Jayaprakash has highlighted the various problems involved in the very elementary and seemingly simple process of getting one's name enrolled in the electoral roll. He observes that as per the present procedures even an educated person must be a motivated citizen willing to spare a lot of "energy, time, money and effort" in order to verify the electoral roll and register. Dr. Narayan diagnosed through Lok Satta, an independent non-governmental organization, with which he has been involved in one of its pilot projects to study this phenomena that 21.7 per cent of the votes polled were false and doubtful and there existed errors in electoral rolls to a tune of 15 per cent in rural areas and 40 per cent in urban areas in Andhra Pradesh. He recommends procedures of removing these errors that are easy to follow. The paper also discusses certain other anomalies of electoral processes e.g. the issue of tendered votes and rightly concludes that though much has to be done to cleanse the electoral process; the first and the foremost is to improve the voter registration procedures.

The following paper is by Yogendra Yadav who in his Article, "Election Reforms: Beyond Middle Class Fantasies" highlights the fact that the object of any serious discussion on electoral reform is the ideal of representation and its relation to the process of democratisation in contemporary India. The challenge is to make the mechanism of election an effective instrument of the democratic will of the people. The agenda for electoral reform must give priority to those disorders or malpractices that create an obstacle in the way of the deepening of the democratic process. The paper examines the election reform proposals and goes at length to assess the first-past-the-post (FPTP) system. The option of proportional representation (PR) has also been evaluated. The paper also discusses the proposal for reform of electoral machinery *viz.* the composition and mode of appointment of the EC, measures to ensure the independence of the EC and set-up of electoral machinery at the state and local level. The various provisions within the Constitution have also been discussed. Issues relating to financial aspects of the election and the caste and community based appeal in the elections etc., have been analyzed and examined effectively.

Sandeep Shastri discusses in depth one of the major issues concerning electoral reforms in India *i.e.* the capacity of the first-past-the-post (FPTP) system to reflect the popular will. Sandeep boldly exposes the acute limitation of the FPTP system by providing tables and charts on the previous performance of the various political parties in various elections. He then goes on to asses the various proposals put forth by successive reform committees and individuals, including the PR system, mixed system, list system and partial list system, negative voting, binary voting, and the second ballot system. The paper concludes by re-asserting that reforms will have to form a part of a comprehensive package and cannot be considered in a piecemeal form.

M.P. Dube in his paper on "Perspectives on Electoral Reforms in India" considers elections the life-breath of democracy. He explains growing corruption, criminalisation and repression in elections as a challenge to democracy. He discusses the various types of electoral systems and discusses these approaches in the context of India. He concludes that the intrusion of religion and caste into politics is playing havoc with the health of the Indian polity. Candidates often emphasise various cleavages in the society; and the party in power mostly misuses official position. Therefore, the author suggests that what is needed is a code of conduct for the political parties and above all, a culture of co-operation and trust on the part of candidates is needed for curing the cancerous malpractices of our democratic system, and for making the national system as a whole more cohesive and stronger.

R.B. Jain's paper "Political Financing in India" traces the history of sources of party finances in India and goes on to highlight the legal provisions for party funding. The paper also examines the various legal provisions within the Companies Act and Foreign Contribution (Regulation) Act etc. With this background it goes on to discuss the merits and demerits of reforms proposed by the Election Commission (1982, 1989) and the various successive governments, and recommendations of the Law Commission (1998). The diverse initiatives put forth by the corporate world like the proposal of the Hinduja Group and the Tata Electoral Trust have also been discussed at length. The author stresses the need for a comprehensive effort to reform political financing in India.

Sanjay Lodha, too, in his article entitled "Election Finance Reforms: Between a Ceiling and a Floor" examines the need for controlling the growing use of money in elections and stresses the fact that this is only possible if an upper expenditure limit (as a ceiling) is fixed and also that all contestants are provided with minimum resources (as a floor). The tug of war between the judiciary and the legislature on explanation of Section 77 of RP Act has been well amplified. The paper has also reviewed the existing laws regarding state funding and parties in various elections of the country. He then goes on to asses the various proposals, like the Proportionate Representation (PR) system, mixed system, list system and partial list system, negative voting, binary voting, and the second ballot system, put forth by successive reform committees and individuals. The paper has also reviewed the existing laws regarding state funding and monitoring of elections. The paper thus seeks to cover the whole debate of election finance reforms in India.

Achal Kumar Gaur in his paper "Testing Median Voter Hypothesis Through Human Development Index: Evidence from Indian Polity", has tested Median Voter Hypothesis with the help of data from some states of India, for the period 1971-95. Empirical results reveal that poorer states like Assam, Bihar, U.P., M.P., Orissa and Rajasthan have been deprived continuously in terms of some major ingredients of quality of human life, like life expectancy, education, safe drinking water, medical and public health etc. This is perhaps one of the root causes for the emergence of regional parties and coalition culture in the Indian polity having a significant impact on Indian electoral system and politics.

Bhaskar Majumder in his paper examines the nature of systems and in particular the electoral system. He believes the task of the ruling coalition is to include the alienated social sections in the political decision-making processes and ensure dynamic stability in the society. Reforms in the electoral system are one dimension of executing the required changes in the social system. Answers to all the questions in a social system are political questions. The task is to understand those questions at the right time and act accordingly.

Rajen Harshe's paper entitled "Electoral System and the Fate of Secular Nationalism," discusses the declining significance of secular nationalism in the political process in India. Placing the challenge of sectarianism and religious bigotry, Rajen situates it in the larger context of the growing challenges to the spirit of secular nationalism in India. He points out that whereas the Sangh Parivar has been transparently communal, the Congress Party has been communal in a pragmatic manner. The 'left forces' too have followed suit. He concludes by stating that it is necessary to explore all possibilities of initiating a new kind of politics that could change the electoral system to suit the times.

Priyankar Upadhyaya's paper on "Electoral Strategies of Ethnic Conflict Management" deals with the major effect the electoral system has in fostering or retarding ethnic conflicts. Priyankar through this paper takes up the task of weighing different methods of representation to reduce ethnic conflicts. Case studies of Lebanon, Cyprus, Nigeria, Guyana, Malaysia, Sri Lanka and South Africa have been evaluated to gain insights into the problem, and he concludes that even though the electoral systems *per se* cannot do much to reduce protracted societal tensions, they should, at the very least, not exacerbate existing majoritarian and exclusionary policies.

Raka Arya in her paper on "Lack of Political Will and Electoral Reforms" has discussed the existing lacunae in the efforts to curb criminals from entering politics and incongruities existent in the Representation of People's Act 1951. Raka has also discussed issues of defection, money power and lack of political will as major impediments to electoral reforms in India.

D.K. Sankaran in his paper "Electoral Reforms in India: An Overview" highlights four areas concerning electoral reforms. These are funding, criminalisation, defection and corrupt electoral practices. The views are shaped by the authors' experience of nearly seven years as Chief Election Officer, Maharashtra and therefore provide a practitioners perspective.

David Annoussamy, former Judge of Madras High Court, in his paper on "Reforms for a Better Representation of the People" assesses the issues of abstentions, re-adjustment of constituencies, election of the leaders, and qualification of candidates. The issue of reserved seats has been examined in the light of the denial of basic civic rights of citizens belonging to other than the reserved categories that lies in the reserved constituency. Similarly the paper also examines the issues of separation of elections for Parliament and States, alliances and symbols.

Clem McCartney's paper "Making the Electoral System Work: Promoting a Democratic Culture through Political Engagement" stresses the importance of political education. The key elements in promoting democratic culture are the existence of an informed, aware and interested public and a political elite committed to these ideals. Also of help can be examination of the experience of other places. The paper looks at one such example of trying to promote such awareness in Northern Ireland. The paper collects the lesson learnt from this experience *i.e.* to promote a culture of dialogue and engagement around the issues that confront the society: dialogue within the society and dialogue with the wider electorate. The scheme also demonstrated the importance of offering a consultant to help a party think through its options.

No discussion on electoral reforms in India can be complete without a discussion on the issue of women's representation in elected bodies. India has been one of the pioneering countries to have reserved no less than 33 per cent of its elected seats in the local councils and has also tabled a bill to reserve similar seats for women at the Center. The paper on "Women's Representation in Legislatures" authored by Madhu Kishwar, Jayaprakash Narayan, Dhirubhai Sheth and Yogendra Yadav and examines the prospects and pitfalls of this bill. Appreciating the need for women's representation in legislatures, the paper cautions the readers about the various lacunae in the Government bill. The authors then go on to present an alternative to the Government bill for women's reservation that will not suffer from the shortcomings of the existing proposal and will ensure the adequate representation of women in elected bodies.

The book also has a list of some useful Internet sites and relevant references of books and journals prepared by Rachana Narayan, which will be a useful tool for academics, politicians and consultants alike.

In Annexure I, the reader is provided with "The Use and Misuse of Administrative Machinery" a copy of the report of the Committee appointed by Sri Jayprakash Narayan on behalf of Citizens for

Democracy for Electoral Reforms and Annexure II provides the text of the "Provisions of the Alternative Women's Reservation Bill" proposed by the Forum for Democratic Reforms. A glossary of main Electoral Systems has also been provided for ready reference.

Anjoo Sharan Upadhyaya

Varanasi
18 April, 2003

Acknowledgements

Special thanks (to the authors of the articles and to *Seminar* for permitting us to use "Distorted Verdicts" by Jayaprakash Narayan); to the participants of the International Seminar and the colleagues of the Department of Political Science, Banaras Hindu University, whose rich contributions were very useful for editing the volume; to Pramod, Rakesh, Vishwanath and Kaushikee for their copious notes of the proceedings; to Srivastava ji and Venkatraman for composing; to Clem McCartney, R.B. Jain and Priyankar Upadhyaya for their useful comments and advice; (to the authors . . . Narayan) to Electoral Reform International Services (ERIS), U.K. for the logistics of the international participants; to Malaviya Centre for Peace Research, B.H.U. for the facilities; to the British High Commission for the bulk of the funding and Banaras Hindu University for the rest of the funding and general help; and to Rachana Narayan for her constant goading and the very willing support.

Contents

Preface vii
Acknowledgement xv
1 Introduction: Deliberations on Electoral Reforms in India 1
— *Anjoo Sharan Upadhyaya*
2 Distorted Verdicts 11
— *Jayaprakash Narayan*
3 Election Reforms: Beyond Middle Class Fantasies 29
— *Yogendra Yadav*
4 Electoral Reforms in India: Need for a Second Look at the First-Past-the-Post-System 64
— *Sandeep Shastri*
5 Perspectives on Electoral Reforms in India 74
— *M.P. Dube*
6 Political Financing in India 86
— *R.B. Jain*
7 Election Finance Reforms: Between a Ceiling and a Floor 113
— *Sanjay Lodha*
8 Testing Median Voter Hypothesis through Human Development Index: Evidence from Indian Polity 128
— *Achal Kumar Gaur*
9 Political Process of Voting and Social Change 145
— *Bhaskar Majumder*
10 Electoral System and the Fate of Secular Nationalism 152
— *Rajen Harshe*
11 Electoral Strategies of Ethnic Conflict Management 159
— *Priyankar Upadhyaya*
12 Lack of Political Will and Electoral Reforms 176
— *Raka Arya*
13 Electoral Reforms in India: An Overview 188
— *D.K. Sankaran*
14 Reforms for a Better Representation of the People 192
— *David Annoussamy*

15 Making the Electoral System Work: Promoting a Democratic Culture through Political Engagement 203
— *Clem McCartney*

16 Enhancing Women's Representation in Legislatures: An Alternative to the Government Bill for Women's Reservation 212
Madhu Kishwar, Jayaprakash Narayan, Dhirubhai Sheth and *Yogendra Yadav*

17 Some Useful Sites and References on Election and Electoral Reforms 231
— *Rachana Narayan*

Annexures

I. Report of the Committee appointed by Sri Jayaprakash Narayan on Behalf of Citizens for Democracy for Electoral Reforms 254

II. Provisions of the Alternative Bill (1) A Bill to Amend the Representation of the People Act, 1951 278

Glossary of Main Electoral Systems 280

Contributors 283

Index 289

1

Introduction

Deliberations on Electoral Reforms in India

ANJOO SHARAN UPADHYAYA

Background

The need for the International Seminar on Electoral Reforms was first mooted by the Banaras Hindu University which prepared a proposal in 1999 outlining some of the concerns about increasing pressures on the Indian electoral system and the need to examine how best to respond to them. The proposal was shared with Electoral Reform International Services, UK (ERIS) who were invited to co-operate. After further discussions and refinement of the proposal an approach was made to the UK High Commission in 1999 and funding was made available to support the seminar. It was agreed that ERIS would identify four international experts to take part in the seminar and Professor David Butler, Dr. Clem McCartney, Mr. Nigel Butler and Mr. Paul Wilder agreed to take part. Academics, activists and politicians from across the country were invited to share the results of their researches and experience to enrich the deliberations of the seminar.

Assumptions

The initial opening speeches, reiterated the organizers' shared assumptions that underpinned the workshop. Professor Butler stressed the belief, which he shared with a number of Indian experts that the electoral system had served India well and that Indians could be justifiably proud of their achievements. In spite of all the pressures and difficulties, which the Election Commission has faced, the operation of the elections and the results have been respected and the electoral process has allowed the orderly transfer of power in the country on a number of occasions.

The Vice Chancellor of the University in his welcome address also supported the belief that the electoral system had functioned effectively but he also reiterated the concerns that do exist and the importance of dealing with those concerns while they were still within manageable limits. Conference Director, the Dean of the Faculty of Social Sciences, and Head Department of Political Science Professor A. S. Upadhyaya, explained the format of the Conference and said that there were three main areas which needed to be considered in the seminar: the overall constitutional principles, legal framework and political context within which the elections operate; the type of electoral system which determines how votes are translated into seats; and technical practices for managing elections and recording votes to ensure honest and fair elections.

Format

The seminar was conceived as a development workshop at which the participants would examine the current situation and identify and agree to the key issues. As a result, strategies for tackling the key issues could be identified and it was hoped that a commitment would emerge to work on resolving the problems identified and in this way strengthen the electoral system. It was intended that the participants should make contributions, which would clarify the current situation in their regions so that a cross-regional comparison could be made of the present functioning of the electoral system. Because of the nature of the proposed contributions, it was decided to take a more thematic approach and on the second day the papers were grouped according to three themes: legislative matters, financial issues in elections (including the cost of running elections and the expenses of candidates) and the social and political context (including issues of fraud, intimidation and violence, the media and ensuring adequate representation of all sections of society). On the morning of the final day, politicians were provided with an opportunity to present their perspective and the final afternoon was an open session to see what common ground existed as a basis for further action.

It was generally agreed that the role of the international guests was to respond to the information and concerns raised by the Indian participants. They took turn to chair sessions, jointly with a local participant and acted as respondents or discussants at which point they could offer their ideas and alternative approaches which they were aware of, from experience elsewhere.

Participants

The seminar participants were a cross-section of those working in the electoral system, politicians, academics and analysts. The seminar was privileged to have the participation of the Chief Election Officer, Uttar Pradesh, Mr. Noor Muhammad, who was not only very patient in sharing his knowledge of organizing elections and dealing with criticisms and complaints but was also very sensitive to the dynamics of the seminar and made a helpful contribution of keeping it focussed. The participation of Mr. P. A. Sangma, the Speaker of the 12th Lok Sabha was also very helpful, confirming that some politicians are reaching the same conclusions as participants from other backgrounds about the areas where reform might be needed.

SEMINAR DISCUSSIONS

Legal and Constitutional Framework

Day two opened with a session on the legal position, which was intended to analyse where changes in legislation might be needed. Included in this discussion was consideration of an alternative system to the current single seat "winner-takes-all" constituencies.

The presentation by Professor G. P. Verma, the Dean of the Faculty of Law at BHU argued that the law governing elections covered all the main areas of concern such as corruption and that the problem was the application of the law and ensuring that it could be enforced. He also thought corrupt practices needed to be put into context because they were only a serious problem in Northern India, where it was particularly problematic because there was little sense that there was anything wrong with vote catching dubiously. He also emphasised the division of responsibility so that the executive carried out elections and the judiciary did have a right to review decisions. Other topics touched on were the possibility of state funding of candidates and the need to ensure proper financial accounting by candidates, maintaining accurate electoral rolls, raising voter awareness and the possibility of compulsory voting, limiting the large number of parties, ensuring neutral government in the run-up to elections, and barring candidates from standing in more than one constituency. A second paper raised the problem of candidates who face criminal charges as there is a general consensus that they should not be able to stand for elections at least if charges are framed against them by Courts in specific offences, but it was not clear at what point in the legal process this disqualification should operate.

The second main topic dealt with in this session was the electoral system. The paper presented by Dr. Sandeep Shastri of Department of Political Science, Bangalore University provided a trenchant critique of the present system. It results in candidates being elected with a small proportion of the votes. However in considering alternatives, a number of considerations were identified. Proportional representation was supported by some of those present, but it was pointed out that some systems, especially the single transferable vote would be unlikely to discourage the further splitting of parties. There were reservations about using a list system because it would be likely to entrench the lack of internal democracy in the political parties. There is a concern about the fragmentation of parties and the weakness of coalition governments, especially when there are a number of small parties involved. The Representation of People's Act has not been able to affect the tendency for new parties to be established. There was some concern about the ability of the electorate to cope with more sophisticated voting methods but it was pointed out that the electorate in other countries has been able to deal with proportional systems of voting. The cost of running elections is also an important issue. Dr. Shastri's own preference was the second ballot system which he believed would ensure that those elected had broader popular support and would tend to result in the election of candidates from the bigger parties. It would also be simple for the voter to operate. The only drawback in his view was that the second ballot would involve extra expense. In the end this option seemed to have support amongst participants.

During the general discussion one speaker emphasised the need to ensure that local elections took place as they were the basic tier of the system. There was concern about the capabilities of some candidates and there was some debate on setting literacy qualifications for candidates. There was also some discussion of the value of giving legal force to the current code of conduct for candidates, which had been voluntarily agreed to by the political parties.

Financial Issues

The second part of the morning dealt with three financial aspects of the election process: the size of the candidate's deposit, the monitoring of the expenses of candidates, and the cost to the Government of running elections.

The size of the deposit is relevant to the multiplication of parties and candidates. The increase in the size of the deposit was generally acknowledged to have been effective in reducing the numbers of candidates to manageable proportions. There was little support for farther increasing the deposit and there was some concern that a high deposit would discourage genuine candidates. The Chief Election Officer pointed to the developing practice of political parties nominating multiple candidates because the deposit was not big and they were then able to spend up to the limit of allowable electoral expenses of all the candidates to benefit the party. An alternative to increasing the size of the deposit is to increase the share of the vote required to retain the deposit because the risk of losing the deposit might be a significant consideration in deciding to stand.

The paper of Dr. Sanjay Lodha from the Department of Political Science, Mohanlal Sukhadia University, Udaipur dealt mainly with the difficulties of ensuring effective monitoring of election expenses. It was agreed that there needed to be more rigorous application of limits on expenses so as to avoid giving special benefit to the wealthier candidate. An essential requirement for more effective monitoring of candidates' expenditure is greater transparency on where finance comes from and how it is spent. Many issues were raised in the subsequent discussion. It was commented that the efforts of the media and NGOs had exposed some practices and this has acted as a check on candidates. Professor R.B. Jain, former Head of the Department of Political Science of Delhi University made the point that the rules on candidates' expenditure are found in three separate statutes and it would be better if there was one comprehensive statute. Underworld money is used in elections but is not accounted for in any way. There is no law on agency, which means that anyone can spend on a candidate's campaign without that expenditure being considered part of the candidate's expenses. This would be an easy change to make if the political will exists. Reference was made already to the practice of parties putting up multiple candidates in order to be able to spend up to the limit of allowable expenditure for each candidate for the benefit of the party as a whole and the preferred candidate.

The Chief Election Officer, Uttar Pradesh also noted that prospective candidates distributed gifts before the elections were called and so this was not taken account of when considering practices during the actual campaign. He also argued that there was already a procedure for ensuring that candidates knew how to complete returns on their expenses and there should be no excuse that they do not know what to do. One suggestion was that the limits on expenditure should rise with inflation. Another suggestion was to limit the areas of expenditure, which were allowed, so that many of the more expensive campaigning practices such as TV advertising would not be available. However a number of participants doubted that organizations such as the media would be willing to lose the potential income from election advertising. It was also pointed out that there was no real knowledge of what expenditure really did make a difference to a candidate's campaign. There is a tendency towards more American style elections with much more national expenditure. At present candidates might be spending money which had no real impact. It was noted that some very wealthy candidates had not been able to get elected in spite of their considerable resources.

The size of the constituencies makes campaigning expensive, especially in widely dispersed populations where road transport is slow. Helicopters become the only way for candidates to be seen throughout the constituency. One suggestion was that expenses allowed should be tailored to the size of the constituency to take account of the extra cost of campaigning in widely dispersed populations. Because of the size of the electorate and the nature of the country the cost to the national and state governments in organising elections is considerable. Dr. Shaibal Gupta of Patna analysed some of the problems in his paper. At the state level this problem can be particularly acute. Some states are virtually bankrupt and if a state is in decline it does not have the basic infrastructure to administer elections such as phones and basic office equipment. The extension of the use of electronic voting machines was referred to a number of times as a means to reduce the difficulties and costs of elections. Although there would be an initial outlay in acquiring machines in the long run it should reduce administration and personnel costs.

Social and Political Culture

The third and fourth sessions dealt with the current social and political context which creates a range of pressures for the electoral process including violence and intimidation, ensuring adequate representation of women, demographic change and the need for a new delimitation of constituencies and so on. Delimitation is of course related to the nature of any future electoral system but in the first instance it was considered within the context of single seat constituencies.

Most of the presentations and discussions in this session focussed on the prevailing political and social culture. It was pointed out that there was a feudal mindset and politics has become communalized. Changes in structures and electoral procedures will not solve the problems as is evidenced by the lack of impact of the Anti-defection law. What was needed was a change in the political culture. He also referred to the hierarchies of political families and the tendency for single seat constituencies to produce governments, which could not command a majority of the popular vote. Another paper advocated the adoption of approval voting. It was observed that the "crisis of discourse on secularisation" is also because the secular nature of the state is not reflected in civil society, which is communal. Professor Pradeep Mathur of the Indian Institute of Mass Communication, New Delhi, argued that the caste card has been overplayed but nevertheless society is not mature enough to look beyond the caste issue. There was a warning not to equate tradition with everything, which was bad, and it was important to remember that many very religious people were very secular in their approach. He cited, Gandhi as one example. But it was argued that emotive issues motivated the electorate.

Another view was that the best way to regulate the behaviour of political parties was through the censure of civil society by rejecting them at the ballot box, but that view did not deal with the problem that the prevailing political culture might not encourage an informed and critical electorate. The electoral system should be appropriate to the needs of the society as it is. For example, different systems could encourage or discourage communal voting. There is a requirement to empower the electorate. Professor Mathur's view was that political education is needed and if there was a better informed electorate, then there would be less need for changes in election procedures. He said that we can not solve problems through changing the system if the voter is not aware and ready to challenge corrupt and other wrong practices. However, it was stressed that it is important not only to propose that society should be different but it is also necessary to explain how change would occur and what practical steps could be introduced to bring about desired changes. A number of measures were highlighted which would help to ensure fair elections including the use of identity cards with photos and the maintenance of an accurate electoral roll. Dr. R. P. Pathak (BHU) in his paper argued for a system based on Gandhi's ideas on local government, by which locally elected representatives would vote on behalf of their communities for candidates to the state and national legislatures.

In the second half of the session, the case was made for increased representation for women in papers by Professor C. Padia and Professor Susheela Singh (both from BHU) but there was no agreed view on how best to achieve greater representation.

On the third day politicians were invited to give their perspectives and the discussion was initiated by Mr. P.A. Sangma, Speaker of the twelfth Lok Sabha. He reiterated and reinforced some of the issues already raised, and stimulated the level of discussion. Mr. Sangma pointed to the change from the first forty years of the State when there were only eight elections while in the last ten years there had been five elections. India had consciously adopted a multi-party system but there had been a huge growth in the number of parties. In the first Lok Sabha there had been twelve parties and in the thirteenth there were forty parties. This has resulted in a loss of stability and a decline in the position of the national political parties. The large number of candidates means that candidates can be elected only a small percentage of the vote. There is a need to try to limit the number of parties. There has been some consideration of proportional representation but this could mean that the member is no longer identified with the constituency and some systems could also further encourage smaller parties. He saw merit in a mixed system combining first past the post with a proportional system.

Another problem arises from the need for a new delimitation of constituencies because the south is proportionally over represented but could the system accept a big shift of seats from the south to the north?

Mr. Sangma mentioned the problem of bribery but more generally he described degeneration in the institutions of the state, which had very limited time for business and for members to raise issues relevant to their constituencies. He said that the last three budgets had been passed without debate. Some States had more ministers than ordinary members and in that situation how could the parliament hold the government accountable. He identified a decline in the quality of members and in reply to a question he recognised the problems caused by illiterate members who could not read relevant papers. In reply to another question he agreed that there should be a retirement age for politicians. Another concern related to disqualification is the issue of barring candidates who were facing criminal charges.

He looked for transformation in the situation coming about through society as a whole influencing politicians and the political parties. He did not think that the quality of politicians could be controlled by laws. However he recognised that the middle classes, intellectuals, business people and professionals were disillusioned with politics and were not voting. On the other hand in a subsequent paper Dr. D.G.A. Khan took the view that political parties needed to be educators of the electorate. Dr. Khan's paper also dealt with the need to maintain the independence of the Election Commission and the Chief Election Officer spoke of the measures which protect electoral officials.

In subsequent discussions it was generally accepted that the middle classes do not vote because they are in fact a privileged class who are not dependent on who is elected. Surveys have shown a consistent pattern across states and regions that the social groups who are most likely to vote are Dalits, tribals, the illiterate and the poor. The lowest level of voting is among women, those from higher castes and urban residents. In the discussion a connection was made to the earlier reference to the impact of emotional issues on voting patterns and the surveys show that the marginalized groups which are less likely to vote are more influenced by emotive issues such as religion and if there are such issues in an election the turn-out by those groups is likely to be higher.

Conclusion: Towards an Agenda for Action

The final session provided an opportunity to clarify if there was common ground on the issues and a clear sense of how the issues could be taken forward. A paper was prepared which listed as far as possible all the issues which had arisen, both major and minor and a quick assessment was made of the views of participants to see where there was consensus and what commitment there was to deal with the issues. It also provided an opportunity to identify those issues which would need further reflection and possible areas which would need further research before it would be possible to identify a clear direction.

2

Distorted Verdicts

JAYAPRAKASH NARAYAN

There has been a vigorous debate on criminalisation of politics and illegitimate use of excessive and unaccounted money power in elections. Several sensible and practical suggestions have been offered. The Election Commission, the Law Commission, and various committees have studied these issues. There is no dearth of solutions. But all efforts at reform have been stymied for want of parliamentary action. Further tightening of Section 8 of the Representation of the People Act, 1951 to prevent persons with criminal record and questionable antecedents from contesting, strict disclosure norms, and public funding in elections require political will and effective legislation. The political parties and successive governments are guilty of inaction in the face of a mounting crisis of legitimacy of the political process on account of criminalisation and use of unaccounted money power.

In this debate the various easily remediable flaws in the voter registration and polling process distorting our elections have been largely ignored. The Lok Satta movement, as a part of its Election Watch campaign for voter awareness, has studied the flaws in voter registration and polling irregularities. Both these can be easily corrected by changes in procedures and rules and do not need new legislation. The answers are simple, once the problems are clearly identified. Correction of registration flaws and elimination of polling irregularities are fundamental to the purity of the election process. What is more, there is no political resistance to these reforms. First let us understand the process in actual operation.

This paper first appeared in Seminar, October 2001, Issue 506.

Every citizen of India age 18 years or above who has registered as a voter is eligible to vote. Citizens declared by courts as mentally unstable and those disqualified for electoral offences are ineligible to vote.

The Election Commission prepares new rolls and revises the existing ones from time to time, normally before every general election to the Lok Sabha and assemblies. They may also be revised on the instructions of the Election Commission before a by-election. Theoretically, additions and changes in the rolls can be made at any time, but in reality accessing them at ordinary times is a painstaking process.

When special revisions are not called for, the voter lists may be checked only at the office of the taluk revenue officer or in the municipal office. And once the elections are announced and the election process is underway, changes are difficult to make. Legally, additions and deletions may be made until just before the deadline for filing nominations. But from a practical viewpoint, it is best to have one's name included or any changes made when the Election Commission calls for such periodic revisions.

Voter lists are prepared for each assembly constituency in the local official language. The list for each assembly constituency is divided into 'parts'. Each part usually pertains to a polling booth. Each assembly constituency (assigned a constituency number) and each polling booth (part number) are numbered for easy access and retrieval of information. The names of voters in each part (polling booth) of the roll are arranged according to house numbers and their names are numbered consecutively. Usually a part of the roll represents a defined geographical area. But sometimes the male and female voters may be segregated, and in such cases there may be two parts pertaining to the same household.

The local revenue official (tehsildar or mandal revenue officer) is normally the person in charge of the electoral registration process. During this process he is called the Assistant Electoral Registration Officer (AERO), and he functions under his superior (sub-divisional magistrate or revenue divisional officer), who is called the Electoral Registration Officer (ERO). The district magistrate/collector/deputy commissioner is the District Election Officer under whose supervision electoral rolls are prepared and published.

In cities of certain states, the electoral registration work may be entrusted to municipal corporation officials. The electoral registration officials prepare the rolls based on birth and death registers, available census data, field surveys, door-to-door enumeration and other available information. The electoral roll contains the name of the voter and details such as the name of the father/husband, age, residential address. Generally the age of the voter is noted as on 1 January of the year in which the revision is carried out. If the voter list is prepared after April, the age as on 1 April is noted.

As soon as the electoral roll for a constituency is ready, the registration officer publishes (displays in his office and such other places as may be prescribed by the Election Commission) the draft by making a copy of it available for inspection and displaying a notice to the public. The Election Commission widely publicizes the release of revised electoral rolls. Two copies of each electoral roll are supplied to recognised political parties free of cost. As per law the draft electoral roll should be displayed at each polling booth (the concerned 'part') in each village for the people to examine. The Election Commission expects all objections to be made at that time. However, the electoral rolls are not displayed everywhere and officers discharge their duties in a casual and perfunctory manner and the people's involvement in the revision of electoral rolls is minimal.

Because it is difficult to make changes to the electoral rolls once the revision is complete, it is best to add or delete names during the update undertaken by the Election Commission. Citizens can then inspect the electoral rolls, and if they find that their names are missing, can file claims for inclusion in Form 6. Citizens should register only in one polling station, generally the one closest to their residence. If there is any objection to the inclusion of a name in a roll, an objection can be filed in Form 7 by any person whose name is already included in that roll. Every change to the details in an entry in the roll (spelling, age, name of father, address, gender, etc.) should be filed in Form 8 by the voter. Similarly, a request for change of polling station (part number) is filed in Form 8A by the voter, and a request for deletion of entry due to death, migration etc., by any enrolled voter in Form 8B. (Table 2.1)

All such objections and requests should be filed before the due date prescribed by the Election Commission. The registration officer then holds a summary inquiry into every such claim and objection after giving notice to the applicant and the public and records his

Table 2.1 : Different Forms for Different Purposes

Form No.	Purpose
6	Inclusion of name
7	Objection to inclusion of name
8	Change of any entry (name, spelling, age, gender etc.)
8 A	Change of polling station within the constituency, change of polling station outside the constituency
8 B	Deletion of entry due to death or migration

decision. The registration officer may also correct the electoral rolls by including names inadvertently omitted, deleting names of persons who died or persons who are no longer residents of the area. The final electoral roll including a list of amendments is then published.

This process appears fair and reasonable. But in reality citizens have little knowledge of the process, nor do they have access to voter lists or appropriate forms for filing claims or objections. Therefore, by default the voter list carries many errors of omission and commission. It is this huge margin of error and inaccessibility of the voter list and the bureaucratic registration process which make our electoral rolls defective.

All such errors could of course be corrected. But this process is cumbersome, non-transparent, inaccessible and generally ineffective. The first difficulty arises with the non-availability of electoral rolls. As explained above, at the time of revision of electoral rolls, the Election Commission publishes (displays) the voter list in select offices. But if the voter wishes to access electoral rolls to verify whether or not his name appears, he has to obtain a copy of the voter list for the polling booth (part)/constituency.

These voter lists are available with the electoral registration officials and are supplied for a fee, usually equivalent to charges for photocopying. Citizens are often unaware of this procedure and do not know where to obtain electoral rolls, the fee payable, constituency number and the part number for which we need electoral rolls and even where the electoral registration office is located.

Moreover, in many states one cannot even pay cash to obtain the electoral rolls. You may have to go to the nearest government treasury office (most people wouldn't know where the treasury is located.

Villagers would have to go to tehsil headquarters) and make the payment by a *challan*, which itself is a long drawn out process. In order to make a payment by challan, a proper application has to be made indicating the appropriate head of account to which the fee is to be remitted.

It is not surprising that ordinary citizens are unable to access electoral rolls by following this tortuous bureaucratic process. If by a miracle, you do manage to get a copy of the electoral roll and if you find that your name is missing, or a dead person's name is included, you will then have to apply in the appropriate form. The forms are theoretically available with the electoral registration officer, but more often they are either not available or when available, not in the local language. Once the form is obtained, the application should be made in duplicate.

How does one register to vote? As with all governmental procedures, inclusion of one's name is a rather painstaking process. To give you an idea of the difficulty involved we narrate below the travails of Ramayya, a farm worker, who decided to check whether his name was registered. Ramayya was one of the few who knew that electoral rolls are available for a fee at the local revenue office and that this fee has to be paid to a particular head of account.

1. He must first go to the tehsil headquarters which may be located 25-50 kms away from his home.
2. He must visit the tehsil office and ask them to provide the following information: (a) the constituency number and the part number relating to his village; (b) the fee to be paid to get a copy of the voter list for that polling booth; and (c) the head of account to which the fee should be remitted.
3. If the tehsil officials oblige him (in our administrative set up it is impossible for Ramayya to obtain all this information in a single day) he will have to go to the treasury. Although the rolls are available at the tehsil office, the payment to get a copy of the rolls is to be made at the treasury which is located in another building, or sometimes in another town not always close by. He must reach before the treasury closes, ask for the appropriate form and fill it. If for any reason Ramayya does not know the head of

account, payment will not be accepted. Usually the fee payable to obtain the electoral roll for a polling station area ('part') will be of the order of Rs. 5 to 10.

4. He takes the challan back to the election registration office (tehsil office) and submits it with a request for a copy of the voters list.
5. If the voter lists are readily available, the tehsil officials may condescend to supply a copy.
6. He then verifies if his name is there (in the meantime the office could close for the day).
7. If he does not find his name, he must ask for Form 6. Though free, most often these forms are not available and when available are not in the regional language (often they are in English). If he manages to get one he has to fill out the four page form in duplicate and file it with the tehsil office (which normally functions as the electoral registration office).
8. According to the rules, once the form is submitted, he should get an acknowledgement. This acknowledgement is the detachable part of Form 6. Even so, an acknowledgement is hardly ever given to anyone.
9. Ramayya then goes home and waits. The rules prescribe that he should expect a response in 10 days. Meanwhile, the electoral registration officer will publish (display) Ramayya's application in his office notice board and ask for objections if any. Objections are to be filed within one week.
10. If an objection is received, the electoral registration officer will conduct a summary inquiry. He might call the objector, and if he deems it necessary send a notice to Ramayya asking him to appear personally. On the basis of this inquiry the electoral registration officer will make a decision on Ramayya's application. The decision has to be intimated to Ramayya in writing. This 'action taken report' is also a detachable part of Form 6, but in reality no one ever receives the report. So until election day, there is uncertainty whether one's name has been included.
11. If the ERO decides to register Ramayya's name as a voter,

> an amendment will be made to the electoral rolls including his name. For any process—inclusion of name, deletion of name, change of name/address/polling booth a similar exercise has to be undertaken. Only the application form varies.

If all the residents of Ramayya's village wish to save time and effort and decide to do this work collectively, the bunch of applications will not be accepted. Each application must be filed personally or sent by post. The above narration is based on *Lok Satta's* direct experience in accessing the voter lists and getting names included or deleted.

One can understand from this how the process in reality is totally inaccessible to the common man. Even an educated person must be a motivated citizen willing to spare a lot of energy, time, money and effort in order to verify the electoral roll and register. No wonder the electoral rolls are flawed.

Many eligible persons are often struck out from the voters lists. This is usually done at the behest of powerful politicians or caste leaders in order to disenfranchise voters who may vote against their wishes. In the last general election in Thane, it was reported that even persons with voter identity cards found their names struck off with a red pen. In the guise of revision or correction, the government/party in power may delete names of people who are not likely to vote for them or add fictitious or ineligible names in order to indulge in bogus voting. This is possible as the administrative machinery in charge of voter registration is controlled by the elected government. But then there have also been instances when ministers, MLAs and even Election Commission officials couldn't find their own names on the rolls.

Pre-poll verification of electoral rolls: As the accuracy of voter lists is an important aspect of the elections, a pilot project for this study was undertaken by Lok Satta during February-March 1999. The available lists, i.e. mother list prepared in 1995 and supplementary lists prepared in 1996 and 1998 were procured. Electoral lists for five parts i.e. three in Assembly Constituency 211, and two in assembly constituency 210, were verified. The study revealed large variations as seen below (Table 2.2).

This pilot verification was limited to Hyderabad city area and its surroundings. Most of the deletions required were due to a change of residence by the voter. Such shifts could be outside the polling station,

Table 2.2 : Sample Verification of Electoral Rolls (1999) in Hyderabad City

AC No./ Part No.	No. of voters in the list	No. of voters verified	Additions required (% to verified voters)	Deletions required (% to verified voters)	Total variations (Additions + Deletions) Col.4+5	% of Variations (Col 6) to voters verified (Col 3)
(1)	(2)	(3)	(4)	(5)	(6)	(7)
210/54	981	825	16 (1.9)	79 (9.6)	95	11.52
210/144	1296	1296	478 (36.9)	300 (23.1)	778	60.03
211/47	4135	1154	205 (17.7)	136 (11.8)	341	29.55
211/229	1638	418	217 (51.9)	136 (32.5)	353	84.45
211/231	572	400	202 (50.5)	182 (45.5)	384	96.0

Source: Lok Satta's Research Data, 2000.

constituency, state or country. (Shifts within polling booth limits was ignored in the survey).

Similarly, about 30 per cent of additions were due to people moving into the area; about 23 per cent were new additions (persons attaining 18 years), 15 per cent due to migration and the rest for other reasons which include omission in the earlier enumeration. It was interesting that supplementary lists were prepared perfunctorily every year since 1995. A 40 per cent plus error of omission and commission was noted in the Lok Satta pilot survey demonstrating that the Election Commission's periodic revisions failed to rectify defects. Similar verifications were conducted by Lok Satta volunteers in most district towns of Andhra Pradesh, and the results showed a recurring and uniform pattern of about 40 per cent error in electoral rolls in most urban areas.

Post-election survey: Immediately after the general elections in 1999, Lok Satta tried to obtain copies of a few 'marked electoral rolls'. These are voter lists available after the polling, in which the names of those who voted are marked by the polling officials. We sought them in order to do a house-to-house survey of each voter shown to have voted in order to 'verify the authenticity of the votes cast. We deliberately chose areas free of violence or complaints of rigging, booth capturing or large scale impersonation. As the election authorities refused to supply copies, political parties were approached for the rolls marked by their agents.

The survey was completed within three weeks of polling. This was difficult, particularly in urban areas, as each voter had to be personally interviewed to verify whether a vote had been cast. The complexity of the survey, the refusal of election authorities to furnish official lists of those who voted, the need for urgency and the limitation of resources forced us to restrict this post-polling survey of voters to only five polling stations. The results of our survey are recorded in (Table 2.3).

This survey was conducted in areas where no rigging or irregularities were officially reported and polling was conducted peacefully. The polling of 53 per cent of votes, which is less than the average polling, indicates that there was no unusual rigging. In fact the number of those who reported to having voted personally was much lower; it worked out to only 41.3 per cent of the total voters registered. 538 voters whose votes were polled were thus listed as doubtful votes. Of these, 190 voters (7.6 per cent of the votes polled) could not have voted in person, whereas the other 348 votes amounting to 14.1 per cent of votes polled pertain to persons residing elsewhere.

It is possible that a few of the voters who had moved into another area of the city might have voted where they were earlier registered. Ascertaining the facts in such cases is both cumbersome and prohibitively expensive. But it is reasonable to assume that many persons from distant areas in a big city might not have voted. It is unlikely that those who shifted to other towns or villages would have visited Hyderabad on polling day merely to vote. The total number of such false and doubtful votes formed 21.7 per cent of the votes polled. Of them, 7.6 per cent were clearly false votes and 14.1 per cent doubtful.

Statewide verification of electoral rolls on sample basis: The variations noted during the pilot surveys (pre-poll and post-poll) were appalling. In addition, variations in different sectors have to be studied to obtain a realistic estimate of errors in the electoral rolls. A statewide sample survey has been planned with the technical advice of statistical experts. Though electoral lists are prepared constituency-wise, the administrative units for electoral registration are revenue mandals (equivalent of taluks/tehsils in other states, but smaller in size) in all districts, and municipal corporation in the city of Hyderabad.

Table 2.3: Post-Polling Survey of Select Polling Station Areas (1999 Assembly and Parliamentary Polls, Hyderabad, AP)

Assembly Constituency/ Polling Booth No.	No. of voters	No. of vote polled	No. not voted or doubtful cases				Total	% of doubtful and 'not voted'
			No. who reported that they actually 'voted'	Residing in the area but not voted	Left the area but residing within the city	Left the city/ country 'voted'		
(1)	(2)	(3)	(4)	(5)	(6)	(7)	(8)	(9)
207/173	1143	625	483	5	91	46	142	22.7
207/176	956	459	377	15	41	26	82	17.9
209/93	725	428	306	20	95	7	122	28.5
209/75	989	495	380	42	72	1	115	23.2
210/426	893	476	399	22	49	6	77	16.2
Total	**4706**	**2483**	**1945**	**104**	**348**	**86**	**538**	**21.7**

Source: Lok Satta—Research and Documentation.

Our earlier experience shows that there is likely to be a greater number of errors in towns and cities than in villages. Keeping this in view, the entire population was divided into a broad category of rural and urban; again the urban areas into municipal corporations and other municipalities. Attention was given to the 'slums' segment in municipal corporations. Normally a sample proportional to population size would have been good enough. But in view of the highly varying error noticed during the pilot surveys in urban areas, a bigger sample was allotted for urban areas.

The objective of the sample survey was not merely to find errors in the list, but to ascertain the reasons for variations to the extent possible.

An effort was made to ascertain the number of first time voters to be registered because of attaining voting age, deletions on account of migration and their inclusion in the rolls elsewhere, and if migrant population went back to their old residences to exercise their vote. We also enquired whether the electoral registration mechanism was satisfactory and whether voters would prefer a user friendly agency like the post office for registration. For deletions, it was proposed to specify reasons like death, migration, foreign emigration and other errors like duplicate entries, fictitious names and so on. The survey conducted by volunteers was spread over a few months. During this intervening period the lists were updated as on 1.1.2000 and 1.1.2001. Hence, lists updated as on date of survey were verified.

The work is incomplete in several districts, but the data collected so far reveals large variations and differences in variations over different strata (Table 2.4).

Lok Satta's findings conform to voter experience at every election. Errors in electoral rolls to a tune of 15 per cent in rural areas and 40 per cent in urban areas are unacceptable in a democracy. It is possible that there are fewer errors in voter registration in other states, but even half this number of errors seriously distorts elections and undermines the legitimacy of the political process. As the sample survey in Hyderabad city after the 1999 polls showed, there is a possibility of bogus voting of up to 21 per cent in urban areas when identity cards are not mandatory. But experience elsewhere shows that identity cards may not be adequate to ensure fair polling for quite some time to come.

Lok Satta organized Election Watch in Kolkatta in 2001 during

Table 2.4 : Verification of Voter Lists in Andhra Pradesh

Particulars of Electoral			Deletions Required (Errors of Commission)					Additions Required (Errors of Commission)				Total Errors	
District	No. of polling stations	No. of voters	Moved out of the area)	Death	Other*	Total	% to voters	Attained 18 years of age	Moved into the area	Total	% to voters	Total number	% to voters regis-tered
Survey of Rural Polling Stations													
E.G.	4	1289	166	36	—	202	15.7	31	50	81	6.3	283	22.0
W.G.	2	2086	37	52	—	89	4.3	24	23	47	2.3	136	6.5
Krishna	1	416	27	13	1	41	9.9	12	3	15	3.6	56	13.5
Prakasam	2	1297	43	38	2	83	6.4	34	12	46	3.5	129	9.9
Nellore	4	3084	87	79	15	181	5.9	60	100	160	5.2	341	11.1
Chittoor	2	1762	143	37	90	270	15.3	47	110	157	8.9	427	24.2
Kurnool	4	4648	488	71	1	560	12.0	82	128	210	4.5	770	16.6
Warangal	2	1399	51	15	4	70	5.0	7	12	19	1.4	89	6.4
M'bnagar	1	344	32	11	—	43	12.5	35	12	47	13.7	90	26.2
Karimnagar	5	3956	549	100	59	708	17.9	78	142	220	5.6	928	23.5
Khammam	2	2016	11	36	12	59	2.9	37	0	37	1.8	96	4.8
Rural Total	**29**	**22297**	**1634**	**488**	**184**	**2306**	**10.34**	**447**	**5 92**	**1039**	**4.7**	**3345**	**15.10**

(Contd.)

Table 2.4 (*Contd.*)

Survey of Urban Polling Stations													
Vizag	3	1298	355	22	17	394	30.4	82	413	495	38.1	889	68.5
E.Godavari	3	419	78	14	0	92	22.0	39	85	124	29.6	216	51.6
W.Godavari	2	1491	121	12	—	133	8.9	46	179	225	15.1	358	24.0
Krishna	3	1919	690	35	0	725	37.8	53	500	553	28.8	1278	66.6
Kurnool	3	1796	419	43	28	490	27.3	62	90	152	8.5	642	35.7
Nalgonda	1	797	273	5	2	280	35.1	34	125	159	19.9	439	55.1
Warangal	2	1863	320	28	30	378	20.3	43	74	117	6.3	495	26.6
Guntur	5	4060	1039	83	92	1214	29.9	209	604	813	20.0	2027	49.9
Hyderabad	5	4459	923	31	42	996	22.3	85	691	776	17.4	1772	39.7
Urban Total	**27**	**18102**	**4218**	**273**	**211**	**4702**	**26.0**	**653**	**2761**	**3414**	**18.9**	**8116**	**44.8**
Rural+ Urban	**56**	**40399**	**5852**	**761**	**395**	**7008**	**17.3**	**1100**	**3353**	**4453**	**11.0**	**11461**	**28.4**

* [under-aged/ineligible/fictitious].
Source: Lok Satta's Research Data, 2000.

the state assembly elections. A 'help line' with 20 telephone lines was widely advertised for voters to lodge complaints. Of the complaints received on polling day, an astonishing 30 per cent claimed that their vote was cast fraudulently by the time they reached the polling station. This happened in an election in which a voter identity card or other forms of establishing identity was mandatory to vote. Collusion or coercion of polling staff and polling agents of opponents, plays a major role in elections. We should, therefore, look at simple, practical solutions to improve the voter registration process to make it transparent, and look for methods of eliminating or limiting voting fraud.

Although voting eligibility is the same for Parliament, assembly, and local bodies, the electoral rolls for local bodies in certain states are different. Not only does it add to the expenditure, it makes revision of electoral rolls expensive and time consuming. A more serious problem is that room for falsification is enhanced. Therefore, there should be common electoral rolls for all elections.

Happily, though errors in voter registration are common, they are also the most easily remediable of defects in our electoral process. All that is required is to evolve a process that is voter friendly. Each polling station contains no more than 700-1000 names. If electoral rolls can be made accessible (displayed) to citizens at all times for easy inspection in a neighbourhood facility, and are available for sale at a nominal price, much of the problem can be corrected.

If the appropriate statutory forms (Forms 6, 7, 8, 8A and 8B) are locally available free or at nominal cost, the voter can present the application, obtain an acknowledgement and await written communication of decision taken on his application. The local public office can be made responsible for acknowledging applications and communicating action taken. All these changes can be brought about by a mere revision of rules and procedures, and no amendment of law is involved. Statutory Forms (Form 6, 7, 8, 8A and 8B) should be available free or for a small fee in the post office. The forms could be made available at the post office and filed, giving details for inclusion or deletion.

There are two public offices locally accessible to all citizens—the village panchayat and the post office. In urban areas, the municipality or corporation is always accessible but it caters to a much larger number of citizens. It would be best if the post office is made the nodal agency for supply of electoral rolls, supply and receipt of statutory forms, acknowledgement of application and communication of action taken reports.

The revenue or municipal office can be the actual decision-making authority in respect of such applications, as is the current practice. All we need is to make the process transparent, accessible and verifiable by citizens locally. There is a post office in every village that is widely regarded as a user-friendly public institution.

The post office has a culture of across-the-table transactions in real time. Any citizen can be given access to the voter list pertaining to the local polling station(s) for inspection to verify the accuracy of entries. All such applications can be received at the post office and an acknowledgement given to the applicant. The post office will then transmit them to the revenue or municipal or panchayat office, as decided by the Election Commission, for enquiry and determination as to whether or not to accept the application. The action taken can be communicated within a period of say one month to the post office, and from there to the citizen.

In order to save public money on postage, applications and action taken reports can be bulk transferred, and the citizen asked to verify the action at the post office. The post office can maintain a register of applications and the action taken reports received from the electoral registration officials. Such a register can be kept open for public scrutiny during office hours. There can be common electoral rolls for all elections—legislative assembly and panchayat or municipality.

The panchayat or municipal offices too can be made nodal agencies for display or supply of electoral rolls, statutory forms, receipt of applications and communication of action taken reports. There can even be change of rules to make the panchayat or municipality responsible for revision of electoral rolls, addition or deletion of names, and correction of entries. In such cases the process will be much simpler as the post office and panchayat will be located in the same village. In case the panchayat's decision is unsatisfactory, there can be provision for an appeal to the appropriate revenue official. Display of electoral rolls on Internet, supply of soft copies of electoral rolls in CD ROMs and availability of statutory forms on internet for down loading are other means by which the process can be made accessible and verifiable.

While this process of accessible and verifiable voter registration through local post offices involves simple and easy changes in procedures and rules, it will mark the most significant improvement in our electoral process at no additional cost. Even though a sizeable percentage of the voting population is illiterate, this will enable the literate population, civil society groups, voluntary organizations, and local political activists to verify the process and check irregularities. The very openness and accessibility of the voter lists and statutory forms will make a marked difference to electoral registration, and improve the quality of electoral rolls.

Measures to curb polling irregularities: While we have outstanding men and women in public service, a flawed electoral process has alienated them from the political and electoral arena. The persons best equipped to represent the people find it impossible to contest if they adhere to law and propriety. Hence we see that parties nominate only 'winnable' candidates who can play and survive in the rough and tumble of what passes off for politics in India today.

In India, winning an election is not about party ideology or manifesto, choice of candidate, campaign strategy and such other traditional democratic methods. Parties and candidates often focus their attention on the polling process for those all-important nine or ten hours when ballots are cast. In order to manipulate the polling process to gain unfair advantage, the candidates only require to master the 'art' of polling manipulation.

Much of the election expenditure in India goes towards illegal activities of buying votes with money and liquor, hiring hoodlums to browbeat and coerce voters and bribing officials and policemen to connive in polling irregularities and rigging. It is the severity of these electoral malpractices that makes it impossible for honest and public spirited citizens to contest and win by fair means. Electoral irregularities do not guarantee victory, as the nefarious practices of one candidate are neutralized by those of the others. But an incapacity to muster muscle and money power and distort the polling process guarantee defeat! That is why though the macro level electoral verdicts seem to be broadly reflective of public opinion trends, at the ground level the picture is altogether different. In order to enhance chances of victory, parties are compelled to nominate 'winnable' candidates who can deploy money and muscle power.

There are exceptions, but they are increasingly rare, and usually unsuccessful. Given this backdrop, regardless of who wins the election, the people are the losers. Even as there is change of players' fortunes in the power game, the process of governance continues to sink deeper into the morass of corruption, incompetence, arbitrariness, injustice and callousness.

Fortunately, there are simple, practical and effective ways of curbing polling irregularities; more significantly, all these measures can be implemented within the purview of the present electoral law. What is required is a change of procedures where needed, and a firm resolve to effectively implement these measures.

Voter identity cards and electronic voting machines (EVMs) have been progressively introduced by the Election Commission. In addition, widespread use of tendered votes as a means of verification of the purity of election process has great potential in checking rigging.

Tendered votes: Where prior identification of voter by verifiable means is not a precondition for voting, there are measures to check false voting and impersonation. In such cases, the polling agent has the opportunity to object to a person casting a vote on grounds of false identity. Such a challenged vote is then decided by the presiding officer at the polling station on the basis of a summary enquiry. However, polling agents cannot be expected to know the voters. Sometimes the polling agents act in collusion with opponents. There are areas where the dominance of one caste or group is so pronounced that polling agents are not available for certain candidates, or when available, are easily intimidated. Therefore, the availability of polling agents is not a sufficient safeguard against polling malpractices. Other measures to curb rigging and impersonation should be considered.

It is common knowledge that many voters go to polling booths and return disappointed on finding their votes cast by others impersonating them. In such cases, the voter can establish his identity by some means or other, and seek a tendered ballot. However, this provision is not widely known. Even if such a tendered vote is cast, under the present rules it has no validity. The sealed cover is opened only in the event of a court order on an election petition. In effect, impersonation is rewarded in elections.

The tendered vote is an indisputable proof of rigging and false voting. No matter what form rigging takes, its one inevitable manifestation is a false vote being cast in the name of another person.

The Election Commission can direct that if the tendered votes exceed say 1 per cent of the valid votes polled in a polling station, there shall be automatic re-polling. If below 1 per cent, the Commission can direct that the tendered votes shall be counted along with the ballots in the ballot box.

If false voting is high, then tendered votes will exceed 1 per cent, and there will be a re-poll. Once it is known that large scale impersonation and rigging, proved through tendered vote percentage, will inevitably lead to a re-poll, it will act as a disincentive. Rigging and false voting by impersonation would be significantly curbed.

Appropriate rules and procedures need to be evolved to apply these measures in respect of electronic voting machines (EVMs). These provisions for re-polling do not need a change in the law and can be incorporated through rules and guidelines.

Much needs to be done to cleanse our electoral process. But the first step is to improve voter registration through greater access to citizens, and simplified procedures. Once the registration process is demystified and made people friendly, millions of public spirited citizens, activist groups and political workers could play a pro-active role to cleanse the electoral rolls. A second step is to recognise the tendered vote as proof of rigging, and ordering a re-poll when such votes exceed a pre-determined norm. In the November 2000 presidential election in the US, one in 200,000 votes in the country affected the outcome in Florida state, and determined the presidency.

It is absurd if we accepted anything less than near perfection in voter registration and fair polling. Much can be effected by procedural changes, and does not require reworking the law. The Election Commission has emerged over the years as a truly independent, impartial constitutional authority enjoying high credibility and respect. Once it addresses these two issues, it will result in significant improvement in our electoral process. A lot more remains to be done to prevent criminals from contesting and check the role of black money in elections. But these vital first steps will pave way to more momentous reforms.

3

Election Reforms
Beyond Middle Class Fantasies

YOGENDRA YADAV*

Discussions on electoral reforms are invariably cast in the familiar discourse on public policy with its customary obsession with details and silence on fundamentals. Its apparent hard realism (no-philosophy-please), high moral tone and capacity to speak for an abstract "public" draws upon a cluster of unexamined and largely unstated presuppositions which derive their truth effect by collaborating in multiple structures of dominance, both global and local. In other words, much of the established common-sense on electoral reform appears balanced, benevolent and realistic only because we are accustomed to looking at it in the glow of power arising out of the fusion of the local elite with the dominant version of the history of global powers. Looked at differently, it is ideology masked in legalese and politics masquerading as public policy. Or so I suspect. The principal ambition of this suspicion is to rehabilitate political common sense as the appropriate mode of thinking about this subject.

Electoral reform is not an uncharted cognitive territory in contemporary India. Since the beginning of electoral politics in the fifties and particularly in the last two decades, this theme has been visited and re-visited by all kinds of travellers; visionary statesmen, tired or temporarily unemployed politicians, bureaucrats-turned-writers, freelance intellectual adventurers, the omnipresent committees and of course, the routine pilgrims—the hack who must knock off his next weekly column and the academic with an eye on promotion.

---

* This paper is an updated version of Yadav, Yogendra (1996): "Electoral Reforms: Beyond Middle Class Fantasies", in *Seminar*, Issue 440, April.

Any design for electoral reform in today's India cannot begin to make sense without reference to this pre-existing and thickly textured discourse which envelop it. Obviously, democracy is threatened not by the 'shackles' of pre-constituted principles but by the fatal temptation to write on a clean slate. At any rate, the practice of advancing one's ideas by way of a commentary, or a tick on the inherited knowledge is not new to our intellectual traditions.

The discourse on the electoral reform serves as a vehicle for every different political urge which needs to be distinguished. On the one hand it expresses a radical democratic yearning for an alternative kind of politics, for overhauling the existing political establishment and for infusing democratic content into the formal institutions of democracy. On the other hand, it serves, as a medium for the middle class will to power, unmediated by the tedious processes of democracy. In this latter form, a call for electoral reform is simply a politically correct name for politics bashing, a morally charming mask for an insidious attack on democracy.

Of late, the urban educated, mostly upper caste, Indian elite (which likes to pass off under this innocuous label, 'middle class'—a rather odd nomenclature for a group which straddles the apex of the social hierarchy in terms of power and privileges) has directed much of its limited energy to acts of public morality and a lot of its unlimited capacity to moralise on the question of electoral reform. Thanks to the stranglehold of this class over the opinion making and disseminating industry in India, its representation largely shapes what is recognised as public opinion on the question of electoral reform. As a result, the discourse on electoral reform has developed linkages with a deep craving for moral action and moral actors in the public arena. So much so that in more ways than one, electoral reform has become a metaphor for morality in politics.

A managerial-bureaucratic perspective has come to dominate our thinking on the subject. Implicit in the official wisdom on this theme from the very beginning, the perspective has of late found expression in the official documents of the Election Commission itself. The theorists and practitioners of public administration have, as always, simply toed the line. According to this perspective, Indian elections are too massive, unwieldy and messy; their 'management' involves policing the relationship between thugs (politicians) and fools (people) under highly charged conditions. The challenge (read "problem") needs to be met with a heavy hand through effective bureaucratic intervention backed by stringent legislation. The point is to teach these politicians a lesson and to educate (read "discipline") the public. The responsibility of doing so has to be shouldered by the bureaucracy.

Closely related, though distinct, is the moralist perspective on electoral reforms; implicit in the writings of some high priests of Indian journalism and politics and often articulated in what Morris Jones had called the 'saintly idiom' of Indian politics. For them electoral reform is the first step in a quest for moral regeneration, for remedying the falling ethical standards of public life. The root cause of electoral malpractice is the decline of values in public life and the end of ideology. The trend can be arrested only by inculcating values in the younger generation, stricter laws and rules for the conduct of elections, use of modern technology and honest officials. It is unclear what the agency of this transformation will be. Apparently the force of pure ideas and the influence of enlightened souls can do the trick.

What unites both these perspectives is an impatience with the messy realities of politics in a newly enfranchised society, contempt for the ordinary citizen, hatred of their rustic leaders, faith in modern technology and the legal system's capacity to set things right. The combination of technology and law is not a coincidence, for these are two privileged expressions of rationality in modern societies. Both these lend themselves to universal application based on uniformity of standards and judgment. Thus a drive for standardisation, or rather cultural homogenisation, underlies the middle class search for a rational, sanitised politics. Hidden behind the ideological mask of I-love-democracy-but-hate-politics and often articulated in the form of a middle class utopia of sanitised politics, it points to a deep fear of politics, the fear of masses taking over and running it any way they like. Needless to stress, this perspective is not unrelated to the middle class fantasy of being the guardian, the philosopher-king, faced with the real fear of power slipping away from it.

Against these two non-political and potentially anti-political perspectives, one needs to establish a political perspective on electoral reform. On this reading any understanding of what electoral reform may do to politics must be informed by what politics does to it. Not just in the most obvious sense of petty politicking that goes on in the name of electoral reform but in the deeper senses of the political. On the one hand we may refer to the political consequences of electoral reform. Here the question is who gets what by changing electoral rules in which way? A related question concerns the negative effects of electoral reform or non-reform on the distribution of power in society: reform for whom? At whose expense? On the other hand, we may refer to the hidden ideological dimensions of the discourse on electoral reform: what is the agenda? Who sets it? And for what purpose? The manufacturing of a shared common-sense which determines the terms for any 'serious' discussion on elections and their reform is, in the final analysis, a political phenomenon which needs to be interpreted politically.

The key to a meaningful political discussion about electoral reform is the ideal of representation and its relation to the process of democratisation in contemporary India. The institution of universal adult franchise kicked off a democratic revolution involving greater and more intense participation along with higher expectations in the game of politics. Yet the institutional apparatus of democracy has not been strengthened in keeping with this greater load; if anything, the intermediate structures, which negotiated the relationship between the people and the centre of power, have weakened considerably. The mismatch causes considerable tension, particularly in the case of the institution of election which has taken on a greater burden in the wake of the collapse of other institutions. The resultant dissociation of electoral mandates from the process of government formation and policy-making has distorted the nature of representation.

This is what gives rise to the challenge of electoral reform. The challenge is to make the mechanism of election an effective instrument of the democratic will of the people, especially those who have so far been excluded from their due share of power. This is directly related to the character of representation, for effective democratisation is achieved through a transition from formal representation to substantive representation. The litmus test for any proposal of electoral reform is its ability to carry forward the process of democratisation. Accordingly, the agenda for electoral reform must give priroity to those disorders/malpractices, which create an obstacle in the way of deepening of the democratic process. Other reforms of an administrative or procedural nature, which any public institution in

India needs at any given time, must occupy a secondary place and be judged in the light of the former.

If electoral reforms are political, the agency to bring it about must also be political. It is unlikely that an enlightened, benevolent and disinterested ruler will institute electoral reform on being convinced of its moral worth. At any rate, such an expectation is alien to the design of modern democracy or its adaptations, based as they are on the mechanism of competitive politics propelled by the calculus of interests. If basic electoral reforms do come about it, it would only be because the ruling establishment believes that it stands to gain by bringing this about, or that it stands to lose considerably popular goodwill by not doing so, or a combination of both. A political perspective would thus require that any proposal for electoral reform must also go into the political agency and the political strategy, which may reasonably be expected to bring it about.

Following the mirror-for-the-prince tradition, proposals for electoral reform have conventionally been presented as a list of recommendation of the state. Instead of adding to that already long list, let me class the proposals into a few areas and then comment on the significant ones in each.

A number of suggestions for overhauling the institutional design of Indian politics have invariably involved corresponding changes in the electoral system. Jayaprakash Narayan's famous proposal for indirect and party-less elections to the Parliament and state assemblies was fundamentally naïve, not just about the likely consequences of an indirect election but, more significantly, about the sociological realities of the Indian village (de Souza, 1992). Similarly a good deal of the charm of the occasional demand for shifting to the presidential system draws upon the fascination for the untried and middle class fantasy for a benevolent dictator.

The only proposal which merits careful consideration is that of replacing the existing first-past-the-post (FPTP) system by some other system of converting popular votes into legislative seats. The outcome of the existing system in the case of Lok Sabha has been summarized in Table 3.1. While no single party has ever won a majority of votes in any Lok Sabha election (Rajiv Gandhi's Congress fell short only by 2 per cent in the 1984 election held in the wake of Indira Gandhi's assassination), the plurality system has produced comfortable and even overwhelming majorities for the leading party in the first eight general

Table 3.1 : Summary of Lok Sabha Election Results, 1952-1991

Year	First Party	Votes %	Seats %	Second Party	Votes %	Seats %	Third Party	Votes %	Seats %
1952	INC	45.0	74.4	SOC	10.6	2.4	KMMP	5.8	1.8
1957	INC	47.8	75.1	PSP	10.4	3.8	CPI	8.9	5.4
1962	INC	44.7	73.0	CIP	9.9	5.8	SWA	7.9	3.6
1967	INC	40.8	54.4	BJS	9.4	6.7	SWA	8.7	8.4
1971	INC	43.7	67.9	NCO	10.4	3.0	BJS	7.4	4.2
1977	JNP	41.3	54.4	INC	34.5	28.4	CPM	4.3	4.0
1980	INC	42.7	65.1	JNP	19.0	5.7	JNPS	9.4	7.5
1984	INC	48.0	76.5	BJP	7.4	0.3	JNP	6.7	1.8
1989	INC	39.5	37.2	JD	17.7	26.8	BJP	11.5	16.2
1991	INC	36.6	45.6	BJP	20.0	22.4	JD	11.8	11.0

Note: Table entries are for the name, per cent share of popular vote and per cent share of Lok Sabha seats respectively for the first, second and the third party in every general election to Lok Sabha.

Sources: Calculated from V.B. Singh and Shankar Bose, *Elections in India: Data Handbook on Lok Sabha Elections*, Volume 1(1952-85) and 2 (1986-1991), New Delhi, Sage, 1986 and 1994.

elections. The last two elections did not produce a legislative majority for one party (the same is bound to be the case in the forthcoming election), but the eventual ruling party did capture a disproportionately large number of seats in relation to its votes. (See Table 3.1)

Over the years the FPTP system has come in for criticism mainly from non-Congress parties, which were at the receiving end of its inequalities. Some version of proportional representation invariably came up as an alternative to mitigate its unfairness. Subsequently, the critique has spilled over into academic and official circles as well. Serious proposals for proportional representation in India go back to a seminar held in 1969 (Advani, 1970; Bhambhri, 1970). The Joint Committee of Parliament on Amendments to Electoral Laws (1971-72) considered and rejected the proposal, but recommended the formation of an expert committee to review it. Jayprakash Narayan, on behalf of an independent organization, Citizens for Democracy, appointed a non-governmental committee on Electoral Reforms

(1974-75) headed by V.M. Tarkunde, which prepared a carefully considered proposal for adopting a variant of the German system. The proposal was supported by S.L. Shakdher (1980:12-13), then Chief Election Commissioner and argued for by L.P. Singh (1986: 109-120) in one of the few serious books on this issue. However, the Committee on Electoral Reforms (1990) of the Government of India, headed by Dinesh Goswami, failed to reach any conclusion on this question (it needs to be remembered that it was a non-Congress regime then); like the JPC of 1972, it also recommended an expert committee.

A perusal of these proposals reveals that no one has made a case for a pure Proportionate Representation (PR) system (see Bhambhri 1970 for an exception). All the proposals recommended a mix of PR and plurality system, close to the one followed in Germany. The precise composition of the mixture varies. The Tarkunde Committee recommended two alternative formula for consideration. The first was the German formula double vote, half of the seats by direct plurality system, 'top-up' on the basis of the second vote modified, if necessary, to change the mix of direct and list seats from 1/2:1/2 to 2/3:1/3. The second involved an innovative suggestion: single vote, polling as in the present system, all candidates who secure a majority of votes to be declared elected directly, the rest of the seats to be filled from party lists according to the proposition of votes for each party (top-up procedure) with some relaxation for independents.

The search for the best electoral system is a never-ending process, for it involves an element of essential contestability by way of multiple criteria (Eunleavy and Margettes, 1995:13). Not surprisingly, therefore, the Indian debate on this theme has remained inconclusive. But there is an additional difficulty here. Because of the narrow terms in which the question has been posed, the PR *vs.* FPTP debate has been reduced to fairness *vs.* stability. Arguments for PR or a PR-mixed system have relied on a rather simple moral reasoning, which equates proportionality with fairness and fairness with justice. While there is an element of truth in this moral reasoning, it is not good enough.

Even if we confine ourselves to moral arguments drawn from democratic theory, proportionality or political equality is just one of the consideration. Accountability of representatives to the electorate is an equally serious moral concern and the PR system would deprive ordinary votes of an instrument to directly punish a non-responsive representative. The German system will increase the size of a Lok Sabha constituency to ridiculous proportions (about 20,00,000 electors per constituency) and thus erode the accountability of the directly elected numbers as well. Moreover, while the PR system reduces the disjunction between popular votes and legislative seats, it is likely to increase the disjunction between popular vote and government formation, thus reducing the voters' capacity to influence public policy.

In any case, a moral argument is not the only aspect to political reasoning. Moral recommendation cannot become the basis for political action without taking into account the full range of their real-life consequences, both the intended and unintended, as far as our empirical cognitive capacity permits us. This basic lesson of political common-sense and elaborate philosophic arguments as applied ethics seems to have been largely overlooked by enthusiasts for PR.

Consider some of the likely consequences of the adoption of the PR-mix system in India. Firstly, no party will get a majority in the Lok Sabha; given the rather poor record of the Indian party system on coalition making, this is a recipe for a series of unstable governments, popular frustration and political upheaval. Secondly, the stranglehold of party bosses on deciding the fate of a candidate would be nearly complete, eroding whatever remains of inner-party democracy in mainstream political parties. Thirdly, while the proportion of minority representation may increase, its character and effectiveness in terms of influencing the ruling party/coalition will suffer. The present system forces constituency-level social coalitions in a competition for political viability. It has the healthy effect of encouraging mainstream political parties to internalize the minority issues and leadership and encouraging minority voters to opt for mainstream parties. The PR system would have the opposite effect as minority voters would become a national constituency unto themselves, an informal version of a separate electorate, for which exclusive minority parties alone would be able to compete. This is not to say that a plurality system has no undesirable consequences, but to suggest that the balance of normative and realist consideration weighs against a change towards a proportionality system in India. (See Table 3.2)

Of late, the voice for a change in the electoral system has grown feeble. The attraction for PR has waned with the end of the era of one-party dominance of the Congress (or even one-party salience)

Table 3.2 : Candidates Elected with Majority of Votes in Lok Sabha Election, 1952-91

Year	Total Seats	Candidates Elected with 50% + Votes			
		Total	Congress	Leading Non-Congress Party	
1952	489	234	181	CPI	7
1957	494	300	229	CPI	14
1962	494	208	151	CPI	17
1967	520	209	99	SWA	23
1971	518	354	262	BJS	11
1977	542	475	128	JNP	266
1980	542	289	205	CPM	29
1984	542	386	296	TDP	27
1989	529	305	112	JD	89
1991	534	207	111	BJP	30

Note : Total seats refer to seats where elections were held.
Source : Same as Table 3.1.

and the rising spectre of a series of hung parliaments. Some major erstwhile champions of proportionate representation have developed a vested interest in the present electoral system (all the existing state governments headed by the opposition parties, the BJP and JD, could only have been formed on the basis of the same disproportionality they once bitterly complained about). With neither a foolproof intellectual argument nor the backing of a viable and enduring political coalition, the overwhelming considerations of familiarity and simplicity are enough to prevent any basic change in the electoral system in the future. Unless a dramatic change takes place or the demonstration effect of the global trend towards a mixed electoral system in the long run is decisive, India will have to live with the present system. And she may not be the worse off for it.

The various proposals for reforms of the electoral machinery relate to:

(a) composition and mode of appointment of the Election Commission;

(b) other measures to ensure the independence of the Election Commission; and

(c) set up of electoral machinery at the state and local level.

In the last few years the controversy regarding the size and the composition of the Election Commission has overshadowed the question of its mode of appointment. The Constitution does not specify any qualification or procedure for consultation to ensure the non-partisan character of the Election Commission, leaving it to democratic conventions. Like in other institutions, this expectation remains unfulfilled. The Tarkunde Committee noted the deterioration which had set in by the mid-seventies.

'In recent years, an impression had gained ground that the Election Commission is becoming less and less independent of the executive than in the earlier years of Independence, because the choice of the Chief Election Commissioner has not always been based on criteria which would command the confidence of all sections of public opinion. The practice of making it a berth for retiring Government officials has, perhaps, been responsible for the feeling that the incumbent so benefited will be beholden to the Government for his office' (1975:3).

The situation has deteriorated considerably since and is best exemplified by the back-room drama and political manipulations over the appointment of the current Chief Election Commissioner. The case for a better mode of selection of the Election Commissioners cannot be overstated. In this context, the recommendation of the Tarkunde Committee and the Dinesh Goswami Committee that the Election Commissioners should be appointed by the President in consultation with the Chief Justice of India and the Leader of the Opposition (or the leader of the largest opposition group in Lok Sabha) needs to be accepted forthwith. The consultation should have a statutory backing. Though not perfect, this method is surely better than what exists.

Too much attention has recently been given to the merits of a single-member or a multi-number Electoral Commision. Now that the 1993 Act and the Supreme Court judgment of July 1995 has made the constitutional position clear, it leaves only the practical considerations of efficiency and smooth functioning to be worked out. Every Chief Election Commissioner has always insisted that a single-member Election Commission is the best way to run it, but a self-serving institutional egotism seems to be at work here. The suggestions of the Tarkunde and Goswami Committees for a regular three member (as opposed to an unspecified multi-member) Election

Commission seems to be a better guarantee of independent functioning. In any case, the real question is not one of numbers but of their role. The recent Supreme Court judgment leaves open a dangerous loophole, which needs to be plugged; the executive may, at any point, fill the Election Commission with as many new members as would constitute a majority. The suggestion of a regular three member Election Commission to be appointed in this manner would be an effective way to prevent such a possibility.

Other issues related to the reform of the electoral machinery do not require elaborate discussion and justification and can, therefore, be listed as follows:

1. Unlike most other constitutional offices, the Constitution does not specify the tenure of the Chief Election Commissioner and other Election Commissioners. The suggestion of the Dinesh Goswami Committee for fixing it at 'a term of five years or sixty five years of age, whichever is later' and in no case beyond ten years in all, appears reasonable.
2. Similarly, their salary and service conditions have not been provided for in the Constitution. Although the experience of the functioning of institutions does not suggest that this issue has any bearing on its independence or otherwise, this change demanded by the Election Commissioner may be affected, if only as a symbol of its parity with other independent constitutional offices. The same is true of the status of the Chief Election Commissioners vis-a-vis the official hierarchy: it is a petty issue but may go towards enhancing the dignity of the office and advance its ability to deal with the ruling establishment.
3. A more serious need is to curb the practice of rewarding the 'well-behaved' Chief Election Commissioner with a plum position after retirement. Not surprisingly, the need to curb it does not figure in the list of reforms suggested by the Election Commissioner at different points. The Dinesh Goswami Committee suggestion should be accepted that there should be a ban on all post-retirement appointments by the government, including appointments

as a state governor.

4. The Election Commission should have an independent secretariat, with powers to recruit and regulate its functioning, as is the case with Parliament and the Union Public Service Commission.
5. At the state level, the Chief Electoral Officer, usually a senior Indian Administrative Service Officer, should exclusively be entrusted with election work and not saddled with other responsibilities as is the practice. The Election Commission should have a veto not only in selecting the CEO as is the case today, but also the Assistant/Joint/Deputy CEO, to prevent the state government from appointing its own favourites in such crucial positions.
6. At the district level, the electoral machinery is supervised by the District Election Officer (usually the head of the district administration), who is appointed by the Election Commission, and conducted by various government officials on deputation. There is need to provide the Election Commission effective control over these officers, including framing of charges, lodging of prosecution and disciplinary proceedings against them for breach of duty during their deputation . The transfer of officers connected with election work should be effected only with the concurrence of the Election Commission.

The Constitution of India along with some basic legislation (particularly the Representation of the People Act, 1950 and the Representation of the People Act, 1951 (hereafter RPA, 1950 and RPA, 1951) provide a fairly comprehensive set of basic regulations concerning elections in India. Like the rest of India's constitutional law, little has been left to the imagination of the practitioners or to conventions. The experience of the last four decades has confirmed the wisdom of this decision; the intense game of competitive politics in conditions of sudden universal enfranchisement leave little space for evolution of conventions. And to the extent that one can expect rules to hold in a game like this, they have done so in India.

This is not to say that these rules have never been stretched, flouted or violated in letter or spirit–the fate of a rule in any game—but to underline the crucial fact that, unlike many other post-colonial democracies, the game has not ended, and the difference between the winner and the looser remains undisturbed. The basic regulations have served as a fairly effective instrument for starting the process of democratisation and letting it work through the dynamics of competitive politics. That is why there has been little demand for any thorough overhaul of these regulations. Even the most elaborate list of proposed changes in the basic regulations (for example, EC 1992) is, in the final analysis, a case of fine-tuning rather than fundamental restructuring. The various proposals for change in the basic regulations fall under four heads.

The basic principle of universal adult franchise, without any discrimination, is one of the central pillars of the Indian Constitution (Article 326). Due to the dynamics of competitive politics, the right to vote is one of the few constitutional rights actually enjoyed by even the ordinary citizens of India. With intensification of democratisation, the importance of having one's name on the electoral roll is understood by every ordinary voter. For many, it is as their only proof of Indian citizenship. In other words, it is the mundane, everyday working of politics, rather than merely the letter of the Constitution, which has made universal adult franchise truly universal, or nearly so.

Looked at from a political perspective, the large number of errors, discrepancies and distortions which routinely characterise the electoral rolls in India need to be divided into three types in a discussion on electoral reform. First, there are the routine, unintended errors arising out of the notorious inefficiency of our bureaucracy. The second category comprises distortions arising out of partisanship of the official machinery, mainly its prejudices against the poor and powerless. In the third category fall the much publicised cases of political disenfranchisement of social communities (like the campaigns for the exclusion of 'Bangladeshi' voters in Assam and other states).

An undifferentiated understanding of these problems in the middle class discourse on electoral reform results in strategies, which are meant to overcome the first category of problems at the expense of the other two. Looked at from the vantage point of democratisation, the real problems are those of the second and third categories. More or less random distortions and discrepancies are a widespread nuisance and can often acquire scandalous proportions, but they do not threaten the democratic character of elections, something that the exclusion of the underprivileged or minorities does. Most of the standard suggestions for improving the electoral rolls can be quickly reviewed in this light. The suggestion to undertake intensive revision every alternate year or to fix four qualifying dates within a year for registration on attaining 18 years (assuming, of course, that everyone knows and celebrates birthdays) might bring about only a marginal improvement. More effective in this context would be the simplification of the procedure for enrolment, amendment and appeal (EC 1992: 9-11, especially points 3.3, 4.3, 11.2). Another useful suggestion is to conduct a selective check based on a rigorous stratified random sampling of, say, one percent of the booths, following the standard procedure adopted during the census (for a model, see L.P. Singh, 1986: 123-4).

In this context the issue of photo identity cards needs to be discussed separately, for it has been portrayed as the final solution to both the problem of defective electoral rolls and polling irregularities. Drawing upon the old fantasy that there are technological solutions to social and political problems, the idea is not new. But it is only in the last decade that the Election Commission has included it on its agenda of electoral reform (Shakdher 1980; 18, EC, 1984: 89, EC, 1992: 11-12). Thanks to the Chief Election Commissioner's obsession in the last couple of years, about 40 per cent of the Indian electorate has been photographed for these cards, whose utility is yet to be tested. That a large number of the identity cards supplied so far (around 15—20%) are defective, has already proved its critics right on at least one score; identity cards cannot, by themselves, eliminate errors of enumeration; they can only laminate them.

It is also doubtful if the identity card can do much to overcome polling irregularities, where the real problem is not an inability to put face to name (anyone who has cared to spend a few days in rural India would know that) but that those who wield local power and can put names to faces, do not like some faces making their appearance at the booth on polling day. Unless the local power structures are targeted the irregularities are bound to remain, identity card or no. However the identity card is going to be a multi-purpose document, everyone insists and what it can achieve is to establish a more effective system of state surveillance of ordinary citizen than has been achieved in the last 150 years of India's tryst with modernity.

It needs to be remembered here that those who live on the margins of society have historically been the victims of such systems of state surveillance. The latest suggestion of the computerisation of electoral rolls (EC, 1992:10) would take this process to its logical conclusion.

The idea that the Indian bureaucracy will suddenly exhibit an extraordinary level of efficiency when it comes to compiling electoral rolls is over-optimistic, to put it mildly. In any case, the future of Indian democracy does not hinge on this. It is far more realistic and urgent to think of eliminating the second and third kinds of problems identified above. And here, the best guarantee is publicity through channels of communication available to the non-literate population.

As it exists today, the entire process of enumeration or revision of electoral rolls is 'open' only to those who can read and write and who make it their daily practice to look for the fine print of public notices tucked away in English language newspapers or the notice board in a dingy corner of some government building. Thus the recent practice of using large hoardings and prominent advertising in local newspapers is a welcome change. This initiative needs to be carried forward to include the non-literate in its ambit. Finally, it needs to be stated that preparation of electoral rolls is not merely a bureaucratic exercise; it is the first stage of political mobilisation. Local bodies are the best guarantee of good electoral rolls.

The absence of any serious restrictions on contesting elections is a corollary of universal adult franchise in a democratic polity. Here again the Constitution lays down the fundamental norm of political equality (Article 14) and very minimal conditions for contesting the elections to the legislatures (Article 173).

These liberal regulations have, over the last four decades, succeeded in drawing a large number of participants into the electoral fray, sustaining its legitimacy as an arena of open contestation. The data presented in Table 3.3 shows a secular trend towards higher participation, including a progressively larger number of independent candidates. At the same time, a consolidation of the party system has meant that the probability of an independent candidate making it to the legislature or even saving his security deposit has fallen sharply over the decades (see Table 3.3).

On a political reading, this combination of higher participation with consolidation of party system would appear ideally suited to a

Table 3.3 : Candidates and their Performance in Lok Sabha Elections, 1952-91

Year of Election	Total No.	All Candidates		Independents	
		Average per seat	% lost deposit	Total No.	% lost deposit
1952	1874	3.8	39.8	533	66.6
1957	1519	3.1	29.4	481	60.1
1962	1985	4.0	43.5	480	79.0
1967	2369	4.6	50.8	864	86.2
1971	2784	5.4	61.4	1134	94.0
1977	2439	4.5	55.6	1224	97.2
1980	4629	8.8	73.8	2826	98.9
1984	5493	10.1	79.8	3878	98.8
1989	6160	11.6	81.2	3709	98.9
1991	8296	16.3	86.1	5230	99.5

Source : V.B. Singh, 1991.

young democracy.

But this is not how it gets depicted in the discourse on electoral reform. The dominant bureaucratic rationality views the capacity of democratic politics to draw out hitherto non-political sectors of Indian society into the arena of competitive politics and thus act as a vehicle of democratisation, as nothing more than a problem. As a result of this discursive twist, a 'multiplicity of candidates' has come to be seen as a malady of the electoral system, which needs to be cured through electoral reform. Ever since this diagnosis gained respectability about a decade ago, various remedies have been suggested to eliminate 'non-serious' candidates:

(i) Ten-fold increase in the amount of security deposit;
(ii) Differential rates of security deposit for independents and party candidates;
(iii) Increasing the minimum threshold for refund of security from 1/6th to 1/4th of valid votes;
(iv) Disqualification of candidates who fail to secure 20 per cent votes;
(v) Denial to independents of special facilities extended to candidates during the campaign period;

(vi) Raising the number of proposers required to validate nomination papers from one to ten.

(vii) Additional requirement of a passport size photograph duly attested by a gazetted officer of the central or state government; and

(viii) Additional requirement of a certificate from an officer that 'he either knows the candidate personally or that the candidate has been identified by someone who he knows personally'.

A poverty of imagination and an absence of political common sense, which runs through these proposals (especially iv, vii and viii above, the last two being the original contribution of the current Election Commission) need not detain us here; I have already said enough about the bureaucratic mind-set and its debilities. We need not go into the details of whether these measures will lead to a reduction in the number of candidates; suffice to note here that all these measures put together cannot achieve this goal presently, unless one is seeking to reverse the trend of democratisation itself.

But it is necessary to respond to the belief that proliferation of candidates including independents constitutes a malady which needs a cure. The arguments for reducing candidates are essentially managerial (difficulties of printing ballots, bigger boxes, confusion of names, and so on) or pseudo-political (fragmentation of the party system). The latter is patently mistaken: the FPTP system and the existing party system has already taken care of the problem of fragmentation. The share of votes polled by independents bears no relationship to their numbers.

Besides, the idea that candidates who stand no chance of winning election are useless to the electoral process and thus nuisance is to take a narrow view of the political process. The electoral arena is a training ground for political socialisation. It is a market place, as it were, where interests are articulated and then aggregated. A large number of independent candidates serve the crucial function of bringing to light issues and sections of society ignored by mainstream political processes. Even if their role is limited to filing the nomination and then withdrawing it, or starting the contest and then 'retiring' midway through the campaign, they have done their job. This has become even more important with the collapse of party organisations and their inability to perform these functions.

Finally, unrestricted opportunity to contest is a virtue in itself, even if it serves no purpose. The legitimacy of a democratic polity hinges, in some measure, on the belief that channels of representation are open to everyone; that a large number of persons take advantage of this opportunity should be seen as a source of strength for Indian democracy.

As for the administrative difficulty caused by multiplicity of candidates, the answer would lie in strengthening the contingent arrangements of the election machinery. Steps to discourage 'dummy' candidates (those who contest in order to acquire facilities for another candidate) are surely in order. The recent experiment of denying facilities to those candidates who have made public declarations to support another is a useful step in that direction. It would be justified, perhaps necessary, to ban the practice of a candidate contesting simultaneously from more than one constituency of the same category.

The drawing and re-drawing of the boundaries of electoral constituencies is not an issue which figures high on the agenda of electoral reform because India has not witnessed the kind of gerrymandering one associates with other democracies. This job was initially undertaken by the Election Commission but later assigned on its recommendation to an independent statutory body, the Delimitation Commission, comprising the Chief Election Commissioner and two serving or retired judges of the High/Supreme Court (according to the Delimitation Act, 1972). Although there have been instances of boundaries which tend to favour the Congress Party, these are not of the order which would put the independence of this mechanism under suspicion.

The problems that do obtain in the existing delimitation are structural in the sense that they do not arise out of instrumental manipulation intended to favour someone or some party: like all structural injustice its victims are too diffused and disorganised to recognise it, let alone protest against it. Two of these merit special attention. First, the embargo on fresh delimitation of constituencies till the first census after the year 2000 placed by the 42nd Amendment 1976 has created several anomalies. It is not known if this embargo furthered the noble cause of family planning (bizarre though it may sound, this was the official reason stated to justify the amendment: if constituencies are carved out afresh on the basis of patterns of population growth, there would be less incentive for family planning measures!), what it did achieve was a differential value of votes for different citizens. In particular, it systematically undervalued the votes of urban centres, which have experienced heavy immigration and, within these centres, the votes of the poor, the slum dwellers and the residents of urban villages who have migrated in the recent waves.

The data for seven Lok Sabha constituencies of Delhi, presented in Table 3.4, illustrate how a whimsical piece of legislation can compromise the principle of political equality with respect to the subalterns. It is futile now to work for a removal of this anomaly; one can only look forward to its lapsing in another five years. (see Table 3.4)

Table 3.4 : Electors in Delhi's Parliamentary Constituencies, 1977-91

Constituencies Name	Electors 1977 (in Lakhs)	Electors 1991 (in Lakhs)
New Delhi	2.70	4.56
South Delhi	3.82	9.03
Outer Delhi	4.40	18.66
East Delhi	5.11	15.82
Chandni Chowk	3.13	3.99
Delhi Sadar	3.09	5.34
Karol Bagh	3.15	5.09

Note : Outer Delhi and East Delhi areas account for the bulk of slums, unauthorised colonies, working class settlements and urbanised villages in the union territory of Delhi.

Source : Same as Table 3.1.

The second problem is not fully unintended and would not lapse automatically. The practice of rotating the reserved constituencies with every new delimitation was frozen in 1976. The continuous reservation of the same constituencies for two decades (in many cases three decades or more) has given rise to a group of beneficiaries, the MPs and MLAs from these constituencies, whose interest lies in preventing any rotation, and who have, cutting across party lines, formed a cartel for this purpose. This stalemate needs to be broken and the principle of rotation firmly adhered to in order to be fair both to non-SC leadership in these constituencies and SC aspirants in the remaining ones. (The rotation may take place only after two or three consecutive-elections on the basis of reservations, so as to give the new SC leadership a chance to stabilise.) It might entail waiting for a new party in power whose interests do not match those of the existing cartel.

Following the unstated principle of politics being a self-regulative activity, there are few restrictions on forming and running a political party in India. Till 1989 there was no formal registration of political parties. In 1989 the Representation of the People Act, 1951 was amended to introduce a provision (Part IV A, Section 29A) for registration of any political party which wishes to contest elections and claim the privileges of a party. It must make an application to the Election Commission, supply basic information with a copy of its constitution and get registered. As of now, the law is rather harmless, for there is little scope for non-registration or arbitrariness.

Formally speaking, the decision of the Commission is 'final' yet such provisions have never prevented the Indian judiciary from extending protection against acts of arbitrariness. The only substantive and controversial aspect of the requirement is that the Constitution of the party must contain a provision that it 'shall bear true faith and allegiance to the Constitution of India as by law established, and to the principles of socialism, secularism, and democracy, and would uphold the sovereignty, unity and integrity of India' [Section 29 A (5)].

At present this clause is no more than a formality, for the law gives the Election Commission no power to verify if the party believes in or acts upon this mandatory clause in the Constitution. Even so, the provision is open to misuse. At any rate, there should be no legal restriction on the ideologies which parties may espouse. The Goswami Committee had rightly suggested that this provision be done away with. But it is difficult to agree with its other recommendation of totally scrapping the requirements of registration. In itself registration is useful, provided it can be detached from the ethos of what was known as the licence-permitraj . Registration should be available as a matter of right, provided some procedural requirements are met.

Proposals for electoral reform have often expressed the need to regulate the functioning of political parties to ensure that they work on democratic lines and to check various maladies which had crept up over the years. It cannot be disputed that the internal malfunctioning of political parties introduces grave distortions in the democratic system. When Chief Election Commissioner, S.L. Shakdher had suggested legislation for norms of internal functioning of political parties (1980:10) some regulations on German political parties come to mind as a model.

Perhaps there is a case here for a minimal external regulation to ensure that the party's own constitution is adhered to and there is a minimal level of democracy in the party. But linking it to registration or eligibility to contest elections can do more harm than good. Given the present condition where abiding to its own constitution is an exception rather than a rule for political parties, such legislation would push the entire party-political activity into the domain of illegal functioning, which would lead to worse distortions. As a rule, political activity should be regulated as little as possible. At most, some minimal requirements of democratic functioning can be made a condition for eligibility for state subvention discussed in the next section.

Generally speaking, the role of money in elections, a standard concern of the discourse on electoral reform in India, belongs to that category of maladies which are systemic in origin. Given the structural relationship which obtains between economic and political power in the various forms of modern politics, it is naïve to view the influence of economic interests in elections as an unfortunate accident which can be removed through strict legislation. The growth of commercial society, accompanied by private property, unequal distribution of wealth and income and consumerism affect not just electoral politics but the entire gamut of social and political relations. Middle class enthusiasts of development, free enterprise and globalisation who express concern over the growing nexus between money and politics are thus applauding the cause while regretting the consequence. A radical democratic concern with eliminating or reducing the general nexus between politics and economic power cannot be confined within the agenda of electoral reform; it must relate to larger questions of transforming the structure of the economy, the model of development and the institutional design of democracy.

At a more concrete plane, the question refers to the direct relationship between the monetary resources of a candidate or party and the capacity to win an election. Although this direct relationship exists in today's India, it is not yet a decisive factor in the election outcome. Those with greater monetary resources do enjoy an edge in registering their presence in the electoral campaign. More importantly, those without resources often fail to cross the minimal threshold of publicity for this reason. But we must refrain from drawing an extreme picture of a direct causal relationship, for candidates and parties with virtually unlimited resources routinely lose the elections to those who cannot match them in these terms. Ruling parties always try to 'buy' votes and huge disbursement often takes place on this account, but the regularity with which ruling parties have lost the elections in the recent past is enough evidence that such tactics are far from successful. The effect of electoral waves has rendered money power far less effective than would otherwise have been the case. Each electoral realignment has been accompanied by the entry of a large number of resourceless candidates to the legislatures.

A complex and differentiated understanding of the role of money in electoral politics would suggest that the practical challenge of controlling its influence involves fixing a ceiling and a flow. The challenge is, first, to devise practical ways of ensuring that no candidate spends so much that it would put other candidates to enormous disadvantage and second, to ensure that every potential winner has the minimum resources to remain viable in the electoral contest. The existing literature shows insufficient awareness of the distinctiveness of the two challenges and the need to meet them separately.

Characteristically, the middle class discourse focuses its attention on the issue of ceiling, or on the existing law related to the ceiling on electoral expenses and ways to enforce it in practice. The Representation of the People Act, 1951 (Sections 10A, 77 and 78) makes it mandatory for every candidate who contests an election to file tax returns of his electoral expenses within a month of the election. It also lays down that the total expenditure should not exceed the 'prescribed limit'. The limit (under Conduct of Elections Rules, 1961, Rule 90) is raised after every decade or so, like the salary revision of government employees. The last revision, hastily undertaken in October 1994 after the current Chief Election Commissioner threatened to actually enforce the ridiculously low limit in operation then, fixes Rs.4,50,000 as the limit for a standard Lok Sabha constituency and Rs.1,35,000 to Rs.1,50,000 for Vidhan Sabha.

In practice, however three flaws have reduced the ceiling to a mockery:

1. The ceiling is invariably fixed so low as to make it impossible to enforce. It represents a clerk's version of the minimum amount it would take to run something like a campaign, if everything was available from government-owned fair price shops. Though there are no rigorous studies on actual expenses, estimates in the 1993 assembly elections show that every serious candidate spent several times more than the legal limit. The minimum amount an honest candidate from a resourceless party and poor family had to spend was more than twice the existing legal ceiling!
2. The existing law does not provide for any cross checking of the returns filed by the candidate. So there is no way to verify whether the returns are true, without recourse to an election petition against the winner. In the assembly elections held in late 1994 and early 1995, the EC tried to arm itself with these powers and enlisted the services of revenue officials and private accountants. It did create a scare and instilled financial discipline among candidates, but a year later nothing is known about the results of this highly publicised move.
3. A notorious amendment to the law brought about in 1974 has rendered the provision virtually inoperative even in a court of law. The definition of 'expenditure' for the purposes of ceiling now excludes any expenditure for the election by 'a political party or by any other association or body of persons or by any individual (other than the candidate or his election agent)'. It means that the sky is the limit to what can be spent, provided the amount can be shown to have been spent by someone other than the candidate.

If the legal provision of ceiling on electoral expenses is to have more than ornamental value, it must be changed in one of the following ways. Either the statutory limit should be scrapped altogether and replaced by a selective ban on certain kinds of expenditure (any bribe to voters in cash or kind, for instance). Or the existing provisions should be amended to provide for (i) much higher ceiling than what currently exists (say Rs. 15 to 20 lakhs for a Lok Sabha constituency); (ii) regular revision of the ceiling before every general election; (iii) all the expenditure, irrespective of who paid for it, to be brought within the purview of this provision; (iv) candidate/agent's authorisation to be necessary for election related expenditure by others; (v) mechanism for routine verification/auditing of the return of expenditure; and (vi) publicity of the returns filed by the candidates in the local press.

The reported suggestion of the Election Commission to increase the ceiling is a good one. An effective legal ceiling can at best be one of the factors which contribute to reducing the direct influence of money on elections. The existence of local party organisations is another crucial factor, for in its absence an election campaign is forced to imitate commercial advertising campaigns which naturally raises the cost. The most effective measures and the only guarantee lies in a political culture of simplicity, so that any ostentatious expenditure can be expected to work against the candidate's electoral prospects.

The other aspects of electoral finance, namely how to ensure that some minimum resource is available to popular or potentially popular candidates, is a neglected area. Not just electoral finance, the entire question of funds for political activities and political activists has merely received occasional comments about the kind of funds that are questionable (black market, corporate or foreign funding). In this respect the public reaction to the hawala scam was no different; outrage over 'bad' money, but little thought about where 'good' money will come from. The consequences of this silence are worse in the Indian case, given the co-existence of extreme economic inequality with democratic processes of change, than in western democracies from where it is borrowed.

In the last two decades, the collapse of intermediary institutions has worsened the position of non-upper class participants in electoral politics. The consequences are familiar: only the well-heeled can contest elections; political parties select individuals who can afford to contest; others must compromise with the local rich; once in power, politicians must develop a personal-political fund. The condition of small parties is similar.

A minimum level of institutionalised funding of political activity in general elections in particular is a pressing need today. A fact, which no one wishes to confront, is that politics needs more (legitimate) money than is available. A serious response to this need has receded as politics/politician-bashing becomes the favourite sport of the middle class. Most suggestions are vaguely made and do not go beyond some meagre assistance in kind (free paper, postage and so on). Though valuable, the Dinesh Goswami Committee report suffers from this limitation.

In this context a proposal for state subvention of elections by Pai Panandiker and Ramashray Roy (1994) merits close consideration. It recommends: (i) State funding of elections on an exclusive basis; (ii) The creation of an Election Fund at Rs.10 per vote polled throughout the country; (iii) A special funding agency or the EC to administer the fund; (iv) The fund to be apportioned on the basis of votes secured by candidates in the election, subject to the ceiling of Rs.1 million per seat contested; (v) The amount to be released to individual candidates (and not political parties) on the basis of nominations made; (vi) 50 per cent to be released as an advance, before elections, on the basis of previous performance; (vii) The minimum threshold for eligibility for state subvention to be 20 per cent of national votes for national or major parties (10 per cent for minor or new parties) or 10-12 per cent votes in a constituency for independent candidates; and (viii) Detailed account of the candidate to be audited by the EC.

The basic framework of a state-sponsored Election Fund to be apportioned according to vote share of different parties/candidates is sound and needs to be accepted immediately. However, a principal objective is to discourage 'non-serious' parties and candidates. I have already argued above why this should not be on the agenda of electoral reform. In any case the logic of the FPTP system is already against them. Instead of reinforcing this systemic prejudice, the Election Fund can be used to encourage healthy functioning. To my mind, the Panandiker-Roy proposal should be accepted with the following modifications:

(a) State funding should not be exclusive; parties and

candidates should be free to raise funds from other sources to an overall ceiling of expenditure.

(b) The amount should be given to parties, which should be left free to disburse it to the çandidates/party offices.

(c) The party must spend at least 50 per cent of the funds during the election campaign and it should be allowed to spend the remaining amount (up to 50%) during the next five years before the subsequent general election.

(d) The entire amount should be accounted for and audited without any restriction on internal budgeting.

(e) The eligibility threshold should operate at the state level and be reduced to the bare minimum (say 2% of the vote share in a state or 5% in a constituency, in the case of an independent) so as to exclude only the dummy candidates or paper organisations.

(f) The payment should be made conditional upon régular democratic election of the highest decision-making body and office bearers of the party (the Election Commissioner and the Supreme Court should have the power to adjudicate any dispute in this regard).

The basic idea is to bring nearly every serious party within the ambit of state funding, provide them with some minimum financial resources to contest election, carry out regular political work in-between elections, and to link this assistance to internal democratic functioning. As for the burden on the exchequer, the Election Fund would have amounted to Rs.27.8 billion in the 1991 election (at Rs.10 per vote polled). It would go up to 35 billion in the 1996 Lok Sabha election (assuming a little over 60% turnout). The amount, especially when spread over a period of five years, is a small fraction of India's annual budget, smaller than the annual grant of a small size ministry. Bigger amounts have changed hands in recent instances of political corruption. Surely this is a small price to pay for encouraging the healthy democratic functioning of political parties, however limited its impact.

This point has been accepted, at least in principle, by all major non-Congress parties. But the casual manner in which this debate has been conducted in the last two months indicates that our political establishment is unprepared to undertake any significant restructuring of the pattern of electoral financing.

Having discussed the major issue of expenditure, we are left with the following categories of problems/proposals related to the election campaign: (i) nature of election appeal; (ii) conduct of candidates/ parties during the campaign; (iii) use of government power/machinery; and (iv) other limitations on campaign.

The question of caste/community-based appeal has attracted attention in the last few years, in the wake of the Mandal-Mandir controversies. The legal-constitutional position is unambiguous on this point. There is no bar on election appeal on grounds of caste and religion (a point confirmed by the Supreme Court). The Model Code of Conduct calls upon the parties not to 'appeal to caste or communal feelings for securing votes', but its provisions cannot be enforced in a court of law. There is definitely a ban, however, on any election-related act which 'promotes or attempts to promote on grounds of religion, race, caste, community or language, feelings of enmity or hatred, between different classes of citizens of India' (Section 125, RP Act, 1951; also Section 153A of Indian Penal Code). Demands have often been raised to make the law more stringent by making any appeal on caste/religion a ground for disqualification. In 1993 the government tried, unsuccessfully, to bring a constitutional and legal amendment to this effect.

On balance, the arguments for changing the existing constitutional-legal position are not compelling. Competitive politics is bound to establish linkages with social cleavages, often accentuating them. The resultant problems can be handled effectively only by a politics of social coalition made through a discourse of integration. If that fails, an institutional arrangement according to the consociational model needs to be worked out. A simple-minded ban can only be counterproductive. In fact, it is likely to become an instrument to block the expression of the legitimate grievances and interest of minorities and backward castes in the political arena.

The issue of an appropriate conduct of candidates and parties during the campaign has already been codified in the Model Code of Conduct outlined by the Election Commission and approved by representatives of all major political parties in 1982. It lays down elaborate guidelines regarding the organisation of election meetings, processions, conduct on polling day and at the polling booth, the nature of election appeal and other general matters. Although the Code has no statutory standing, its guidelines are a reiteration of the existing legal provisions and can easily be enforced by the law and order machinery.

But the last section of the Code of Conduct, dealing with misuse of official machinery and power by the ruling party, needs to be given statutory force. These guidelines (Section VII, Code of Conduct) deal with combining official visits with election campaigning, misusing official transport, monopolising public facilities, issuing advertisements to highlight the government's image, discretionary grants or payments and announcement/initiation of new schemes. As of now the Election Commission can do no more than issue public warning to the state authorities.

Seshan tried to make it more effective by linking its non-observance to cancellation of elections. And it did work sometimes, though there have been cases of the Chief Election Commissioner clearly exceeding his brief, or the 'punishment' being invited by the ruling party, keen to avoid/postpone an inconvenient by-poll. The Dinesh Goswami Committee has already recommended that this part of the Code be brought on the statute book and its violation be made punishable. In addition to the point mentioned above, it includes a ban on the transfer of election-related officials before or during the election period without the consent from the Election Commission. These recommendations are uncontroversial in so far as no political party has opposed them. Even the Congress has demanded the implementation of these provisions in states where it has faced elections without being in office. It must form an essential part of the legislative package for electoral reform.

However, several recent suggestions for ensuring a 'clean' campaign go against the spirit of democratisation. The Election Commission's suggestion on reducing the campaign period from three to two weeks falls in the category. It says something about the bureaucratic mind-set that the only consideration in deciding upon this period is the time required for printing ballot papers. It does not concern anyone that this period is meant for political campaign, canvassing and accountability. That, given the size and the electorate of a parliamentary constituency (comprising about 500 villages), a period of less than three weeks is just not enough for serious campaigning. The reduction in campaign time would make the vote more dependent upon distant media images and also reduce direct accountability of the parties and candidates. But that perhaps is a sign of progress in the register of middle class sensibilities.

Before the state assembly elections of 1994-95, the Chief Election Commissioner issued a series of fresh instructions about the campaign. These included restricted hours for campaigning, ban on cut-outs or wall-writing and several other ways of saving public 'inconvenience'. Apparently, the 'public' in question is urban and middle class and state regulation is the only way to help it. If we take a wider political view of its interests these new regulations appear in a different light. It may be relevant to note that campaigning in urban working class areas or a place like the walled city in Delhi can begin only after the Chief Election Commissioner's deadline has expired. Or that wall-writing is one of the cheapest media available to small parties and poor candidates. But the middle class drive for clean politics has little patience with such trivial considerations.

The bankruptcy of the managerial perspective on electoral reform is nowhere as evident as in its approach to counter polling and counting irregularities on which the discourse on electoral reform focuses. Unable to come to terms with the fact of brute power leading to these irregularities, the middle class discourse turns to technology and law, the two privileged instruments of modernity, as the solution to all ills. It does not and cannot come to terms with the fact that the real problem lies with the way technology is used and the way law is enforced which itself derives from the nature of the social structure and the relationships of power.

Besides, the sense of scandal, which surrounds any discussion on polling and counting irregularities, leads to a loss of perspective on the extent to which these irregularities and manipulations routinely characterise Indian elections. But there is no reliable estimate of the extent to which these irregularities affect the popular character of the electoral outcome. While these irregularities are significant enough to cause concern, they are still not on a scale which may differentiate India and a majority of third world democracies.

Not withstanding allegations to the contrary, there are few cases where a candidate gets elected despite the fact that the voters did not want to vote for him. The instances where a party came to power mainly by rigging a general election are still fewer: all elections held in Jammu and Kashmir (except 1977), many elections in the insurgency-prone states of the North-East and West Bengal in 1972. In recent years electoral outcome in several districts of Bihar, eastern U.P. and Telengana has become suspect. Despite all these qualifications, it is necessary to insist that in a minimal procedural sense, India continues to have fair elections. So much administrative and policy attention has been focussed on details of polling and counting that it is difficult to add any more than the following remarks:

1. It would be naïve to expect the voting machine to solve the problems of irregularity in the electoral process, for these problems are a function of local power structures which do not admit of technological solutions. However, the government has spent a fortune in acquiring the machines, it has already been tried out and the necessary legal change carried out. With such effort invested into it, the machine is perhaps worth trying if only to dispel its mythical charms.
2. It would be helpful to give the Election Commission some additional powers under RP Act :

   (a) It should be free to act on a report of electoral malpractice from any source besides the Returning Officer;
   (b) The power to declare polling in an entire constituency void and order re-poll should be formally given to the Election Commission;
   (c) The Election Commission should be empowered to establish investigative and prosecution agencies to deal with electoral offences; and
   (d) The Election Commission's instructions regarding booth capturing should have statutory force.

3. In some respects the existing law related to electoral offences needs to be strengthened, though an indiscriminate raising of penalties for all the offences recommended by the Election Commission (1992: 30-34) should be resisted. Some provisions which need to be included or made stricter are:

(a) Increased penalty for officers at elections acting for candidates or influencing voting;
(b) Ban on carrying of firearms and lethal weapons on polling day;
(c) Ban on plying of mechanically propelled four wheelers on polling day;
(d) Impersonation to be made an electoral offence leading to imprisonment;
(e) Booth capturing to be made a cognizable offence leading to more stringent punishment.

4. The Election Commission should encourage and facilitate free observation and investigation cf polling and counting by the media, human rights groups of long standing, non-partisan NGO's and international observers. A system for 'accreditation' of such groups should be evolved.
5. The earlier practice of booth-wise counting should be revived both as a measure to counter polling/counting irregularities and as feedback necessary for the democratic process.
6. As in Bangladesh, it should be made constitutionally mandatory to hold by-elections within a specified period, say six months, of a seat falling vacant.

Needless to emphasise, these steps in themselves cannot be a guarantee of free and fair polling. These can strengthen the hands of poll officials, if they want to ensure free and fair poll. But measures of electoral reform which ultimately depend on the good intentions of the bureaucracy are bound to fail when it comes to systematic discrimination against marginalised groups. In the last instance, irregularities arising out of local power structures can only be met by counter political mobilization. All said and done, the Indian People's Front (now CPI-ML) in central Bihar and the BSP in some parts of U.P. have done more to enfranchise the Dalits than all the legislation on electoral reform put together.

This brings us to the final and most difficult question: assuming that the arguments offered above for bringing about a certain type of reform are good and workable, who will bell the cat? And how? The difficulty arises partly from the failure of modern political theory (except in its Marxist variant) to address the question of agency with the requisite care and rigour. Standing as they do on the boundary shared by moral reasoning and causal analysis, such questions require the highest skill of political judgment which must combine ethical sensitivity and sociological realism. In its absence, a non-response takes over. Like other vexing questions confronting contemporary India, this seems to have happened to the intellectual responses on the question of electoral reform as well.

But the real source of the problem is located in the self-referential character of the question. Modern societies are organised around the principles of primacy of politics. In the proverbial last instance the decision concerning any question of public importance must emerge out of the political arena. This raises a simple question: if politics regulates everything else, who regulates politics? The question does not admit an easy answer. It is the political counterpart of the theological query about who made God, if He made the universe. Like the theologian, a theorist of modern politics must also come up with one variant or another of the principle of self-regulation: that which regulates everything else must also regulate itself. The deep silence or exuberant fantasising which often characterises the discourse on electoral reform, when it comes to the question of agency, should be seen as a way to come to terms with the assumption of self-regulation of politics.

The insistence that we must come to terms with the self-regulatory character of politics, however, does not mean that we can do no more than naïvely hope for self-discipline by the politician. An acceptance of the self-regulation of politics need not reduce us to a state of helplessness, for there are ways or processes through which politics can be regulated without depending upon the notorious incapacity and unwillingness of the politicians to regulate themselves. A careful thinking about the relative merits or otherwise of the three main routes and their possible combinations alone can lead us towards an answer to the difficult question of the agency for electoral reform.

The first and most obvious alternative is the legal one. The idea that the world of politics can be reformed by an elaborate set of strict laws has always tempted middle class reformers. But more laws do not always mean greater morality. If anything, the relationship is closer to its opposite; since any law for its enforcement must depend on the very class it seeks to regulate. Besides, to expect the political class to enact such legislation of its own accord is to be over optimistic. In any case, there are aspects of politics (like inner-party organisation, leadership attributes, political culture) which simply cannot be dictated by law. This is not to say that legal-constitutional changes are entirely useless—some have already been suggested above—but merely to suggest that law cannot be the principal instrument of electoral reform.

The other alternative is the regulation of politics by the citizen. In the last instance, political norms can be instituted only if citizens are prepared to uphold them and punish the transgressors. The fear of losing the next elections has proved a more effective deterrent than court summons or an elusive conscience. There are other relatively less effective instruments of regulation such as protest, agitation or a popular movement. In other words, the real solution to the ill of electoral politics lies in more politics, electoral or otherwise.

However, regulation by the citizen suffers from the problem involved in all determination in-the-last-instance, namely that the proverbial instance never arrives and we are forced to live infinitely in the no-man's land of last-but-one-instance. Besides, there are practical difficulties. Voting is a complex judgment which tends to overlook legitimate but secondary considerations (as long as empowerment of backward classes is the primary agenda, considerations of rigging or even misgovernance will remain irrelevant in Bihar). The vote by itself is insufficient to attend to the secondary preferences of the voter. Besides, it is of no use when seeking remedy for a denial of the right to vote itself.

Those who are not satisfied with legal remedies and cannot wait for the ultimate regulation by the citizen to happen, those who seek to be effective here and now, must look for a third alternative which lies in strengthening the intermediary political institutions and the institutions of civil society. The former would cover the entire gamut of political institutions which mediate between the citizen and the state and whose collapse has accentuated electoral malpractices in the first place. Strengthening of party organisations, evolving norms for inner-party democracy, developing conventions on career mobility and retirement from politics, institutionalising 'white' money in parties and innovating non-legal forms of inquiry and punishment in a party are some ways of removing the current ills of electoral democracy.

These need to be supplemented by checks and regulation from outside the world of politics. The crucial task here is to expand the effective reach of media, civil liberties organisations and non-party movement groups beyond the cultural ghetto of the urban middle classes.

A strengthening and transformation of these crucial institutions of civil society is a prerequisite for the discourse on public scrutiny. Human rights reports and investigative journalism to be accessible to the subalterns in their own register of sensibilities. An effective intervention in this arena would go a long way towards developing a political culture in which the current democratic upsurge can be anchored. It may also serve to rescue the transformative potential of the discourse on electoral reform and prevent it from being hijacked by the anti-politics of the English-speaking elite.

References

Advani, L.K. (1970): 'Indian Electoral System—A Plea for Reform', *Journal of Constitutional and Parliamentary Studies*, IV(4), October-December.

Advani, L.K. (1984): 'Electoral Reforms: Imperative and Urgent', *Journal of Constitutional and Parliamentary Studies*, XVIII (1-2), January-June.

Bhambhri, C.P. (1970): 'Electoral Reform and Party System in India—A Plea for Proportional Representation', *Journal of Constitutional and Parliamentary Studies*, IV(4), October-December.

Bhambhri, (1990): Committee on Electoral Reforms (Dinesh Goswami Committee), Report of the Committee on Electoral Reforms, Legislative Department, Ministry of Law and Justice, GOI, New Delhi.

DeSouza, Peter R. (1992): 'For and Against Participatory Democracy', in Nageshwar Prasad (ed.), *J.P. and Social Change*, Radiant, New Delhi.

Dunleavy, Patrick and Helen Margetts (1995): 'Understanding the Dynamics of Electoral Reform', *International Political Science Review*, 16(1), January.

——, (1983): Election Commission of India (EC), 1984, First Annual Report, New Delhi.

——, (1992): Election Commission of India (EC), Proposals of the Election Commission for Electoral Reforms (Forwarded to GOI in February 1992), New Delhi

——, (1993): Electoral Politics in Pakistan. National Assembly Elections, Report of SAARC-NGO observers, Vikas, New Delhi.

——, (1995): Ministry of Law, Justice and Company Affairs, Manual of Election Law (A Compilation of the Statutory Provisions Governing Elections to Parliament and State Legislatures). 2 Vols. Delhi Controller of Publications, GOI.

Pai Panandiker, V.A. and Ramashray Roy (1994): *Financing of Elections*, Centre for Policy Research, New Delhi.

Prasad Bimal (ed.) (1980): *A Revolutionary's Quest: Selected Writings of Jayaprakash Narayan*, Oxford, Delhi.

Shakdher, S.L. (1980): Electoral Reforms for India, The Voters' Council and Citizens for Democracy, Delhi.

Shakdher, S.L. (1984): 'Electoral Reforms', *Journal of Constitutional and Parliamentary Studies*, XVIII(1-2), January-June.

Sheth, D.L. (1991): *Crisis of Representation*, Seminar (385), September.

Singh, V.B. (1991): 'Multiplicity of Candidates in Elections: A Case for Upward Revision in Security Deposits', *Indian Journal of Public Administration*, XXXVI(3), July-September.

Singh, L.P. (1986): *Electoral Reform: Problems and Suggested Solutions*, Uppal, New Delhi.

Swami, Praveen (1995): 'Seshan Tamed: Supreme Court Blow to the CEC's Ways', *Frontline*, 11 August.

— —, (1975): Tarkunde Committee, Report of the Committee on Electoral Reforms, *Citizens for Democracy*, Delhi.

4

Electoral Reforms in India

Need for a Second Look at the First-Past-the-Post System

SANDEEP SHASTRI

Electoral reform initiatives need to primarily focus their attention on ensuring greater democratic intensity and providing ways and means for a more authentic articulation of the citizen's voice. Reforms in the electoral system need to aim at ensuring more effective forms of representation. The pressing need for electoral reforms in India, has now been voiced for several years and has found a prominent mention in the election manifestos of all the major political parties. The Tarkunde Committee, Dinesh Goswami Committee and the Law Commission have made several useful suggestions in this regard. While, an activist Election Commission has, in recent years, contributed significantly to sanitising the electoral process, the implementation of comprehensive electoral reforms is long overdue.

In this context, a second look at the first-past-the-post system (FPTP) becomes vital. In its recommendations, the Election Commission has drawn attention to the need to initiate a national debate on the present electoral system, 'so as to have a broad national consensus on this very fundamental subject'[1]. The Law Commission too, in its proposals, has opined that the deficiencies of the FPTP system 'have become too evident in recent years, particularly on account of the increase in the number of political parties contesting elections'.[2]

It is interesting to note in this regard, that in the 1999 general elections, the election manifestos of both the National Democratic Alliance (NDA) and the Congress while reiterated their firm commitment to electoral reforms were silent on the specific question of the need for a second look at the electoral system. The NDA manifesto states that it will 'introduce necessary electoral reforms on the basis of the recommendations of the Goswami Committee, the Inderjit Gupta Committee and the Law Commission so as to deal with the malaise of defections, corruption and criminalisation of politics'.[3] The Congress manifesto speaks of the party's commitment to introduce 'comprehensive electoral reform bill... based as much on the ideas put forward by citizens organisations as on ideas by political parties in Parliament and ideas put forward by the Election Commission in recent years[4].

Under the FPTP system it is noticed that the electoral verdict is not effectively mirrored in the composition of the House. This system permits a candidate to win an election from a constituency merely because he/she polls the highest number of votes and the fact that he/she secured less than 50 per cent of the valid votes polled is of little electoral significance (see Table 4.2). A candidate wins the election not so much because of the 'majority behind him, but because he has managed to split the votes against him'[5]. Multi-cornered contests are largely responsible for this trend. As a result, the present electoral system has resulted in an alarming and disproportionate gap between the percentage of votes polled and the percentage of seats won by the various political parties. Ruling parties at the centre have come to power as a result of a 'manufactured majority'[6], as in all the Lok Sabha elections, on no occasion has the party that formed the government after the elections, polled more than 48 per cent of the votes (see Table 4.1). The percentage of seats won by the ruling party has always been significantly higher than the percentage of votes polled by it. The FPTP system has also permitted political parties to rationalise the election results according to their political convenience. A party which emerges as the ruling party after a poll, makes a strong claim to have secured the voters' mandate, even as it underplays the fact that the percentage of votes it has polled is substantially lower than the seats secured. On the other hand, the party that fails to secure a majority, focuses on the relatively high proportion of votes it has polled and highlights the seats won/votes polled distortion in the ruling party.

An in-depth analysis of the results of three successive Assembly elections in Karnataka points to the limitation of the FPTP system.

Table 4.1 : Percentage of Votes polled and seats won in the Lok Sabha elections by the Party which formed the government immediately after the poll

Year	% of Votes polled	% of Seats won
1998	25	33
1996	20	30
1991	37	45
1989	18	26
1984	48	77
1980	43	67
1977	41	54
1971	44	68
1967	41	54
1962	45	73
1957	48	75
1952	45	74

Table 4.2 : Percentage of Winners who polled less than 50 % of valid votes in Lok Sabha elections

Year	% of winners who polled less than 50% of valid votes polled
1991	53
1989	45
1984	31
1980	46
1977	12
1971	31
1967	58
1962	56
1957	52
1952	61

In the 1989 Karnataka Assembly elections, the Congress party secured 176 of the 224 seats (79%) even though it polled only 44 per cent of the votes. The Janata Dal on the other hand, secured only 24 seats (11%) in spite of polling 27 per cent of the votes. More than 109 of the 176 Congress (62%) victors polled less than 50 per cent of the valid votes and the combined votes of the candidates in the 2nd and

Table 4.3 : 1989 Karnataka Assembly Election: Winners securing less than 50 % of valid votes polled

	C	J	B	O	Total
46-50	43	2	—	4	49
41-45	35	4	1	3	43
36-40	23	10	—	3	36
31-35	7	2	3	2	14
26-30	1	—	—	1	2
21-25	—	—	—	—	—
	109	18	4	13	144

C: Congress, J: Janata Dal, B: BJP, O: Others.

3rd position were higher than those of the winner (see Table 4.3; also for details see Shastri and Vinod, 1991). Similarly, in the 1994 Karnataka Assembly elections, though the Janata Dal secured 115 of the 224 seats (52 %) it polled only 33 per cent of the votes. On the other hand, while the Congress won only 36 seats (16%) it polled as much as 27 per cent of the votes. As many as 76 of the 115 (66%) Janata Dal MLA's won by securing less than 50 per cent of the valid

Table 4.4 : 1994 Karnataka Assembly Election: Winners securing less than 50 % of valid votes polled

	C	J	B	O	Total
46-50	4	22	7	8	41
41-45	4	14	5	5	28
36-40	10	20	6	10	46
31-35	8	8	9	—	25
26-30	3	12	4	4	23
21-25	2	—	1	4	07
	31	76	32	31	170

C: Congress, J: Janata Dal, B: BJP, O: Others

votes and the combined votes of the candidates in the 2nd and 3rd position were higher than those of the winner (see Table 4.4, also for details see Shastri, 1995). In the 1999 Assembly elections, though the Congress secured as many as 132 seats (59%), it polled only 41 per cent of the votes. The BJP and the Janata Dal (United)—who were poll allies—secured over 34 per cent of the popular votes polled but won only 63 seats (28%). As many as 72 of the 132 Congress

Table 4.5 : 1999 Karnataka Assembly Election: Winners securing less than 50 % of valid votes polled

	C	B	JU	JS	O	Total
46-50	28	6	3	1	2	40
41-45	18	7	3	1	3	32
36-40	11	10	2	3	4	30
31-35	10	6	1	3	4	24
26-30	3	2	2	1	—	8
21-25	2	1	—	—	2	5
	72	32	11	9	15	139

C: Congress, B: BJP, JU: Janata Dal (United), JS: Janata Dal (Secular), O: Others.

MLA's (55%) secured less than 50 per cent of the votes polled (see Table 4.5).

In view of the glaring anomalies that have arisen as a result of the first-past-the-post system, there is an urgent need to replace the system with a more suitable one. Several suggestions have been made in this regard.

The Tarkunde Committee (Committee to suggest Electoral Reforms appointed by Jayaprakash Narayan on behalf of the Citizens for Democracy) in its Report, categorically stated that the FPTP system did not 'lead to a fair reflection of the popular will in the legislatures (and) .... The seat-vote distortion in India has reached grave proportions'[7]. The Committee went on to add that the objection to the distortion caused by the FTPT system were neither academic nor abstract but because it had led to 'concrete evils and ... created a situation where there is danger of people losing faith in democratic institutions'[8]. The Committee spoke of the possibility of adopting the 'Mixed system' —a combination of the PR and plurality system—which would result in the total strength of each party (directly elected + elected from the list) being roughly proportionate to the votes polled by the party. However, the Committee also acknowledged the weaknesses of the system and called for a widespread public debate for a consensus to emerge[9]. The Committee on Electoral Reforms (1990) headed by Dinesh Goswami also favoured an exhaustive debate on the electoral system and recommended the appointment of an expert committee for this purpose.

The Law Commission of India, in its recent proposals on 'Reform of the Electoral Laws' has suggested that the strength of the Lok Sabha be increased from the present 550 to 688 (138 additional members, a 25% increase). The additional 138 members could be elected as per the List system. These 138 seats could be divided state-wise as per population (smaller states being clubbed together). After the elections for the 550 direct seats have been completed, the total number of votes secured by each recognised political party in a state should be calculated and the additional seats allotted to a state (from among the 138) be proportionately divided between the recognised political parties on the basis of the total votes polled by each of them in that state/group of states. Prior to the election, every recognised political party must publish a state-wise list of their nominees under the list system.

The proposals made by the Tarkunde Committee and the Law Commission seek to combine the benefits of a Proportional Representation (PR) and FPTP system. However, it must be realised that any PR system increases 'the disjunction between popular vote and government formation'[10]. Further a List system or partial List system increases the control exercised by the party leadership and given the lack of internal-democracy in most political parties, such a system may result in party dictatorship. Under the FPTP electoral system, minorities and social groups are able to forge social coalitions in a competitive political environment. Under a PR system, the proportion of representation of various groups may increase but the 'character and effectiveness' of this representation is likely to suffer and may also result in minority voters becoming a 'national constituency'.[11]

Yet another proposal for reforming the electoral system has been put forward by the Ex-Vice President of India, Late Shri Krishna Kant (this suggestion was first made by him when he was the Governor of Andhra Pradesh). He has made out a case for a system of negative voting. A negative vote provision—wherein a voter would have the benefit of an extra column on the ballot paper stating, none of the above—would, he felt, be a legal channel for the expression of dissent[12]. In the convocation address at the National Law School of India University, Late Shri Krishna Kant once again pleaded for the 'rejection vote' and emphasised that it was not a negative solution as negating, the negative aspects of the political process becomes positive, non-violent action for cleansing the process of power. Parties too would be forced to field the best among the people.[13] However, the negative vote suggestion may at the most, serve as a negative solution to the problem and will in no way positively contribute to strengthening the electoral system.

The 'binary voting' option has also been suggested as an alternative to the FPTP system. Under binary voting, each voter has both a positive and a negative vote—the positive vote for the most preferred candidate and the negative vote for the most disliked candidate. The negative votes, a candidate secures are subtracted from the positive votes in order to decide the winner. The binary voting system would compel political parties and contestants to make an effort to not merely secure the support of the majority but also ensure that no antagonism is generated against them. It is argued that this system would result in the dissolution of vote banks and 'only those who truly synthesise the total spectrum of public opinion will succeed'[14].

Both the negative vote and binary voting system seek to find a solution to the middle class apathy to the electoral process. Voter apathy in middle class urban pockets is a clear trend witnessed across several elections in India. In Karnataka, every Assembly and Lok Sabha election held since 1983, has seen Bangalore city district registering the lowest voter turnout. In the 1999 elections, if the State recorded a turnout of over 67 per cent, the constituencies in Bangalore city registered a turnout of 53 per cent. Voter apathy in urban areas is reflective of the 'middle class' attitude towards politics in general and elections in particular. Urbanites tend to point out to the futility of the electoral process and the lack of credible choices with which they are presented to explain their disinterest in electoral politics. In reality, the impact and utility of the electoral process for the urban voter is limited as they (urbanites) rarely seek the assistance of elected representatives to solve their problems as they have access to other avenues in this regard[15].

A more meaningful and practical alternative appears to be the second ballot system. Under such a system, if no candidate secures more than 50 per cent of the valid votes polled in the first round of elections in a constituency, a second run-off is held between the top two contestants within a week. As a result the candidate who wins the election from a constituency secures a majority of the votes polled. Adopting the second ballot system appears to be the most effective alternative for overcoming the defects of the first-past-the-post system. Candidates would have to take their election campaigns more seriously, and electoral victories would not merely be achieved by dividing the opponents' votes on caste or religious lines or concentrating on securing the votes of one segment of the voters. Those elected could then be termed as being genuinely representatives of the constituency from which they have been elected from[16]. Further, in a competitive party system, a second ballot vote would encourage the polarisation of political forces and contribute to the emergence of a bi-polar alliance system.[17]

The merit of the 'second ballot system' becomes clear if the examples of the three elections cited earlier (1989, 1994 and 1999 Karnataka Assembly elections) are examined. In 1989, 144 of the 224 MLA's elected (64 %) secured less than 50 per cent of the valid votes. 109 of these 144 MLA's (76 per cent) belonged to the ruling party. These 104 accounted for nearly 60 per cent of the ruling party MLA's. In 1994, 170 of the 224 MLA's had secured (76%) less than 50 per cent of the valid votes polled and as many as 76 of them belonged to the ruling Janata Dal (45%). More than 66 per cent of the Janata Dal MLA's (76 of 115) secured less than 50 per cent of the valid votes polled. In the Assembly elected in 1999, as many as 139 of the 224 MLA's have secured less than 50 per cent of the valid votes polled (62%) and 76 of them are from the ruling Congress (55%). More than half the ruling party MLA's (72 of 132) secured less than 50 per cent of the votes in the constituencies they represent. The 'second ballot system' would require the holding of a second run off in these constituencies.

If the second run off system were to be applied to the 1999 Karnataka Assembly elections, only 85 of the 224 constituencies would have decided on their representatives in the first round. The proportions of seats each party would have secured at the end of the first round is significant as it reflects the overall voting percentage in the election (see Table 4.6). Further, in the 139 constituencies where a second run off would be required, a clear polarisation is obvious. With the Congress being one of the contestants in 116 seats and the BJP-Janata Dal (U) alliance contesting 99 seats. The Janata Dal (S) which would be a contestant in 27 seats would also be a crucial player in terms of swinging the support either in favour of the Congress or the BJP led alliance (see Table 4.7). As mentioned earlier, the second run off system would clearly expedite the process of political polarisation and contribute to the emergence of a 'bi-polar alliance system'. Such a system could help mirror voter preferences more effectively. While endorsing the utility of the second ballot system a caveat needs to be added. This reform cannot be considered in isolation and would have to form a part of a comprehensive package of electoral reforms that the system needs today.

Table 4.6: 1999 Karnataka Assembly Election: Seats Secured by Parties in the First Round in the Event of Second Run Off System

Total Seats : 224	Decided in First round: 85
Congress	60 (132)
BJP	12 (44)
Janata Dal (U)	8 (19)
Janata Dal (S)	1 (10)
Others	4 (19)

(Seats actually secured under FTPT system in brackets.)

Table 4.7 : 1999 Karnataka Assembly Election: Contestants in Second Round in the Event of Second Run Off System

Total Seats: 224	To be Decided in Second round: 139	
Congress		116
BJP	66	99
Janata Dal (U)	33	
Janata Dal (S)		27
Others		36

Notes

1. Election Commission of India, *Electoral Reforms: Views and Proposals*, Nirvachan Sadan, New Delhi, p.15.
2. Law Commission of India, *Reform of the Electoral Laws*, New Delhi, p.9.
3. National Democratic Alliance, 1999, For a Proud, Prosperous India: An Agenda, p.7.
4. Indian National Congress, 1999, *Manifesto*, p.53.
5. Ramachandran, Raju, (1991): 'Myths of Parliamentary Democracy', *Indian Express*, 6 August.
6. Rae, Douglas. W., (1967): *The Political Consequences of Electoral Laws*, Yale University Press, New Haven , p.74.
7. _____(1991) 'Report of the Committee Appointed by Sri Jayaprakash Narayan on behalf of Citizens for Democracy for Electoral Reforms', *Indian Journal of Public Administration*, New Delhi, 37:3:595.
8. *Ibid*, p. 596.
9. n 7, p. 597.
10. Yadav, Yogendra (1998): 'Electoral Reforms: Beyond Middle Class Fantasies', in M.P. Singh (ed), *Ideologies and Institutions in Indian Politics*, New Delhi: Deep and Deep, p.418.
11. *Ibid.*
12. Kant, Krishna (1992): 'Consensual Nationalism', *Mainstream*, Annual: 27-36.
13. *Indian Express*, 31 August 1998.
14. Indiresan, P.V. (1991): 'Electing Representatives, Responsible and Responsive Legislators', *Indian Journal of Public Administration*, New Delhi, 37:3:294-301.
15. Shastri, Sandeep (1999): 'Beyond Vital Statistics', *Deccan Herald*, 20 October.
16. Shastri, Sandeep (1992): 'Indian Constitution: Is a Fresh Look Really Necessary', *Mainstream*, 30:30:9-12,17.
17. Shastri, Sandeep (1999): 'Parlimentarism *vs.* Presidentialism: Problems and Prospects in the Indian Context', in Khanna. D.D. *et al.* (eds) (1999): *Principles, Power and Politics*, McMillan, pp. 291-316.

(Further Reading)

Shastri, Sandeep and M.J.Vinod (1991): 'Dynamics of Electoral Politics: A Case Study of the Karnataka Assembly Elections 1989', *Indian Journal of Social Sciences*, 4:3:389-406

——, (1995): *Towards Explaining the Voters Mandate*, Vinayaka, Bangalore.

——, (1999): 'Parliamentarism *vs.* Presidentialism: Problems and Prospects in the Indian Context' in Khanna.D.D.(ed), 291-316.

5

Perspectives on Electoral Reforms in India

M.P. DUBE

Free competitive elections are regarded as the key to representative democracy. Elections are the life-breath of a democratic polity. Consequently it becomes essential to ensure free, fair and peaceful elections, where the verdict of the people finds full expression. Ancient Greeks voted by placing pebbles (psephos) in an urn, giving rise to the term psephology, or study of elections. Freedom opened a new chapter in our history and led to the establishment of a modern political system for the governance of the country. The founding fathers had envisioned a socio-economic revolution that alone could ensure a rightful and honoured place for India in the community of nations. They aimed to achieve the unity and integrity of the nation, socialism, secularism and the development of the democratic values—adult franchise, regular elections, accountability of political leadership by a constitution which they drafted in meticulous detail. Pt. Nehru, the first Prime Minister had great faith in democratic values. He evolved and developed democratic institutions and practices. But soon an erosion of these institutions and the decline of the political process began as a consequence of the excess of the populist and confrontational politics that began in the last quarter of the 1960s. Today the normal political process has been grossly distorted. The political legitimacy and morality of the political leadership is suspected by the people. There is gross decline of democratic commitment. Growing corruption, criminalisation, repression and intimidation have gravely perverted the democratic process. Very often there are complaints of booth capturing, tampering with ballot boxes, impersonation and extensive use of money and muscle power.

Time and again, the plurality system which has been adopted for the Parliamentary, Assembly and municipal elections has been criticised for not reflecting the people's will. The proliferation of political parties and a lack of credible opposition to the ruling party has brought our democracy to naught. We cannot afford to allow this state of affairs to continue. This brings to the fore the need for wide-ranging electoral reforms and an electoral code to be followed by parties and candidates at the time of election.

Electoral System

The countries of the world have various types of electoral systems. They can be analysed in three dimensions. The first, the method of calculating votes or electoral formula—the three main methods are plurality, majority and proportional; second, the size of the constituency or district magnitude—constituencies may be single-member, multi-member or national; and third, the extent to which the voter enjoys choice of candidates.[1]

The plurality and majority methods are almost always combined with single-member constituencies. In contrast to the plurality method, the majority method offers choice of candidate since it allows each party or bloc to present multiple candidatures without fear of splitting the vote. The plurality method is used in Britain and in democracies that have been at one time under British rule. The majority method is currently used only in Australia (alternative Vote) and in France (Second ballot). Some writers think that the plurality method is a means of securing stable and effective government, since it exaggerated the representation of large parties while systematically under-representing small parties that were not territorially concentrated. The relationship can be shown by what is known as the 'cube law' : the seats of party A stand in respect to the seats of party B as the cube of the votes cast for party A stand to the cube of votes cast for party B. The electoral system gives a bonus of seats to the party which is ahead, even though it may be ahead by only a small fraction of the popular vote. And the further it is ahead in popular votes the greater does this bonus tend to become.

The method of proportional representation aims to bring about the representation of voters in proportion with their members. It is not the name of a single method of election. It is a generic term for a wide variety of methods that are based on the belief that no vote should be lost and that every minority/majority group should get duly represented in the legislature. The two main varieties of this system are: party list system, which is widely used in European countries and the single transferable vote (STV) which is used in American cities and Eire. Under the list system each party offers a list of its candidates up to the number of seats to be filled for each constituency. In this system representation of opinion is secured through parties so that an effective method of election should secure the proportional representation of parties. It is for the party rather than the elector to decide which candidates should carry the party banner in the legislature. The STV is the preferential method of voting in multi-member constituencies without ordered lists. A voter's first preference is transferred if it cannot be used to help elect the candidate of his first choice either because this candidate has no chance of election, or because the candidate has more votes than are needed to secure election. The number of votes necessary to secure election is calculated by means of the Droop Quota.

In general, in deeply divided or plural societies where there are ethnic, religious, territorial or tribal cleavage, plurality and majority methods will work less successfully than in homogeneous ones, which have a national culture unified both ideologically and ethnically. Plurality and majority electoral methods also work less well in multi-party systems. It was, indeed, for protecting minorities in ethnically heterogeneous societies that many of the earliest moves towards proportional representation occurred. In linguistically and religiously divided societies majority elections could clearly threaten the continued existence of the political system. The introduction of some element of minority representation came to be seen as an essential step in a strategy of territorial consolidation.

Proportional representation is widely appreciated for its mathematical accuracy in reflecting public opinion. This system favours higher levels of female representation and representation of ethnic minorities. As a consequence of the multi-member element present in almost all proportional systems, there is less incentive for bribery, extravagance and gerrymandering.[2]

In India, under the British rule there existed constitutional barriers to political and social union since the introduction of separate electorates in 1909 and, in fact, since the introduction of functional representation in municipal councils in 1885. The franchise was restricted by property, educational and other qualifications to approximately 15 per cent population of the country, and the resulting electorate was split into no less than thirteen communal and functional compartments for whose representatives seats were reserved in the various parliamentary bodies. The founding fathers of the Indian Constitution aimed to create a basis for the social and political unity of the country by providing for universal adult franchise. Alladi Krishnaswami Ayyar said: 'The Assembly has adopted the principle of adult franchise with an abundant faith in the common man and the ultimate success of democratic rule, and in the full belief that the introduction of democratic government on the basis of adult suffrage will bring enlightenment and promote the well being, the standard of life, the comfort, and the decent living of the common man.'[3] In his book, *Unity of India*, Jawaharlal Nehru wrote in 1938 that an assembly constituted by direct election would represent the people as a whole and would be far more interested in the economic and social problems of the masses than in the petty communal issues which affect small groups.

As to electoral system some members of the Constituent Assembly had apprehension that proportional representation might lead to political fragmentation in the body politic, and to elimination of intimate contact between the voters and his representatives, that it would be conducive in reflecting the social cleavage which is ethnic, religious, territorial and tribal in nature and that the nature and process of this system are complicated and would be unintelligible to the vast majority of voters who continue to be illiterate. For these reasons the Assembly adopted the first-past-the-post rule, as it was regarded as a means of securing stable and effective government. The framers of the Constitution were enamoured with the plurality system, a system that apparently served the nation well for the initial twenty years of Independence. Rajni Kothari had called these the years of the 'Congress system'.[4]

Distortions in the Electoral System

However, over the years since 1967 several serious distortions in the electoral system have been identified and several members from the opposition ranks had attributed their diminished national presence to these distortions in the existing system. That our electoral system has a number of proven and demonstrated weaknesses is beyond doubt.

Firstly, the plurality system has enabled a minority party, i.e. one that does not command the confidence of the majority of voters in the country, to secure an absolute majority of seats in parliament. And wherever there are multi-cornered contests - and that is the case in most of constituencies - the winning candidate represents a minority while the majority goes unrepresented.

Secondly, a major electoral malady is the proliferation of political parties and the resultant lack of a credible opposition to the ruling party. Before the passing of the Anti-defection Act in 1985, the country witnessed several bizarre incidents of defections and open market operations' in the sale and purchase of MLAs in several states. The phenomenon of '*Aya Ram*' and '*Gaya Ram*' and the unique political culture of the country have caused a multiplication in the number of parties. According to an amendment of the Constitution (52nd Amendment, which introduced the Anti-defection provisions as 10th Schedule of the Constitution) if one-third of the members of the party decided to defect, it would not be called defection. The Supreme Court in a landmark judgement held the 52nd Amendment valid. It, however, struck down its clause 7 on the ground that it barred judicial review which is violation of the basic structure of the Constitution. The act confers greater immunity for a greater sin and the law punishes a small fry but not the big fish. And this is exactly what has happened in the splitting of Janata Dal by Chandrashekhar in 1999, Ajay Singh's split from Janata Dal in 1992, Laloo Prasad's split to form Rastriya Janata Dal and the split in the Bahujan Samaj Party in the U.P. legislature. Moreover there is no time limit for the Speakers/Chairman to take a decision. If somebody is declared a defector then he can go to a High Court and the Court procedure can be dragged on till new elections are held to the House or very likely the House itself gets dissolved earlier. In the meantime a stay is easily obtained from the Court and the legislator in question can continue to be a member of the House, though perhaps without right to vote. He certainly does not suffer as a defector. This has resulted in the multiplicity of parties and the multiplicity of candidates. There is a deplorable splitting of votes. The present system in fact encourages party fragmentation, resulting in confusion and chaos in the minds of the voters.

Thirdly, the tendency of the plurality method in India, instead of building a national culture unified both ideologically and ethnically, has more often emphasised ethnic, religious, communal, caste, linguistic, regional and tribal cleavages. Today communal hatred, linguistic fanaticism and regional loyalty are threatening to tear apart the fabric of national unity.

Fourthly, extensive use of money power to influence elections is undoubtedly the most serious of all problems that has led to the cancerous growth of corruption in the body politics. Public meetings, banners, posters, house to house canvassing, use of transport and mass media require very huge amount of money. Here the use of big or black money has gone beyond all proportion. In India candidates are subject to a limitation or ceiling on expenditure but the political party sponsoring him or his friends, relatives and supporters are free to spend as much they like for his election. Consequently, the object of imposing the ceiling has been frustrated and the provisions in this regard have been wholly emasculated. In the famous case of Kanwarlal Gupta *vs.* Amar Nath Chawla, the Supreme Court set aside the election of a ruling party M.P., Amar Nath Chawala because more money was spent on his campaign than was permitted legally. After the decision the ruling party by an amendment limited the period for which a candidate was required to furnish the details of expenditure (between the notification of the election and the polling), thus making it easy for him to spend any amount he wished before, or to repay those who spent money on his behalf after the prescribed dates. Another amendment limited the details of expenditure to money spent by candidate personally.

Fifthly, party donations continue to be the most contentious issue. Section 293A of the Companies Act 1956, limits company donations to political parties to five per cent of the average net profit of the company as determined under the law during the three years immediately preceding the financial year. But as a matter of fact, these restrictions apply to the Board of Directors only, as companies, in general meetings, can donate any amount (that may run into crore rupees or more in the case of flourishing companies) out of their profits. Moreover, party donations are no longer expressions of political sympathy, but are often made as under-cover payments for specific benefits, which repay the investment many times over.

Further, the political parties are under a statutory obligation to file a return of income in respect of each assessment year in accordance with the provisions of the Income Tax Act. The parties, which have not been filing returns for several years, have *prima facie* violated the statutory provisions of the Act. The Income Tax authorities have been remiss in the performance of their statutory duties, having failed to take appropriate action against the defaulter political parties.

Finally, booth capturing, tampering with ballot boxes, impersonation and extensive use of muscle power, use of official machinery and resources by candidates and persistent use of state-owned audio-visual media for pro-government news and subtle image-projection of the ruling party leaders are serious distortions that have attracted wide public attention and concern.

The Tarkunde Committee Report and its Aftermath

Today it is almost universally conceded that our electoral system has a number of proven and demonstrated weaknesses. With the aim of making elections cheaper, freer and fairer, the problem was studied by several committees in the past, but their recommendations were soon forgotten or shelved. The Election Commission in its reports suggested changes in law and procedure of elections in the interest of administrative efficiency and public convenience. Some of the suggestions advanced in these reports were accepted by the government in modified form and converted into law by amending the election law during the year 1956, 1966, 1974, 1978, 1988 and 1989. Consolidated proposals for reforms in the system were sent by the committee to the government in 1971. The proposals were referred by the government to the Joint Parliamentary Committee on Amendment to the Election Law that submitted its report in 1972. The reports of the Jagannath Rao Parliamentary Joint Committee and Election Commission's reports met with the same fate. In August, 1974, Jayaprakash Narayan, on behalf of the Citizens for Democracy, appointed a committee headed by Mr. V. M. Tarkunde, to go into all aspects of the matter and submit a report. The Tarkunde Committee report focussed mainly on the use and misuse of administrative machinery, money power in elections, and alternative systems of representation. Some of its main recommendations were: the government should function as a caretaker government from the time of dissolution of Parliament/Assemblies until the polling day and take measures to avoid misuse of government machinery during that period. In order to minimise the role of big black money, the Committee recommended that 'all recognised political parties should be required by law to keep full and accurate accounts, including their sources and details of expenditure. The accounts should be audited by Chartered Accountants nominated by the Election Commission and should be open to public inspection on moderate charges. It also recommended the adoption of the 'mixed system'. The report maintained that, in the constituencies where no candidate gets an absolute majority of the valid votes, the seats in those constituencies should not be filled by this direct election but by persons from the top of the lists of the recognised political parties submitted by them in advance of the polling, roughly in proportion to the votes they poll so that the popular will may be fairly reflected. The Committee suggested that certain facilities like printing, postage and telephone be provided free of charge to all candidates. It also suggested that the present limit of election expenses should be doubled; security deposits should be increased; and the voting age should be reduced to 18 years. Despite these recommendations no breakthrough was made by the ruling parties because of the advantages accruing to it—whichever party happened to be in power was eager to perpetuate its temporary advantage. Consequently the steps taken by them were half hearted and ineffective.

During the last quarter of the 1980s, suddenly, the long-pending electoral reforms were projected by the opposition as part of its political programme. Lest it should be outdone, the Congress Working Committee, at its meeting in Delhi in the third week of October 1988, adopted resolutions of far-reaching significance in relation to election reforms. In a bid to steal the thunder of the opposition, on December 10 the Congress (I) government circulated to Members of Parliament two bills. The first was the Constitution 62nd Amendment Bill, 1988 to lower the voting age to 18 years. The bill proposing comprehensive changes in the People's Representation Act, 1950 and 1951, enjoined political parties to register with the Election Commission and subscribe to socialism, secularism and democracy. The electronic voting machines would be introduced and there were extensive provisions against booth capturing and abetting by government servants. It also aimed to prevent frivolous candidates from contesting elections to the Upper House. A specific provision was included to bring electoral officers under the discipline of the Election Commission during the election period.

Both the bills were passed by the Parliament after accepting one amendment to the second bill, which added misuse of religious places as one of the offences inviting disqualification of a candidate contesting an election.

In 1990, the government constituted a Committee comprising prominent members of the national and state parties and experts in election law, headed by Dinesh Goswami, the then Law Minister, to suggest suitable electoral reforms. The Committee submitted its report in May 1990. Accepting some of the Committee's recommendations, the government introduced four bills in the Rajya Sabha in 1991. Of the four bills, only one, relating to the terms and conditions of service of the Chief Election Commissioner and other Election Commissioners was passed by the Parliament. Meanwhile, the Lok Sabha was dissolved and the other bills lapsed. The Act prescribed a term of six years or till the age of 65, whichever is earlier, for the office of the Chief Election Commissioner and six years or the age of 62 years for an Election Commissioner. In terms of salary and other monetary benefits, the Chief Election Commissioner was equated with a judge of the Supreme Court and Election Commissioner with a judge of a High Court.

In October 1993, the Act was amended through Presidential Order to make the Election Commission a multi-member body with the appointment of two Election Commissioners. The President's order was converted into an Act in the same year.

These election reforms are only piecemeal measures. They are not going to curb the damaging role of big money and distortions in the electoral system unless we reform the electoral system as a whole, including the whole political culture. Vested interests, criminals and amoral politicians would make full use of their ingenuity to circumvent any penal or regulatory provisions of law. Thus the electoral system needs to be reviewed as a whole; wide-ranging changes are to be made in order to make it free and fair.

Needed Reforms

Today, the mood is of disillusionment and despair all around. How does one get out of this morass? The need is to restore the normal constitutional process, and rebuild the lost political consensus. Investigation of the history of electoral systems has shown that many democracies altered their electoral systems to proportional representation as a part of strategy of national integration—an alternative to monopolisation of influence or civil war-and of neutralizing the threat to their systems by the entrenched linguistic, religious or ethnic minorities. They reformed their systems in order to accommodate changes in the political system which had already occurred. It is beyond doubt that proportional representation reflects social cleavages more faithfully than plurality or majority methods. Plurality and majority methods, by contrast, tend to stress some cleavages while suppressing some others. Moreover, proportional representation far from necessarily causing a multiplication in the number of parties is merely recognition of the fact that there is already a multi-party system in existence.

In a country like India, with multi-faceted diversity and a multi-party system, proportional representation may be adopted in order to obviate the defects of the present system. Since to my mind the single transferable vote system might be unintelligible to the ordinary voter it is suggested that the Additional Member System (mixed system) should be adopted in which the single-member constituency element is combined with PR, the additional members being derived from a party list. Here the voters will be allowed two votes. One by way of 'approval voting' for a simple plurality election in single-member constituencies, the other for a proportional representation election among party lists. In 'approval voting system' people will be allowed to vote as many candidates as they wish, but only one vote will be cast for each approved candidate. The candidate with the most approval votes will win. This system will give voters more flexible options that will encourage a larger turnout. Moreover, the system is simple for voters to understand. In this system intellectuals and scholars will find opening. It may help political parties to keep away the corrupt ways of raising party funds. Not only electability but ability would prevail in elections. Women, tribes, other weaker sections and social workers would get the chance of being elected. In order to discourage the formation of splinter parties, there should be introduced a threshold either on the basis of the percentage share of the total national vote or on the basis of the number of the direct seats already won. Furthermore, in order to secure stability, as in Germany, a 'constructive vote of no-confidence' should be provided in our Constitution.

The need to ensure the credibility of the Election Commission becomes acute when the Commission appears to be beholden to the executive, as when there is a practice of a Chief Secretary doubling as the state's Chief Electoral Officer. In order to restore the dignity and authority enjoined for it by the makers of the Constitution, the Chief Election Commissioner and other Election Commissioners should be appointed by the President in consultation with the Chief Justice of India, the Prime Minister and the leader of the opposition.

State funding of elections has been widely recommended as a means to prevent the increasing influence of money power. But here one thing to be noted is that in countries where state funding is in operation, it has neither rid political parties of their financial burdens nor cleansed public life; dubious methods are adopted to spend more (in addition to state funds) in elections. It is desirable to give state aid in kind and not in cash. Helpful in this regard would be use without charge of public places and buildings for election meetings, free printing of certain number of posters, circulars and tax exemption on publications, free postage of electoral communications, a limited amount of petrol and diesel and sufficient time on radio and television for party broadcasts.

The Representation of the People Act (Second Amendment), 1996 makes several provisions such as: (1) reduction of 20 days now available between the date of withdrawal of candidature and the first date of poll to 14 days; (2) observers getting statutory recognition with certain specified duties assigned to them; (3) sentence for insult to the national flag and prevention of singing the national Anthem entailing disqualification for standing for election for six years; (4) adjournment of election and non-countermanding as at present only if a candidate set up by recognised political party dies; (5) ban on the sale and distribution of liquor 48 hours before; (6) grant of holiday on the poll day for industrial workers and of other establishments; (7) holding of by-elections within six months.

There is need for regulation of the functioning of political parties and their adherence to their constitutions, both in letter and spirit. It should be mandatory for political parties to maintain accounts of the funds received and the disbursement made under various heads. The accounts so prepared should be audited by authorised neutral auditors. Further, funds spent by others for a candidate should form a part of his election returns.

The switch to Electronic Voting Machines for party list elections, and multi-purpose identity cards is desirable. Voting machines will limit the malpractices of stuffing ballot boxes, mismarking and miscounting; it will put an end to the possibility of tampering with ballot boxes during transit and storage; furthermore, the delay in the declaration of results and the cost of holding elections will be minimised. A multi-purpose card will entitle one not only to vote in elections, but to avail of other services like rations, health facilities and so on. Consociational democracy is particularly suitable for the governance of plural societies, that is societies which are deeply divided by religious, ideological, linguistic, regional, cultural, racial or ethnic differences, which form clearly separate and easily identifiable segments. This type of democracy should be made the creed of governance in our country. The principles of executive power-sharing or grand coalition, high degree of autonomy for the segments of the plural society, proportionality and the minority veto should be adhered to the formation and functioning of the governments.

Today, the intrusion of religion and caste into politics is playing havoc with the body politic. Candidates most often emphasise the various cleavages in the society. Official power is sometimes misused by the party in power. Therefore, what is needed is not the five-star consumerism but a sense of service and dedication to the people. In order to make elections free and fair a code of conduct must be formulated for the political parties. Above all, a culture of co-operation and trust on the part of candidates is needed for curing the cancerous malpractices of our democratic system, and for making the national system as a whole much more cohesive and stronger.

Notes

1. Rae, D.W. (1971): *The Political Consequences of Electoral Laws*, Yale University Press, New Haven.
2. Rokkan, Stein (1968): 'Electoral Systems', *International Encyclopaedia of Social Sciences*, Vol. V, pp. 6-21.
3. CAD, XI, 9, 835.
4. Kothari, Rajni (1987): *The Hindustan Times*, Jan. 11.

6

Political Financing in India

R.B. JAIN

The present paper is a modest attempt to discuss some aspects of political financing in India—the largest, the most populous and the most enduring democracy in the Third World—and to analyse the efforts that have been made in India to regulate political financing, and develop alternative strategies for preventing the misuse of money power for electoral and political gains.

Nature of Party System in India

Political parties and the party system in India have been greatly influenced by the cultural diversity, social, ethnic, caste, community and religious pluralism, and shaped by the traditions of the nationalist movement, the contrasting style of party leadership, and clashing ideological perspectives.[1] The two major categories of political parties in India are national and regional, and are so recognised by the Election Commission of India on the basis of certain specified criteria. As of today, there are six national parties (seven after the split in the Janata Dal in August 1999) and 38 regional parties operating in the Indian political scene and recognised as such by the Election Commission of India.[2]

Despite the dominant role played by the Congress Party since Independence leading to the characterisation of the party system as the one-party dominant system in the first three decades of the republic, there has been an increasing trend towards a fragmented and splintered multi-party system thereafter. This has contributed to the instability of the governments and frequent elections, almost on an annual basis (between 1996-1999, there had been three General Elections), putting heavy strains on the availability of party finances for elections leading to a variety of corrupt and irregular practices in party and campaign financing. This has been a matter of serious public concern in recent times.

Sources of Party Finances in India

There are a number of sources for party finances in India—membership dues, public donations, contributions by corporate groups, public meetings, and so on. Amongst the national parties, the Congress Party has been the best financed. Although the party in its 1992 organisational elections claimed a membership of 25 million, but its active membership was less than one million. Besides membership dues, additional contributions are secured from wealthy supporters and solicited in fund-raising campaigns. During the emergency period of 1975-77, the corporate sector was subjected to virtual extortion by the Congress Party and the auxiliary Youth Congress. They were forced to take out expensive advertisements in the souvenir programme of the party's annual session. A major portion of income that pours into the coffers of the political parties is from "black money"—that is unaccounted income. "And it was the black money connection between business and politics that helped to perpetuate the system of controls that so long strangled the Indian economy, as politicians traded influence in return for business' contributions".[3] In the 1980s, the Congress Party was alleged to have been the beneficiary of kickbacks in return for government contracts for major arms purchases from abroad, most notoriously the $ 1.3 billion Bofors contract. The party in power has an obvious advantage in raising money for election campaign, and the Congress Party's long control of the center and most state governments gave it a tremendous advantage. Dependent upon the "Permit Raj", the corporate sector contributed richly to the Congress Party. Some of the business houses, taking no chance with a volatile electorate, have contributed to each of the major political parties, right and left. The opposition, however, generally has had far less access to financial support than the Congress Party.

In the beginning of the Indian republic, under the first prime minister, Jawaharlal Nehru, companies were permitted to donate funds to political parties. Predictably, industrial houses and shrewd businessmen took out "political insurance coverage" with all the parties. However, in the late 60s when big business houses began donating to the rightist Swatantra Party, which strongly supported free enterprise, Indira Gandhi's centrist government and the ruling Congress Party, socialists became concerned. The socialists proposed an official bill in the Lok Sabha demanding a ban on company donations. Mrs. Gandhi's government responded by banning company donations and blocking the flow of funds to the opposition. Under the new law, only the ruling party received company donations, though it was done under the table.

This decision, "played ... hell with the system and also with business ethics and morality".[4] Funds were still needed to win elections, but since they could not be gotten lawfully, other methods of raising money were discovered. The late Lalit Narain Mishra, a former Union Minister, A. R. Antulay, former Chief Minister of Maharashtra, and others showed Mrs. Gandhi some of these methods and became her fundraisers. Licenses and permits were unabashedly hawked. Dubious foundations and organisations were created with a view to raising and soliciting funds. Leading industrial houses, known for their impeccable business morality initially refused to join the new cult, but eventually buckled under in the race for survival. Several ministers made big money in the process, and the electoral system itself was debased.

The party in power, by virtue of its control over permits, licenses, and import controls, has access to enormous slush funds not available to others. In place of donations made by businessmen to the ruling party in the 1970s, there are now kickbacks, or commissions for foreign trade, and on orders for equipment, machinery, and essential supplies. Enormous amounts are kept in secret accounts abroad for both personal and party interests. Although the ban on company donations was removed by Prime Minster Rajiv Gandhi in 1985, the damage done to political life in the last decade, with repeated allegations and counter-allegations of bribery and kickbacks (as in the Bofors affair), has been irreparable.

The income of parties from membership dues fluctuates considerably; party membership is largest immediately before elections, because of the mass recruitment of bogus membership arranged by various sections of political parties to strengthen their bargaining position in the competition for party tickets. The candidates themselves are also expected to make sizeable contribution to the party election fund, and tickets are occasionally awarded for a major commitment of financial support. This practice varies considerably from party to party and from seat to seat, for there are clearly a number of candidates from the Congress as well as from other parties without any major source of private income. Levies are also made on the salaries of parliamentary and assembly members. Each of the political parties also derives some income from publishing newspapers, books and pamphlets, and the most active have been the Communist parties. In addition to several newspapers, the Communist Party of India (CPI) also operates a publishing house and a chain of bookstores once subsidized by the former Soviet Union. Indeed, it is widely assumed that the former Soviet Union financed the CPI and the Communist Party (Marxists) is alleged to have at one time received support from China.

Election time makes captains of industry and the corporate sector groan in discomfort and disgust, forced as they are to pay "protection money" to political parties indulging in no less than blatant extortion. Payment is in hard cash or involves providing campaign vehicles, guest houses and the like. In addition, like the majority of victims of extortion, businessmen too simply grin and bear it. What annoys businessmen most is that the demand for "election funds" is another way for politicians to line their own pockets. It is anybody's guess what percentage of the funds raised goes to the party, and what percentage is split among the party functionaries. Until the parties are forced to set their accounts in order and regulation of funding is firmly in place, there is little point in expecting business and industry to heed the former Chief Election Commissioner, T. N. Sehsan's exhortation not to contribute to election coffers of political parties.

Legal Provisions for Party Funding

In India, there is no single comprehensive legislation regulating the finances of political parties. In fact, there are no restrictions on the political parties or groups as to the sources or manner of raising funds and contributions from individuals or corporate establishments for furthering their political activities. The Peoples' Representation Act of 1951, which otherwise prescribes the regulations for conducting elections in India does not contain any provision regulating the flow of funds to political parties. It does, however, prescribe the manner of keeping accounts of election expenses, filing of return of election expenses, and prescribes what constitutes corrupt election practices and electoral offences.

As mentioned earlier, the political parties in their own constitution do prescribe the amount of subscription dues of different category of their memberships and also general provisions for receiving contributions/donations and mobilising resources for achieving their objectives. The Constitution of India also does not contain any provision in this regard, except that the political parties are mentioned in the Tenth Schedule of the Constitution which contains certain provisions relating to the disqualification of members of Parliament on account of defection from their original party affiliation. Thus, there is no regularity in receipt of financial subscriptions/contributions by the political parties of all hues or ideology except that some political parties have more stable membership than others and thus have better financial support.

Business in India has no systematized method for giving contribution to political parties. Contributions are provided in several ways—through company contributions, through individual contributions and through industry groups. The only piece of legislation that regulates such contributions is the Indian Companies Act of 1956, as amended in 1960 and further amended in 1969, and 1985. Between 1960 until 3 April 1970, a company in India was permitted, under Section 293A of the Companies Act, to contribute money to political parties provided its memorandum of association authorised such contributions. Such contributions were limited to Rs. 25,000 or 5 per cent of the average net profit of the company for the preceding three years, whichever was greater. The companies were required to disclose such amount in their annual profit and loss accounts. The company donations were banned by the then government of Mrs. Indira Gandhi in 1970 and remained so until Rajiv Gandhi lifted the ban through the Companies (Amendment) Act, 1985. Under Section 293A of the new provision of the Act, a company, except government company, which has been in existence for at least three years can contribute amounts directly or indirectly to any party or for any political purpose to any person provided that the amount so contributed in any financial year does not exceed 5 per cent of its average net profits during the three immediate preceding years. Such contributions also include any donations or subscription to any publication, brochure, tract, pamphlet or the like, published by a political party. No contribution can be made by a company unless a resolution authorising the making of such contribution is passed at a meeting of the Board of Directors. Every company is required to disclose in its profit and loss account the amounts contributed by it to the political party. If any company makes any contributions contravening these provisions, it is liable to be punished with fine and the officer of the company concerned may be imprisoned for up to three years and be also liable to a fine.

The Indrajit Gupta Committee on electoral reforms which reported in December 1998, was in favour of the continuation of the ban on donations by Government companies for political purposes, but left the decision on any ban on donations by other companies and corporate bodies for political purposes to be decided by Government and Parliament in their collective wisdom. The question whether election expenses of political parties and other bodies or associations and individuals should be included or not in the accounts of election expenses of candidates might also be decided by the Government/ Parliament in their collective wisdom. However, apparent contradiction between the provisions of Section 77 (I), Explanation (1), Representation of the People Act, 1951 and section 171 H, IPC, needs to be resolved. Periodical revision of election expenses may continue to be done by the Central Government, in consultation with the Election Commission of India as at present.[5]

Although company contributions represent only a fraction of the total business donations to political parties, they have been the most controversial. The Indian courts, have questioned the practice on several occasions. By and large, political contributions stemming from business in India have been individual, not collective. They are made directly to selected MPs to ensure access to bureaucracy or ministers for the purpose of obtaining an industrial license, permit or other such benefits. In its relationship with political parties, business uses its most potent resource -money. Business finances elections. It also finances the various party meetings, which by tradition are held in rural settings. Substantial amounts are required to build and provide facilities to house and feed the delegates to such meetings. The major functions of political contributions are to support ideologically acceptable parties, to ensure easy access to potential decision-makers, and to try to influence the nomination process. Thus, while political contributions may ensure access and may aid in securing individual benefits, they do no guarantee that the business voice will dominate and determine public policy.[6]

Another piece of legislation which regulates party funding in India is the Foreign Contribution (Regulation) Act, 1976. Section 4 of the Act provides that any candidate for election, member of any legislature, political party, or officer, or organisation of a political nature shall not accept any foreign money, contribution or hospitality except with the prior permission of the Central Government. Under Section 14 of the Act, the Central Government has powers to inspect any account or record maintained by any political party, person or organisation or association, if it has any ground to suspect that any provision of this Act has been contravened. The Act also provides punishment by disqualification for a term extending to five years or with a fine or with both, if any person, political party, or organisation is found contravening any provision of the Act.

Except for the above provisions in the Indian Companies Act and Foreign Contribution (Regulation) Act, there are no other legal provisions regulating the flow of funds to political parties. Thus, political parties in India are by and large, free to raise and mobilise financial resources as and how they deem fit. Their capacity to mobilize financial resources depends very much on their mass support, political strength and their continuance in political power.

The increasing costs of periodic elections and the huge sums of money spent by vote seekers have become issues of serious concerns in the Indian polity. If the misuse of money power, muscle power, and state power in the electoral process could be minimized through reforms, it would be a great step towards breaking the stranglehold of corruption that has so completely enveloped Indian society. Laws limiting election expenditure do exist in the Indian polity, but are blatantly abused, making such legal provisions meaningless.

Candidate's Election Expenses: Ceilings and Regulations

In 1950, the Representation of People's Act fixed the ceiling on a candidate's election expenses. In 1956, however, the law was liberalised through an amendment and expense ceilings were varied from state to state, ranging from Rs. 20,000 to 1,50,000 for candidates to the Lok Sabha (the lower and popular house of the Union Parliament) and from Rs. 5,000 to Rs.50,000 for candidates to the State Assembly.

Other changes introduced in 1956 were as follows: (i) the period for maintaining the accounts was limited to the interval between the dates of notification of the poll and declaration of the results; (ii) the period of disqualification for a false declaration was raised from five to six years; and (iii) a candidate was required to declare by oath before a magistrate as to the correctness of the election expenditure returns. After 1956, the ceiling on election expenditure has in practice come to be virtually disregarded as most MPs and members of the Legislative Assembly invariably made false statements regarding election expenses before taking the oath of office.

In 1974, an amendment of the Act further diluted the effectiveness of the ceilings, by stating that any expenditure connected with the election of a candidate by political party, by an association or body of persons, or by an individual (other than the candidate or his election agent), would not be considered to be an expenditure of the candidate.[7] Later several loopholes appeared in the implementation of the Act, which allowed the display and use of money without fear of punishment, making the enforcement of the ceiling a hopeless exercise. Such liberalisation may have been justified in the early stages of India's government, but now five decades of democracy should provide the maturity necessary to abide by the more stringent rules followed in other established democracies. As contributions are curbed by such rules, they cannot be used to organise lavish campaigns, and indulging in an assortment of malpractices.[8]

Reforms Proposed by the Election Commission (1982)

In 1982, the Election Commission recommended a package of corrective reform proposals: (1) the inclusion of all election expenses incurred within the expense ceiling, whether made before, during, or after the election; (2) the reinstatement of the declaration about the correctness of the nature; (3) the prohibition of incurring election expenses by any person or by any club, association, society, etc., other than the candidate or his election agent; (4) an increase in the period of disqualification of a proven, false declaration from three to four years; (5) the granting of power to the Commission to scrutinize the return, and, if necessary, to disqualify. The package also permitted the political parties to spend money on a candidate provided that the expenditure was incurred by the candidate.[9] The government disregarded these proposals.

The Election Commission issued another report during 1986-1987, which conveyed to the Parliament its "serious concern" over the use of money during elections. The Commission noted that "even though the electorate has not been, by and large, swayed by such display and use of money power, so long as there is no fear of punishment, those having money power will persist in using it".[10] Since the government still refused to include election expenditures paid by other organisations and individuals within the expense ceilings of the candidates, the Commission's proposal to increase the candidates' expense limit from Rs. 1,50,000 to Rs. 2,20,000 for the Lok Sabha, and from Rs. 50,000 to Rs. 70,000 for the Assembly, would have become an exercise in futility.[11]

Post-1989 Elections Reforms Proposals

The ninth general election in India, held in November 1989, which were described as the "greatest show on earth", once again demonstrated the free verdict of an "illiterate" electorate for a change of government. The elections were testimony to the vast Indian electorate which refuses to be taken for granted and demands that a party holding office is judged by its performance record and its response to complaints or criticisms. This clear verdict against the establishment, deposing the almost uninterrupted forty-year rule of the Congress-I at the Centre and toppling the so-called "dynastic rule", was made despite the most violent election campaign to date. Apart from poll violence, in which more than 110 people lost their lives in three days, there were instances of capturing booths, stuffing ballot boxes, burning jeeps, mishandling election staff, and free use of arms.

The ninth general elections have also earned the dubious distinction of being the most expensive elections in India's history, estimated at Rs. 100 billion.[12] This does not include the expense of administering the elections, which could amount to another billion.

The ceilings placed on candidates' election expenditures became a farce, compelling every elected MP to sign an almost unbelievable declaration that he or she spent less than Rs. 20,000 or Rs. 1,50,000 on the election campaign, depending upon the size of the constituency. Even taking into account the loopholes that money spent by the candidates' parties and friends was not to be included, there can be little doubt that all the candidates spent more than was permitted.

It was in this context that, immediately after the new government (led by the National Front leader, V. P. Singh) assumed office, the Chief Election Commissioner, R. V. Peri Sastri, made a strong plea for more stringent punishments, including imprisonment and disqualification, for booth capturing during elections. Because poll reforms were a priority of the Singh Government, a comprehensive reform package, providing for limited state funding of elections, eliminating non-serious candidates, and strengthening the Election Commission to make it "truly independent", seemed possible.[13] Public funding was seriously regarded as a key method to reduce the role money plays in politics. Regular audits of party funds and assurances from parties that they comply with the rules framed by their respective constitutions were also contemplated.

The package also was expected to incorporate certain other important measures suggested by the Commission but not favoured by the previous government, such as the delimitation of constituencies. With many of the urban constituencies becoming unwieldy because of a steady influx of people, the Election Commission had suggested redrawing the constituency boundaries so that they were uniformly representative. Similarly, the continued reservation of certain constituencies for certain communities (some for thirty years) has given rise to discontent among candidates belonging to other communities, who have to look for some outside constituency to contest. The Commission also favoured rotation of the reserved seats from time to time.

Finally, the new package was expected to give legal sanction to a model code of conduct, expedite disposal of election petitions, and see to the installation of electronic voting machines. Despite the earlier unanimity on the advantage of laser machines, they were not deployed in the 1991 polls because non-Congress-I parties suddenly revised their opinion and voiced apprehension that the machines could facilitate the rigging of elections.[14]

The new package of reforms was debated by the high-powered

Committee on Electoral Reforms headed by then Law Minister, Dinesh Goswami. Based on the Committee's recommendations, three bills on electorate reforms were introduced in the Rajya Sabha (the upper house of the Union legislature) by the Law Minister himself on 19 May 1990.[15] Two of these bills were aimed at amending the Constitution to lay down the procedure for the appointment of the Chief Election Commissioner and to de-limit the constituencies based on the 1981 census. The third bill sought to amend the Representation of the People's Act of 1950 and 1951. Among the other provisions of the bill, one important item was to put electoral expense back to its pre-1974 position, so that the total expenditure by party or candidates would be required to remain within the ceiling. The bill also proposed a modest beginning toward the state funding of elections, making available to candidates copies of the electoral rolls, a certain amount of fuel for a certain number of vehicles, and payment to the candidates of recognised political parties for rental charges of microphones.

The bills could not get through Parliament as the V. P. Singh government fell and went out of office in November 1990. But even if the bill had passed, they did not vest the Election Commission with the power to scrutinize the accounts of election expenses filed by the candidates. In the absence of that, the proposed provision for assistance to candidates constituted only a fraction of the money which candidates and political parties usually spend in elections. Nominal assistance to candidates could hardly be considered a major electoral reform.

Reforms Efforts Under the Rao Government

Arrangements to reduce the influence of big money in elections have yet to receive real government attention. The root of the problem is the huge amount of unaccounted money at the disposal of political parties. This can be checked only with compulsory auditing, a step the Singh government failed to take. The successive Chandra Sekhar government hardly had any time to move in this direction before it also fell, paving the way for the Tenth general elections in May 1991. Even the successor government of P. V. Narasimha Rao was not able to take any concrete steps in this direction.

In February 1992, the Election Commission of India submitted a proposal to the Government of India recommending two specific measures to regulate the election expenditure of the political parties and the contesting candidates. These were:

1. Every political party registered with the Commission should publish its accounts annually and such accounts should be audited by agencies specified by the Election Commission.
2. No association or body of person (except a registered political party) or individual should be permitted to incur any election expenditure without the written authorisation of the concerned candidate or his election agent, and if so authorized, such expenditure should be included in the return of the election expenses of the candidate concerned. Any person violating these provisions should be liable to punishment of one to five years imprisonment and a fine. The Commission had also recommended that the person so convicted should be debarred from contesting another election for six years.

The government, however, did not respond to these proposals.[16] Instead, the Rao government introduced two Bills in the Lok Sabha on 29 July 1993. One was to amend the Representation of Peoples' Act (RP) 1950, and another a Constitution Amendment Bill. While the amendment to RP Act provided for government approval on the issuance of some types of notifications by the Election Commission, the Constitutional Amendment was intended to give equal powers to all the three Election Commissioners (the Election Commission was made a multi-member Commission of three Commissioners in 1993) so that disputed decisions can be taken by majority vote. In the midst of a controversy, the government made a hasty retreat, and despite the fact that one of the bills was even referred to a Committee of Parliament, which submitted its report later, the two Bills were eventually withdrawn by the Minister of State for Law, H. R. Bhardwaj in both the Lok Sabha and Rajya Sabha on 13 June 1994.[17]

However, bowing to an increasing pressure from all quarters for fixation of realistic limit on election expenditure and on the recommendations of the Chief Election Commissioner, who wanted the ceilings on election expenditure to be raised four-fold, the government through a notification in October 1994 raised the expenditure ceilings three-fold to a maximum of Rs. 4,50,000 for a Parliamentary constituency and Rs. 1,50,000 for a state Assembly constituency.[18]

In December 1994, the Standing Committee of the Parliament has again suggested that as a measure of electoral reforms, each candidate fighting an election should by law be required to declare his or her assets at the time of filing the nomination paper for the contest. This recommendation, if had been accepted by the Government and incorporated into the RP Act, would have curtailed money power and minimised corruption by the legislature. The Standing Committee also made a number of other recommendations for electoral reforms.[19] But the government which subsequently went out of power after the 1996 Elections could not take any action in this matter.

The Supreme Court Judgement—4 April 1996

In a landmark judgment to curb use of black money and to bring transparency in the election funding, the Supreme Court on 4 April 1996 ruled that the expenditure incurred by a political party on a candidate in an election would fall within the prescribed ceiling of expenses if the source of the money was not revealed.

The court held that political parties not maintaining books of accounts and not filing income tax returns could not take advantage of the provision exempting the expenditure incurred by political parties on their candidates. According to the court if a political party deliberately chooses to violate or circumvent mandatory provisions of Income Tax Act and Representation of People Act and goes through the election process with the help of black and unaccounted money, the said party, ordinarily, cannot be permitted to say that it has incurred or authorised expenditure in connection with the election of its candidates in terms of Explanation 1 of Section 77 of the RP Act.[20]

The ruling was given by the division bench comprising Mr. Justice Kuldip Singh and Mr. Justice Faizen Uddin while allowing a public interest petition by "Common Cause", a registered society, headed by Mr. H. D. Shourie. The petitioner was seeking strict enforcement of Section 293A of the Companies Act, 1956, Section 13A of the Act, 1961 and Section 77 of the Representatives of Peoples' Act, 1950 as these provisions of law were being violated by the political parties with impunity.

It is the virtual immunity enjoyed by the political parties, through the acquiescence of the government for obvious reasons, that led to the flouting of the ceiling, with the candidate's own expenditure passed on as the party's and the parties themselves under no compulsion to explain where the crores of rupees they pumped in came from. This dispensation should change immediately with the Supreme Court's additional clarification that Article 32A of the Constitution empowers the Election Commission to seek details of the expenditure incurred or authorised by political parties for the election of their candidates.[21]

Although this judgment has restricted a candidate's unlimited discretion in dubbing the extra expenses beyond the ceiling as money spent by his friends or well wishers, or his party, it has not really made any substantive check on his election expenses, if the contributors were willing to reveal the source of their funding.

Raising Ceilings of Election Expenses

In its notification issued on 31 December 1997, the then government of Mr. I. K. Gujral raised the ceiling on election expenditure between Rs. 6 lakhs (0.6 million) to Rs. 15 lakhs (1.5 million), but this was not to include the expenditure incurred by political parties or well wishers of the candidates.[22] For the larger Lok Sabha constituencies (that is, all the constituencies in 19 of the 25 states and Delhi), the ceiling is up from Rs. 4.50 lakhs (0.45 million) to Rs. 15 lakhs (1.5 million). The six smaller States, which will have a comparatively lower ceiling, are Goa (Rs. 8 lakh), Arunachal Pradesh (Rs. 10 lakh), Sikkim (Rs. 10 lakh), Manipur (Rs. 13 lakh), Mizoram (Rs. 12 lakh) and Meghalaya (Rs. 13 lakh). In the case of Union Territories, the raised ceiling ranges from Rs. 6 lakh to Rs. 12 lakh. In respect of Assembly elections, the Government has revised the expenditure ceiling from Rs. 1.50 lakh to Rs. 6 lakh for States with larger Assembly constituencies. The hike in ceiling on election expenditure follows the Election Commission's approval given to the Government's proposal.[23] But in raising this limit, the government has ignored the Election Commission's main point (i.e. the ceiling to include the expenditure incurred by political parties and contributions from friends and well wishers). On its part, Nirvachan Sadan (the name of the office of the Election Commission of India) under the Chief Election Commissioner, Dr. M. S. Gill has preferred to let it pass. Thus, though there may now be more visibility of the amount spent by the candidate, the expense incurred by his/her party continues to go unchecked.[24]

However, now the Election Commission's revised format for filing returns of election expenditure, will make 'fudging of accounts' somewhat difficult as the candidates have to give details of expenditure incurred under various accounts. In addition, these are to be tallied with returns filed by political parties. Under the revised format, a candidate has to furnish details of the expenditure incurred not only by him but also by those supporting him—the political party which has set him up, any other political party (allies), any other organisation, association or body and any other individual. He or she has also now to spell out the amounts spent by each under various heads like public meetings, campaign material (handbills, posters, video and audio cassettes), vehicles used and visits of party leaders. Candidates can, therefore, no longer palm off large chunks of their expenses as simply those incurred by others. The names, the amount spent and the purpose must be specified. Not only this, the candidate had better tally these with those filed by his party, lest there be a discrepancy[25].

The political parties too have to furnish specific details in another format. A party has to state (i) its opening balance as on date of announcement of elections; (ii) total receipts from all sources, donations etc., received in cash and by cheques; (iii) total expenditure from date of announcement to date of completion of election—both in cash and by cheques; and (iv) the closing balance after elections. This apart, the parties have to give details of expenditure on 'general party propaganda' (that is, publicity, travel expense of leaders, cars, helicopters, aircraft etc.) and other expenses such as maintenance and running of campaign finance. However, one of the negative effects of this format is that it is likely to make it relatively easy for any loser candidate to seek disqualification of his rival elected candidate on grounds of exceeding the prescribed expenditure limits, leading to some unnecessary and frivolous litigations.[26]

State Funding of Elections

No reform effort to curb the use of money in elections can be effective unless means are devised to block the undisclosed sources of funds to which some parties or groups have easy access. In addition to compulsory accounting and receipts and donations by recognised agencies, state funding of elections, based on the pattern of the Federal Republic of Germany has often been suggested as a means of reform. State funding would provide assistance to political parties— funding proportionate to their percentage of votes polled in the preceding election. Many public figures, even some former Chief Election Commissioners, have recommended this strategy. The short-lived Charan Singh government 1979-80 was almost ready to implement this proposal when it was vetoed by the then President Sanjiva Reddy.[27]

Later in a study on the same subject, L. P. Singh, a former member of the Indian Civil Service (ICS) and a former Home Secretary of the Government of India, had observed that state funding of elections was essential for wider economic and social considerations and equality of opportunity among political parties in elections.[28]

Law Commission's Recommendations (1998)

In September 1998, The Union Law Commission in its report on "Reform of Electoral Laws" has advised state funding of elections limited to recognised political parties. It advised the government "to supply free of cost to candidates of recognised political parties such number of copies of the electoral roll, diesel or petrol for vehicles" to be used for electioneering. The government should also supply microphones and other equipments. It also suggested steep increases in the security deposit made by the candidates in order to discourage non-serious candidates to contest elections.[29] However, no action was taken as the government preferred to wait for the report of the all-party Committee on State Funding of Elections, consisting of eight members under the chairmanship of the former Union Home Minister and CPI leader, Mr. Indrajit Gupta, appointed on May 22, 1998 to report on the issue of State Funding of Elections.

Indrajit Gupta Committee on State Funding of Elections (1998)

The Indrajit Gupta Committee on State Funding of Elections, which submitted its Report to the Union Home Minister on 14 January 1999 favoured state funding of polls as it would not only help strengthen the democratic roots, but would also help in removing corruption and black money and other malpractice from the elections. State funding of political parties and their candidates would also tend to provide a level playing field even for those weaker political parties which may not have easy access to big business or industrial houses or may not enjoy patronage of such big donors because of their political ideologies and the policies or philosophy which they seek to pursue. State support to such parties would afford them with a reasonably equal opportunity of contesting elections with a fair chance of success against those parties who have superior financial power.[30]

The Committee, however, did not suggest any government help in cash as the Indian electorate had by now exceeded 60 crores, and the number of political parties was very large with 7 recognised National parties and 43 recognised State parties, apart from nearly 675 registered and unrecognised political parties. Nevertheless the committee thought that it should be possible to meet the 'essential expenses' involved in the elections. In view of limited financial resources and budgetary constraints, the government has to evolve its own system of State funding of elections. Examining the legal implications of the State funds being provided only to the recognised political parties and their candidates, and not to others, the Committee has noted that in view of the Supreme Court's judgement in Ramakant Pandey *vs.* Union of India and others (AIR 1993 SC 776) that the candidates of recognised political parties form a class by themselves and any discrimination made between them and others does not violate the equality clause in Article 14 of the Constitution of India, and thus any favour shown to the recognised political parties for providing state assistance was not inconsistent with the constitutional provisions.[31]

Agreeing with the opinion that any cash subsidies are capable of being misappropriated or used for purposes other than those for which the same was granted, the Committee recommended that State subvention may be given only in kind, in the form of certain facilities to the recognised political parties and their candidates. These could be: rent-free accommodation for the national headquarters of a recognised national party; rent-free telephone with STD facility; specified number of free telephone calls; sufficient free time on the State owned TV channels of Doordarshan and All-India Radio for their election propaganda over the electronic media. (In the scheme of election related telecasts/broadcasts over DD and AIR already in operation during the last general election, the Committee suggested a modification that the parties be permitted to use their allotted time for their propaganda in the manner they like and not necessarily for political speeches alone). Candidates of recognised National or State party should be provided with a certain specified quantity of petrol or diesel for vehicle used by them in their election campaign, a certain specified quantity of paper for printing their election literature and postal stamps of a certain specified amount to enable them to communicate with the election authorities and also with voters, five copies of electoral rolls of their constituency, set of loudspeakers and microphones and one telephone at his main campaign office in the constituency during election campaign period, minimum arrangements for the candidates' camps on the day of the poll and supply of refreshments and food packets to the counting agents inside the counting halls.[32]

Difficulties in State Funding

State funding of elections in India requires the government to raise adequate resources and involves a number of prerequisites. Such funding proposals also must assume a level of integrity which may not be attainable by the present day party leaders and members. Public funding may only supplement the resources now being deployed in elections and in party work. A report on West Germany's experience noted that "state funding of elections has neither rid political parties of their financial burdens nor cleaned public life",[33] party managers find various methods of raising additional money for their campaigns and candidates.

Many electoral reform efforts in India have not supported the state funding proposal, but have suggested instead that certain facilities, like printing, postage and telephone, be provided free of charge to all candidates. In 1988, the Congress Working Committee panel on electoral reform did not favour state funding, but proposed some financial support to print posters and organise meetings, and free postal services and advertising in newspapers and on television. This assistance would provide about Rs. 5,80,000 to each candidate sponsored by recognised political parties.[34] The 544 Lok Sabha candidates would receive a total of Rs. 980 million. The legitimate expenses of party-sponsored candidates could be met by the Government, but it would not be possible to provide such assistance to independent candidates.

There are a number of precedents, in countries such as Austria, Finland, France, Italy, the Netherlands, Norway, Sweden, the United States, and West Germany, for granting assistance in cash and in kind to political parties or their candidates. However, in India, this type of subsidisation is highly complicated by the enormous electorates of Assembly and Parliamentary constituencies, the multiplicity of parties, the inchoate nature of their organisation and financial management and the competing demands on the scarce government resources. As a result, the government has been dismissive of a public funding proposal, arguing that would aggravate the problem. Thus, the proposals did not find acceptance by the Gadgil Committee on Electoral Reforms in 1988 and subsequently, were not taken up for consideration by the government. While the opposition parties felt that state funding would end the dependence on the rich and the corrupt, the ruling Congress-I Party argued that it would not prevent parties from collecting money from other sources, putting an extra burden on the state, and increasing the number of independent candidates in the field.[35] It remains to be seen to what extent the recommendations of the Indrajit Gupta Committee (1998) found acceptance with the new government which came into power after the 13th General Elections in September/October 1999. Following an intensive discussion with the leaders of the political parties on September 13, 2001, the Government introduced on March 19, 2002, the Election and Other Related Laws (Amendment) Bill, 2002, based on Indrajit Gupta Committee Report. This Bill, which is intended to provide for State Funding of Elections, is pending before the Standing Committee of Parliament on Home Affairs.

Establishing an Electoral Trust

During the year 1997, the chief of the London-based multi-billion Hinduja Group, Mr. S. P. Hinduja proposed a viable transparent system to fund political parties and elections by individuals as well as corporate houses. The Hinduja Group has favoured a levy of 2 per cent of total income tax paid as surcharge on all assesses towards the election funds. Mr. Hinduja also suggested that the Government should set an annual target of Rs. 3009 crore and progressively increase it. Alternatively, it was stated that an election cess of Rs. 100 be levied on every individual tax assessee and Rs. 1,000 on corporate assesses.

In a third option given by the Hindujas, it was stated that owners of houses should pay 5 per cent of house tax towards election cess.

Mr. Hinduja further suggested that there should be an upper ceiling imposed for voluntary contributions. It should be Rs. 10,000 per individual and Rs. 1 crore per corporate house. This he thought would bring about transparency in funding of political parties and will tackle the problem of black money. On the question of spending the election fund collected from corporates and individuals, Mr. Hinduja favoured 50:50 allocation for Central and State elections. Funds available should be distributed on an equitable basis to all the constituencies barring North-Eastern states and Jammu and Kashmir. As per Hindujas' proposal, all national and state parties recognised by the Election Commission were to be made eligible for these funds. Any short fall should be made up by the Union Government on an ad hoc basis. On precautionary norms, he also maintained that parties violating election rules, candidates convicted or inducted for malpractices should be barred from utilising such funds.[36] However, nothing came out of these proposals.

At the same time, Mr. Ratan Tata, Chairman of India's largest business conglomerate—the house of Tatas, made a beginning by setting up a poll trust to fund political parties. The Tatas, who took a firm decision a few years back not to pay to any political party have now planned to form a trust which would channel the 100-odd group companies' contributions to political parties based on their past performance at the hustings. Tata Sons Director, S. A. Sabavala hoped that the trust should be functioning by the 1996 General Elections.[37] The keywords, of the Trust, as Mr. Ratan Tata later explained were 'non-discriminatory', 'non-discretionary' and 'transparent'.

The setting up of the trust has indeed raised many questions. Whether it will be workable at all? What is the structure of the trust and how transparent will it be? Are political parties inclined towards it and will they accept the funds? How will the trust decide about the funding—will all political parties get the donation? Above all, what happens to the interests of the shareholders who have a large share in these companies? Will they allow almost 5 per cent of the profit to be donated?

Explaining the whole idea behind the poll trust, Mr. Dinesh Vyas, a senior advocate and the Chairman of the trust based in Mumbai maintained that the very idea behind the fund was to make a transparent system of election funding, which simply means, no hush-hush or under the table dealings are to take place. First of all the Tatas will not be controlling the donations or the trust at all. The trust will function independently under the trustees. The Trustees are not Tata employees, but eminent citizens. In fact this trust is not meant only for the Tata companies, but all other companies, who wish to donate in this fund.[38]

The percentage to be donated by the company will be decided by the board of directors of each company. The contributions will be governed by the provisions of Section 293A of the Act, whereby companies will have to seek the approval of their boards to make any contribution. According to Company's Act, five per cent is the limit for corporate sector donations for political party funding. So the companies under the Tata group are expected to make donations within this limit. The donation does not have to be five per cent of the average profit made by that company in the last three years. It can be anything below that. A formula has been worked out for the distribution of funds in two parts. Half the amount will be given on the number of seats won by a party in the Parliament in the last election and the remaining on the basis of the results of the current elections. Mr. Ratan Tata himself has said earlier that there would be no personal prejudices of the trustees to affect the fund distribution and in no way will the funds be used to purchase favours.[39]

The electrifying launch of the Tata Electoral Trust in 1997 received rapturous applause from the industrialists and the political parties. It also bolstered the morale of people who are against using black money for the electioneering. At the eve of the 12th Lok Sabha Elections in January 1998, the Tata Electoral Trust was looking for an initial corpus of Rs. 50 crores. It has decided to receive a minimum contribution of Rs. 50,000 from individuals or corporates, and all transactions to be done in cheque and accounts audited by a certified chartered accountant. The objective of this electoral trust is to strengthen the democratic forces with a clean electoral process and to create an environment whereby donations can be made to political parties in a transparent, non-discriminatory and non-discretionary manner to help achieve a political framework for overall economic and social development of the country.

The investment policies of the electoral trust would be governed by the Bombay Trust Act so that the idle funds with the trust on any given day are suitably invested for maximising the returns for the next polls.

The trust will have two kinds of funds. The trust funds will be utilised to meet all expenses incidental to the administration of the trust. The distribution funds will not belong to the trustees but will be held by them in trust for the purposes of distributing the same to political parties. The trustees are independent persons of eminence but have no discretion in the matter of disbursement of the distribution funds. According to the formula designed for division of distribution of funds for a particular election, the Chairman of the Trust, Mr. Dinesh Vyas said, that in the first phase, one-half of the distributable amount will be disbursed on the basis of the seats held in the last parliamentary elections and the balance after the completion of the said elections. However funds will not be distributed to those political parties which held less than 5 per cent of the seats in the last Parliamentary elections, and which, in the opinion of the trustees, do not adhere to true democratic principles; encourage terrorist and/or secessionist activities, which can harm the overall development of the country and welfare of the people. The Trust will strictly go by the registration norms of the Election Commission as far as those parties are concerned which are dividing the nation on the basis of religion and caste.[40] The Electoral Trust currently provides for distribution of funds only for the Lok Sabha Parliamentary Elections.[41]

Despite the initiative taken by Mr. Ratan Tata in creating a trust for funding political parties and ensuring that these details are shown in the balance sheets presented to shareholders, for many companies in India, election funding is still a secret affair. Many do not write a cheque for the political party and many pay in cash through black money. There are other reasons why companies do not want to give out their donation figures. Shareholders may not approve of companies giving their money to political party they do not support. Also given that the government still has considerable bearing on business, there is always the fear of political vendetta associated with this practice.[42]

In the Indian context, many scholars have also suggested the creation of an election fund with several tax concession through contributions from the industrialists' which would directly disburse election funds to political parties.[43] But, as has been argued by Srivatsa Krishan:

> It would be too much to expect Indian industrialists to put their money in a labelless coffer, merely for the sake of clean democracy. They give money not out of any altruism, but only to get patronage and favours in return. If this direct nexus between money to a particular party/candidate and favours in return is broken by introducing a common electoral fund, it can be confidently argued that no industrialist would contribute to it. This is also true because in such operations secrecy is paramount, which would be automatically violated if white money is given to a fund. Further, beyond all this, no company will even agree to show these expenses in its balance sheets, for such money always comes from the infamous suitcases. The Bharatiya Janata Party (BJP), which recently stipulated that it would only accept donations through cheques, is faced with a sudden drop in funds mainly because industrialist, who would be otherwise willing to donate money are unwilling to play the ball now.[44]

Proposal for the Creation of a Government Controlled Election Fund

The Indrajit Gupta Committee recommended the creation of a separate Election Fund for meeting the expenses on State funding of elections. To begin with, the Central Government may contribute Rs. 600 crores annually, at the rate of Rs. 10 per elector for the total electorate of about 60 crores in the country, towards the corpus of the fund. The State Governments all taken together, may also contribute proportionately a matching amount of Rs. 600 crores annually, in accordance with the present financial arrangement between the Centre and States whereby all capital expenses on election items are shared by them on 50:50 basis.[45] The recommendation is still in limbo, and it remains to be seen to what extent the new Government which has come into power after the September 1999 elections remain committed to such reforms.

Concluding Observations

The foregoing analysis of the situation in respect of political finance in India, the world's largest democracy, very clearly stresses the need for a proper regulatory framework for party funding and independent monitoring mechanism to ensure an effective, fair and equitable participation of all political parties in a multi-party democracy. Despite conducting 13 general elections since Independence in 1947, which have been regarded by foreign observers as generally free and fair, the Government of India has not been able to enact one single piece of comprehensive legislation regarding the regulation of company donations and contributions to the parties' coffers. Most of the regulatory measures that govern contribution to political parties exist at different places such as Section 293A of the Indian Companies Act, 1956, and Sections 4 and 5 of the Foreign Contribution Regulation Act of 1976, or in the rules on the Ceiling of Expenditures of Elections to be observed by the candidates contesting for Parliamentary or Assembly polls prescribed by the Government of India from time to time. The Constitution of India mentions political parties only in Schedule X of the Constitution which regulates only the defection of candidates from one political party to another. In the absence of such regulations, a number of corrupt practices as described above have emerged for mobilising contributions to party and election funds. Even though the public is quite aware of the havoc that money plays at the time of elections and has become seriously concerned about it — thanks to a concerted one-man crusade launched a few years ago during the 10th General Elections by the then Chief Election Commissioner T. N. Seshan — to clean the election process and provide for free, fair and inexpensive elections, little has been done by the government by way of enacting appropriate legislation and regulations in this regard.

It would thus seem that in any democratic system, particularly in a multi-party democracy like India, there is a need to regulate political financing through a comprehensive legislation, which should among other things make both donor and receiver of political funds accountable; provide for compulsory auditing of party accounts (or else immediate de-recognition); publishing of audited party accounts; enhancement of penalties for filing false or incorrect election returns — a six months imprisonment and automatic party disqualification to contest an election for five years for an incorrect statement; state funding of elections in cash and kind; regulation of corporate funding through a system of tax concessions to obtain transparency in the flow of funds, and partly through limits placed on such contributions; encouragement of smaller contributions by individuals and political groups; provision for reasonable ceilings on election expenses; repeal by an appropriate notification of the 1974 Amendment of the RP Act, a separate judicial tribunal to ensure strict compliance and above all, through the establishment of a strict monitoring mechanism under the control of the Election Commission of India with panel provision for any violations of the code or rules in this regard.

Notes

1. For a detailed discussion on this subject, see Robert L. Hardgrave Jr. and Stanley A. Kochanek, *India: Government and Politics in a Developing Nation*, (Forthworth, Hartcout Brace, Javanovich College Publishers, 1993), pp. 236-308. Also see, Sudha Pai, 'Transformation of the Indian Party System', in *Asian Survey*, Vol. 36, No. 12, December 1996, pp. 1170-1181.
2. See *The Hindustan Times*, 5 August 1999, p. 12, col. 6.
3. See Stanley A. Kochanek, 'Briefcase Politics in India: The Congress Party and the Business Elite', *Asian Survey*, 27 (December 1987), pp. 1278-1301, as quoted in Hardgrave and Kochanek, n.2, pp. 330-331. In 1993; a stock broker, Mr. Harshad Mehta had made a public statement that he had delivered a suitcase containing Rs. 6.4 million in cash to the then Prime Minster, P. V. Narasimha Rao's residence as political contribution to gain some favours.
4. See Inderjit, 'Poll Expense Ceiling Now a Farce', *Economic Times* (New Delhi), 11 July 1989, p. 8.
5. See Government of India, Ministry of Law, Justice and Company Affairs, Legislative Department, Committee on State Funding of Elections (Chair: Indrajit Gupta) Report (New Delhi, December 1998) pp. 57-64, hereafter cited as Indrajit Gupta Committee Report.
6. See Stanley Kochanek, *Business and Politics in India* (Berkeley, University of California Press, 1974), pp. 230-239. Also see his, '*Briefcase Politics in India*', n.3.
7. See, The Representation of the People (Amendment) Act, 1974, No. 58 of 1974, 21 December 1974, Clause 77, Explanation 1.
8. News item, 'EC Move on Expenditure Rejected', *The Times of India* (New Delhi), 3 July 1989, p. 1.
9. *Ibid.*, p.1.
10. *Ibid.*, p.1.
11. Inderjit, n.4.
12. See, 'The Price of Power', *Sunday* (Calcutta), November 26 and 2 December 1989, p. 59.

13. See the statement of Dinesh Goswami, Law Minister in the National Front Government in The Hindustan Times, 17 December 1989, p. 1. See also the news item 'Panel on Electoral Reforms Soon', *The Hindustan Times*, pp. 1 and 10.
14. *The Times of India* (New Delhi), 5 January 1992, p. 1.
15. For details of the recommendations of the Committee, see *The Statesman* (New Delhi), 10 May 1990, p. 1; and *The Hindustan Times* (New Delhi), 8 May 1990. See also S. P. Singh, '*Need for Poll Reform*', *The Hindustan Times*, 9 May 1990, p. 11.
16. See, 'Press and Fair Poll', Editorial, *The Hindustan Times*, 5 February 1993, col. 4-8.
17. For details, See *The Hindustan Times*, 13 June 1994, p.12, col. 4-8; p. 13, col. 3-8; 15 June 1994, p. 13 col. 1-2 and 2 July 1994, p.12, col. 4-8.
18. As reported in *The Hindu*, 22 October 1994.
19. See, *The Hindustan Times*, 15 December 1994, p. 13, col. 23.
20. See, *The Hindustan Times*, 5 August 1996, p. 1, col. 1.
21. See, editorial 'Some Accountability', in *The Hindustan Times*, 6 April 1996, p. 11, col. 12.
22. In Indian terminology a lakh is equal to 0.1 million (100 thousand) and a crore is equal to 10 millions.
23. See, *The Hindustan Times*, 1 January 1998, p.1, col. 4.
24. See, *The Hindustan Times*, 4 January 1998, p.3, col. 5.
25. See, *The Times of India*, 6 November 1998.
26. *Ibid.*
27. See, S. C. Gangal, 'Not by Law Alone', *The Hindistan Times*, 8 August 1988, p. 9.
28. Singh, L. P., *Electoral Reform: Problems and Suggested Solutions* (New Delhi, Uppal Publishing House, 1986), p. 108.
29. See, *The Statesman*, 18 September 1998.
30. Indrajit Gupta Committee Report n. 9, pp. 22-24.
31. *Ibid.*, pp. 25-27.
32. *Ibid.*
33. As reported in Gangal, n. 32.
34. News item, 'State Funding of Poll Opposed', *The Hindustan Times*, 18 October 1988, p. 8.
35. 'Electoral Reform Belie Expectations', *The Hindu* (New Delhi), 9 July 1989, p. 8.
36. See, *The Hindustan Times*, 17 September 1997, p. 12, col. 6-7.
37. As reported in *Financial Times*, 8 November 1994.
38. See, Vimmy Sahay, 'Above Board', Sunday Magazine, *The Hindustan Times*, 31 August 1997, p.7, col. 1-5.
39. *Ibid.*
40. *The Hindustan Times*, 17 January 1998, p. 15, cols. 2-4. Also see The Times of India , 14 August 1999, p.17, cols.7-8.
41. See, *The Hindustan Times*, 12 February 1998, p. 15. cols. 3-4.

42. See, *The Times of India*, 25 July 1999, p. 12. cols. 3-8.
43. See, D. R. Pendse, 'Polls and Reforms', *The Hindustan Times*, 7 October 1993, p. 11, col. 1-4.
44. See, Srivatsa Krishna, 'Electoral Financing' *The Hindustan Times*, 23 June 1994, p. 13, col. 7-8.
45. Indrajit Gupta Committee Report, pp. 57-64.

7

Election Finance Reforms
Between a Ceiling and a Floor

SANJAY LODHA

The last decade of the 20th century was characterised by tremendous political churning in India. In a short span of ten years in the post-1993 period general elections apart from various state assembly elections and elections to local bodies have significantly altered the nature and contents of the Indian political system. So much so that political analysts have described this as heralding the entry of the Indian polity into the 'third electoral system'. The three Ms of Indian Politics: Mandal, Mandir and Market, unleashed new political alignments, and in fact altered the size and composition of those who choose: the voters. Together these forces caused frequent elections and with each election their relative significance also underwent transformations. Moreover, what could be regarded as the most redeeming feature of this political turmoil is that the wave of democratisation brought to the forefront of the Indian political system hitherto marginal social groups *i.e.* dalits, women, tribals and the rural masses.

Frequent electioneering at various levels, while galvanizing the participatory urge, also exerted a heavy financial pressure on the political class. Those in power used/abused their office and authority to amass resources and those waiting in the wings resorted to other unscrupulous means. The significance of money and muscle power in the political arena assumed unprecedented proportions as was vividly displayed by a series of scams and criminalisation of politics. With both the legislative and the executive weakened due to the emerging coalition culture the mantle of cleaning the muck fell on the judiciary. The much-hyped 'judicial activism' however is yet to deliver. In such a scenario the Election Commission, which was considered as just another wing of the administration to complete the formalities of the election, took charge.

Under the stewardship of Mr. T.N. Seshan the Election Commission became hyper active and the Chief Election Commissioner was the most talked about person in any election, making his presence felt on the government, parties and the people. A model code of conduct was made to operate, firmly revealing the hitherto undiscovered and untapped power of the Commission. Even after Seshan's exit the activist role of the Commission continues and its role as a wing of the states may not now be taken for granted. If one overlooks the excesses of the 'Seshan Effect', Mr. Seshan must be credited with the success in bringing to limelight the issue of electoral reforms. People from different walks of life have now joined the debate reflecting upon various aspects. Broadly speaking there are three perspectives in this debate. First of all, there is the managerial-bureaucratic perspective which believes that the electoral exercises in India have become 'too massive', unwieldy and messy and it is only through bureaucratic intervention backed by stringent legislation that the challenge can be met. Then there is the 'moralist' perspective which looks upon the whole task as a quest for moral regeneration necessary to remedy the declining ethical values of public life. In both these perspectives electoral reform has become a metaphor for morality in politics. Both look upon the participatory upsurge in Indian politics with contempt and decry the decentralisation of politics in favour of states and regional political parties. And both put their faith in modern technology (photo identity cards, electronic voting machines, media channels) and the legal system (Election Commission, Law Commission, Joint Parliamentary Committees) to set the house in order. As a counter to these 'non-political and potentially anti-political perspective' is a political perspective. This perspective refuses to equate electoral reforms with moral or social reforms. The challenge is to make the mechanism of election an effective instrument of the democratic will of the people, especially those who have so far been excluded from 'their due share of power'. As such the agenda for electoral reform according to the political perspective, must give priority to those disorders/malpractices, which create an obstacle in the way of deepening of the democratic process

Each of these perspectives has a message and without taking away from the supreme importance of the political perspective it would not be proper to regard the other two as 'middle-class utopia of sanitised' and 'sanity politics'. While the political perspective rightly calls for reforms to translate formal representation into substantive representation, the other two perspectives, to the present author, deal with the mechanisms that are essential to achieve the goal set by the former.

The need for reform of election finance regulations and for controlling the growing use/abuse of money in elections as well as in the over-all political arena has to be located in the context of the three perspectives cited above. The task here is two-fold: 'administrative-managerial' in the sense that a flagrant display of money power can be monitored and controlled only if an upper expenditure limit (as a ceiling) is fixed and a foolproof mechanism developed to enforce this limit; the task is 'political' too in the sense that equality of opportunity should be ensured to all contestants by providing each with minimum resources (as a floor) necessary to make the contest viable.

Election finance reforms pertain to a number of themes: limits on expenditure; limits on contributions from individuals and organisations; public/state funding of elections and parties; reporting and disclosure of election, party and candidates' finances in some form as an administrative prerequisite for enforcement of such curbs. Each of them needs a thorough investigation.

Limits on Expenditure

Limits on expenditure have been more common than limits on contributions. These relate to expenditure of parties and candidates on election campaigns. The Representation of the Peoples Act (RPA), 1951 (Sections 10A, 77 and 78) makes it mandatory for every candidate who contests an election to file tax returns of his election expenses within a month of the election. It also lays down that the total expenditure should not exceed the prescribed limit. The 'limit' under Rule 90 of the Conduct of Election Rules, 1961 is raised after every decade or so. The last revision was undertaken by the Government of India in 1998 raising the limit of Parliamentary constituencies from Rs.4.5 lakhs to Rs.15 lakhs and in the case of State Assembly from Rs.1.5 lakh to Rs.6 lakh. Rule 90 further explains that mere non-disclosure of expenditure is not a corrupt practice but it amounts to expenditure in excess of the prescribed limit in contravention of Section 77 (1 & 2) of the RPA, 1951. Section 123(6) of the Act defines incurring of excessive expenditure as a corrupt practice.

The issue of 'limits on expenditure' has two aspects: the amount to be limited and delimiting those who spend. It is an open secret that the candidates invariably spend more than the limits determined in 1998. For Assembly elections candidates spend more than the Parliamentary limit and for the Parliamentary elections the expenditure is several times more than the legal limit. It is therefore of importance that the limit should be realistic without being unjust to those whose resources are limited. There should be regular revision of the ceiling before every general election. More important is the question as to whether expenses incurred by a political party or by any body or association or an individual (other than the candidate and his election agent) in furtherance of election prospects of a candidate falls within Section 123 Clause 6 read with Section 77 of the RPA, 1951. The Election Commission has been recommending that the limit should be all inclusive embracing the expenditure incurred by a political party or supporters on behalf of a candidate. This was also the view expressed by the Supreme Court in the famous Kanwarlal Gupta *vs.* Amarnath Chawla (1975) case. The Apex Court ruled, 'Now if a candidate were to be subject to the limitation of the ceiling, but the political party sponsoring him or his friends or supporters were to be free to spend as much as they like .... The object of imposing a ceiling would be completely frustrated and the beneficent provision enacted in the interest of public and genuineness of the democratic process would be wholly emasculated.'

As a consequence of the Supreme Court judgment, the RPA was amended (1975) so as to nullify the judgement. Explanation 1 to Section 77 of the RPA was appended, by which unauthorized party and supporters' expenditure in support of the candidate did not count in election expenses incurred by a candidate, for the purpose of ceiling, making the limit, an exercise in futility. This explanation has come under severe criticism by the Supreme Court in various judgments [C. Narayana Swamy *vs.* C.K. Jaffer Sharief (1994); Ghadakh Yeshwant Rao *vs.* Balasaheb Vikhe Patil (1994) and Gajanan Bapat *vs.* Dattaji

Meghe (1995)] whereby the Court has described it as unjustified and unethical and reiterated the need to delete it. However the Parliament has not moved in the matter. In 1990 all the political parties had agreed to the deletion on the basis of which the then Law Minister Dinesh Goswami prepared an amendment bill providing for the deletion. In more recent times the Indrajit Gupta Committee on state funding saw representatives of major parties opposing the deletion. The Law Commission in its Report on the "Reform of Electoral Laws" also emphasised that state funding, partial or total, be not done until and unless explanation of Section 77 is deleted. Moreover, the explanation remains untouched and therefore the sky is the limit.

The Supreme Court in its judgement of April 1996 in the Common Cause *vs.* Union of India case relating to election expenditure, expressed the view that any expenditure incurred by a political party or supporters of a candidate will be excluded from the expenditure of a candidate only if, that expenditure has been shown in the account of the party/body/association/individual concerned and that account has been duly audited and submitted to the Income Tax authorities. Otherwise, such expenditure shall be presumed to be that of the candidate. The Election Commission in a proposal submitted to the Court of India in 1992 recommended that no association or body of persons (except a registered political party) or individuals should be permitted to incur any election expenditure without the written authorisation of the concerned candidate as his election agent and if so authorised such expenditure should be included in the return of the election expenses of the candidate concerned. For every registered political party the Commission recommended annual publication of accounts other than that incurred during election canvassing and auditing of such accounts by agencies appointed by the political parties. It has to be understood that in a democratic system the political parties have to be active between elections also. Functions of interest articulation and aggregation as well as political socialisation are permanent in nature. As such, apart from the ceiling fixed for election expenditure, a ceiling on routine expenses should also be decided. This may be inclusive of the election expenditure and allocated on a constituency basis.

Limits on Contribution

Most of the serious writings on electoral finance reforms, including reports by committees and state agencies, give a lot of importance to fixing a ceiling, not giving sufficient thought to where the money is going to come from, who will receive the money and what should be limits on such contributions. The issue thus relates to both donors and recipients. At the same time the donors should also be subject to certain limits; how much they can contribute per party, per candidate or per year.

In India, parties even from the pre-independence period have collected funds from membership dues and private contributions. There were limits on election expenditure since the RPA, 1951 and, until 1969, company contributions as corporate financing was legal. In 1969 a law was brought into force banning any company contribution to elections. This was an outcome of the growing nexus between black money and political fund raising. The Santhanam Committee (1964) in its report admitted that the existence of a large amount of unaccounted black money was a major source of corruption. The report stated "the public understanding in the prevalence of corruption at high political level has been strengthened by the manner in which funds were collected by political parties, expectedly at the time of elections and it was therefore essential to have a law requiring political parties to keep proper account of their receipts and expenditure".

Until 1979 political parties were required to pay income and wealth tax but this condition was waived in April 1979 provided they filled annual returns including audited accounts and identities of donors. Moreover, it is common knowledge that not many parties paid any taxes in the pre-1979 period nor have most of them taken any interest in filing annual returns in the post-1979 period. Most complied only when forced to do so by the Supreme Court in February 1996. In this exercise, while several reported no income, the three major parties Congress, BJP and Janata Dal declared a suspiciously low combined income of under Rs.170 million. In 1985 the Indian Companies Act was amended permitting companies to make contribution to charitable and other funds up to 5 per cent of their average profit of the three previous years. However, the overwhelming majority of contributions have continued to be through black money since going through the front door means party identification and also wrangling with shareholders. Efforts by the Dinesh Goswami Committee (1990) to introduce a bill on electoral reforms making unauthorised spending a penal offence lapsed and no serious fresh attempt was made thereafter.

The Confederation of Indian Industry (CII) in 1993 set up a Task Force on the issue of corporate contributions to election finance. The group recommended that such contributions to election finance be made tax-deductible and that board decisions should require confirmation by shareholders. The CII also advocated fund raising by a cess of indirect taxes or by contributions by industry to an election fund managed by the state from which funds should be distributed to parties by formula. In fact a beginning was made in this direction in 1997 with the establishment of an electoral fund, started by the Tatas. It will be some time before the outcome of such an exercise becomes clear.

The Election Commission itself does not approve of a total ban on donations by companies to political parties. In a report entitled Electoral Reforms (1998) the Commission mentioned 'After all the political process the activities which a political party legitimately engages itself involve heavy cost which has to be met by funds coming through certain channels.' Moreover, if trade unions and other organisations are allowed to contribute to political parties there seems to be not much ground that companies should be banned from making donations to political parties. Efforts should be made to create an atmosphere where there is more transparency in financial dealings rather than take extreme measures that would only drive these activities underground and away from the public gaze. Therefore, the Commission is of the view that in a democracy, companies may be allowed to contribute for political causes. The Commission cautioned that such contributions should be limited to a reasonable level and undertaken in a transparent fashion

State Funding of Elections

In about five decades of Indian experiment with electoral politics the role of money has been growing with each passing election. All efforts at fixing a ceiling and ensuring that parties and candidates stick to such a ceiling have not succeeded. Nor has the state machinery been any successful in controlling private contributions. There is increasing concern about the nefarious role of unaccounted money being used in the political arena. More and more people committed to cleansing the political milieu, are now advocating the introduction of state funding of elections. As opposed to curbs being exercised from without on a cash flow, which is beyond the control of a machinery trying to ensure its proper use both vis-á-vis the limit, the contributors and the manner of its use, state funding offers an alternative which might possibly provide checks at the beginning point rather than at the end point. Funding of elections or political activity by the state is also important to ensure that some minimum resource is available to popular candidates. At present only the affluent can contest elections; political parties select individuals who can afford to contest; others must compromise with the local rich; once in power, politicians must develop a personal political fund. As such a minimum level of institutionalized funding of political activity in general and elections in particular is a pressing need today. 'Politics needs more legitimate money than is available'. It is therefore, essential to provide a level floor to all.

Beginning with Germany in 1959 some form of public funding of elections and/or parties is a feature existing in at least 22 countries. There are 4 types of public funding, not mutually exclusive: (i) direct grants to political parties/candidates not tied to identified expenditure; (ii) specific grants earmarked for particular items of expenditure; (iii) provision of certain services by the government or government owned organizations; and (iv) indirect subsidies like tax credits to donors or tax exemptions to parties/candidates. State subvention as it exists broadly reveals three patterns.

(1) In Germany, Austria, Denmark, Italy and the Scandinavian countries public funding is the primary source of financing where assistance is given to the parties on the basis of the number of votes/seats secured at elections. This pattern is coupled with legal requirements that force intra-party democracy in Germany and transparency in Scandinavian states;

(2) Australia, New Zealand model where only the candidates are given limited public subsidy—subsidy usually in the

form of specific grants as state-sponsored services. The candidates are accountable to public authority for observance, reporting and disclosure of limits on expenditure mainly for the campaign period; and

(3) State assistance may be given in kind mostly by way of some services like free postage, free use of public premises for meetings, and free or concessional time on broadcasting/ telecasting media like in Ireland and UK.

In all the three patterns, parties and candidates are allowed to raise private contributions also but have to observe the monitoring limits on contributions and expenditure and meet the requirements for reporting and disclosure. There are however, difficulties, both procedural and substantive in the implementation of state subvention in the electoral arena. The main design difficulties are as to who should receive the subsidy and how and when it should be made. The most serious problems are definitional *i.e.* how to define major and minor parties and distinguish the serious from the 'frivolous' candidates seeking nomination just to obtain some free funds. Questions also pertain to issues of fairness, cost administration and enforcement. The major objectives of state subsidisation of the electoral area are to reduce costs, check illegal money, provide equality of opportunity and ensure a healthy, transparent, accountable and democratic functioning of the political parties. However, even in countries that have adopted this model, election spending has not necessarily come down. On the contrary, expenditure increased. Public subsidy has also failed to eliminate corruption and the latest scandal in Germany involving Helmut Kohl is a glaring example. It would also be naïve to believe that there is a direct causal relationship between more resources and victory.

In spite of these problems and difficulties it is believed that public funding, limits on expenditure and contributions and transparency requirements have checked the nexus between politicians and wealthy donors and put a brake on the growth of election expenditure. A minimum level of institutionalised funding is therefore beneficial. The paper seeks to review the existing laws in this regard and the limits and possibilities of state funding of elections in India.

India is not alien to the concept of state funding of elections.

During the constituent assembly debates, one of the members Mr. K.T. Shah suggested that the expenses of election be borne by the state. The government did not oppose this principle but maintained that it would impose an unbearable burden on state exchequer. In 1971 a Joint Parliamentary Committee headed by Mr. Jagannath Rao including the then Law Minister Mr. M.R. Gokhale reported that the electoral system's dependence on money power could be removed "only if it is accepted that all election expenses ought to be legitimate charge on the public fund". The Tarkunde Committee (1974) and the Goswami Committee (1990) advocated partial state intervention in kind as against cash. Earlier, Charan Singh, who was heading the caretaker government in 1980, wanted to implement state funding but the then President vetoed this move stating that it would be improper for a caretaker government to implement such an important decision.

The proposals for state intervention by Pai Panandikar and Ramashray Roy (1994) also merit consideration. They recommended:

(a) State funding of elections on an exclusive basis;
(b) Creation of an election fund of Rs.10 per vote polled all over the country;
(c) A special funding agency like the Electoral Commission to administer the fund;
(d) Funds to be distributed to different candidates on the basis of votes secured, subject to a ceiling of Rs.10 lakh per seat;
(e) The amount to be released to individual candidates (and not to political parties), on the basis of nominations made;
(f) 50 per cent to be released as advance, prior to elections on the basis of previous performance;
(g) Minimum threshold for eligibility for state intervention to be 20 per cent of national votes for national or major parties (10% for minor or new parties) or 10-12 per cent votes in a constituency for independent candidates;
(h) Submission of detailed accounts by the candidates to be audited by the EC.[1]

E. Sridharan (1996) a recognised expert on the subject feels that the Scandinavian 'maximalist' option of funding parties will be a huge drain on the state exchequer. It is also not feasible as political parties are not constitutionally recognised entities. Further, the lack of internal party democracy, weak loyalties, frequent defections/splits, and absence of transparency are also reasons why this option is inappropriate for Indian conditions. Unrealistic expenditure limits will not be enforceable especially as the party system evolves towards an ever-growing number of parties. Sridharan therefore opines that India will have to go in for a 'mixed' pattern providing for state funding along with reforms advocated by the minimalist model. Funding should be given directly to candidates to ensure internal party democracy. It should be in kind for better monitoring and implementation and should be adequate to eliminate the possibility of illegal private donation. To raise the fund Sridharan rejects both the prevailing views of cess on excise and an election tax on industry. Both these options involve an official nexus between industry and election funding. Moreover, industries may not welcome the idea of a tax. It will also lead to unhealthy politicisation of industry. He therefore, recommends that the development fund which has been allotted to MP for the development of their constituency should be abolished (because of its unfairness) and a part of the funds (Rs. 400 billion over a five year period) be used for state subvention of elections. Sridharan suggests that since growing multi-polarity will increase competition and cost in the political arena 'collective action' by political parties in favour of state funding will be in their overall interest.

Yogendra Yadav (1995) another advocate of the idea of state funding accepts the Panandikar-Roy proposal with the following modifications:

(a) State funding should not be exclusive; private fund raising should be allowed subject to an overall ceiling of expenditure.

(b) Instead of direct payments to candidates, funds should be given to parties which should be free to disburse it to candidates/party offIces.

(c) Parties must spend at least 50 per cent of the funds during the election campaign and remaining 50 per cemt during the next five years before the subsequent general election.

(d) The entire amount should be accounted for and audited without any restriction on internal budgeting.

(e) Eligibility threshold should operate at the state level and be reduced to bare minimum (say 2% of the vote share in a state or 5 per cent in a constituency in the case of an independent) so as to exclude only the "dummy" candidates.

(f) Payment should be made conditional upon regular democratic election of the highest decision-making body and office bearers of the party (the Election Commission and the Supreme Court should have the power to adjudicate any dispute in this regard).[2]

Ironically, the Election Commission for its part has not maintained a consistent view on the subject. Till 1980, the Commission advocated state funding. However, in recent years it has shown dissatisfaction with the idea of direct cash subsidy and has instead suggested indirect state funding. The Commission in its report "Electoral Reforms: Views and Proposals, 1998" impressed upon the Government the need to keep the Commission informed and also involve it through a process of dialogue relating to state funding. In fact the Commission evolved a scheme on its own in 1998 whereby recognised political parties are given much more time on state-owned electronic media on an equitable basis, free of any charges.

The Law Commission under the Chairmanship of Justice B.P. Jeevan Reddy in its report on the "Reform of Electoral Laws" has supported the proposals for introducing partial state funding as recommended by the Indrajit Gupta Committee. The Commission has emphasised that state funding, partial or total, should not be introduced until and unless explanation of Section 77 is deleted and the provisions suggested by it on political parties (Part II-A in the 1951 Act) including Section 78-A are enacted simultaneously. The main purpose of Part II-A is to ensure internal democracy in political parties by asking them to have a constitution, internal elections, audit of accounts, etc.

The basic idea is to bring nearly every serious party within the ambit of state funding, provide them with some minimum financial resources to contest election and carry out regular political work between elections and to link this assistance to internal democratic functioning. However, even as all major non-Congress Parties have accepted state funding in principal, their response has been very casual. It is clear that the political establishment is unprepared to undertake any significant restructuring of the pattern of election financing.

Monitoring Election Finance

Any proposal relating to election finance reforms will not carry much meaning until and unless stringent rules and regulation relating to enforcement, auditing, disclosure, etc., are implemented. State funding requires the parties and candidates to be accountable to public authority for observance of limits on expenditure, and reporting and disclosure. Greater transparency is essential to make the whole system creditable.

The Indian Electoral Law under Section 77 of the RPA, 1951 requires that all candidates should disclose the correct account of all expenditure incurred in connection with the elections and that they are bound to submit the accounts for the period between the day on which they have been nominated for election and the day of the declaration of the result thereof. Failure to do so within the time limit can lead to disqualification of membership of the Parliament or State Assembly, which is enforced by the President of India, after seeking the opinion of the Election Commission. According to Section 10(A) of the Act, the Commission itself has the right to disqualify a candidate, if it is satisfied that a candidate failed to submit an account of the expenses in accordance with the rules. The Commission scrutinizes the account and in case of default issues notification of disqualification only after providing ample opportunity to the candidates to represent their case.

The Supreme Court in a number of cases has exhorted the Election Commission to supervise the maintenance of income and expenditure incurred by political parties and also to disclose the funds received by them. The Law Commission of India has also stressed the need for monitoring expenditure incurred by political parties, without which the problem of excess expenditure cannot be checked. The Election Commission itself in 1992 lamented the inadequacy of existing law in placing curbs on the unscrupulous use of money in election. It recommended that every registered political party should publish its accounts annually and such accounts should be audited by agencies appointed by the Election Commission. Moreover, it also suggested that no body of person or association (except a registered political party) or individual should be permitted to incur any election expenditure without the written authorisation of the candidate or his election agent and such expenditure should be included in the return of the election expenses of the candidate concerned. Violation of this provision should be liable to punishment of one to five years' imprisonment and a fine.

The existing law, however, does not provide for any cross checking of the returns filed by the candidate. So there is no way to verify whether the returns are true, without recourse to an election petition against the winner. In the assembly election held in 1994-95 the Commission tried to arm itself with these powers and enlisted the services of revenue officials and private accountants. It did create a scare and instilled financial discipline among candidates but the findings of this exercise were not made public. What is, therefore, important is that the accounts of parties and candidates should be made publicly available to the press and political rivals. In this regard right to information can be of great value if and when it is provided. Moreover, all aspirants to public office should be compelled to make public the official record of income, assets and liabilities for the past 10 years at least whenever they contest an election.

The paper has sought to cover the whole debate of election finance reforms in India. The need to curb unscrupulous practices has never been more urgent. While state subsidy is one instrument to achieve the goals, equally important is strict monitoring and verification mechanisms. Greater vigilance by intermediary institutions and the civil society sector is essential. What is urgently needed is a method to firm up the existing law enforcement machinery, make it work faster, more impartially and more transparently. Mere changes in statute books but with the same set of rules, same bureaucracy, the same law enforcement agencies will not stem the rot. What is perhaps more disturbing is the structural relationship between economic and political power in the present day India which is assuming new proportions in the wake of globalisation and the rise of the middle classes. In such a situation any genuine concern for eliminating the nexus between politics and economic power cannot be confined to the agenda of electoral reform. Much larger questions are involved here. But a beginning has to be made somewhere and it may well be with reforming the financial sector's involvement in the electoral process.

Notes

1. V.A. Pai Panandikar and Ramashray Roy (1994): *Financing of Elections*, Centre for Policy Research, New Delhi.
2. See, Yadav, Yogendra (1998): "Electoral Reforms: Beyond Middle Class Fantasies", in M.P. Singh (ed) *Ideologies and Institutions in Indian Politics*, Deep and Deep, New Delhi.

Reference

Sridharan, E. (1996): 'Reforming Political Finance', *Seminar*, October 2001 pp. 29-36.

8

Testing Median Voter Hypothesis Through Human Development Index

Evidence from Indian Polity

ACHAL KUMAR GAUR

Median Voter Hypothesis: An Exposition

The median voter hypothesis (MVH) which is an important tool of formal political theory was introduced by Black (1958), Bowen (1943) and Hotelling (1929). The prime argument behind the hypothesis[1] states that if political opinion on a particular issue may be viewed as lying in a single dimension, then competition among political candidates will force them towards the position held by the 'typical' median voter McFachern, W.A. (1978). For example, the MV hypothesis, which is extensively examined and tested by scholars including G.K. Turnbull and S.S. Djoundurm (1994), Romer, T. and Rosenthal, H. (1979a, 1979b, 1982), Inman, Robert, P. (1978), Holcombe, R.G. (1980, 1989), states that public fiscal behaviour reflects the preferences of voters with the median income in the jurisdiction. Thus, the level of public expenditure, which is a vital organ of fiscal policy, should correspond to what is acceptable to voters with median income [Romer, T. and Rosenthal, H. (1979b) and Plot, C.R. (1967)]. However, the logic of social justice asserts that the preferences of the voters having income below the income of median voters should also be satisfied through the expenditure policy of the Government.

There is a global consensus among politicians, social thinkers and policy makers [Sen, A.K. (1985, 1987), Sen, A.K. and Dreze, J. (1995, 1998)] that the ingredients of the quality of human life such as life expectancy, education, drinking water facilities, poverty eradication measures must be improved not only for median jurisdictions but also for those having much less income than the median jurisdiction. In the present paper, an attempt has been made to test MVH for nineteen major Indian states. For this purpose, the inter-state Human Development Index (HDI) for education as well as medical and public-health attainment have been constructed for the period 1971-95. Section II of the paper deals with some salient features of the Indian political structure during past fifty years. In Section III, an attempt has been made to test MVH with the help of some of the major ingredients of the quality of human life data *i.e.* inter-state comparison of expenditure pattern governing education, medical and public-health, life expectancy, urbanisation, access to safe drinking water. Section IV presents major findings of the present study.

Indian Political Scenario: Emerging Dimensions

The post-independent political scenario of the Country, from the general election of 1952, may broadly be divided into three periods. The first four general elections from 1952 to 1967 fall under the first phase of electoral system that witnessed one party dominance—*i.e.* the Congress Party—which means that the elections during this period were not competitive in the true sense. Electoral loyalties were determined at the national level and the voter, of course, did not vote as an individual, but rather as a member of a political community. The beginning of the second phase started during the general election of 1967 when Congress and the Savarna jatis (the so called higher castes) were challenged for the first time. The next five general elections between 1971 to 1989 may be taken as the second phase of the Indian electoral system from the electoral victory of Mrs. Indira Gandhi in 1971. The effective participation of 'middle' Castes and Other Backward Castes (OBC) into electoral politics, which made it competitive in the true sense, was major feature of Indian polity during this phase.

The three Ms—Mandal, Mandir and Market—are perhaps the major ingredients of the ensuing third phase of the Indian polity. In essence, the implementation of the Mandal Commission's recommendations for OBC reservation, the Bhartiya Janata Party's (BJP) Rathyatra which ultimately resulted in demolition of Babari Maszid and the first phase of New Economic Policy introduced by

Narasimha Rao's Government in 1991, have led to a new type of political mobilisation. These changes have resulted in a transition in the electoral system and have allowed various latent forces to surface in electoral politics.

The dynamism as well as the versatility of the Indian electoral system has revealed several distinctive features. For example, the aggregate volatility between Lok Sabha elections during 1977-1998 has declined sharply from 23.8 per cent in 1977-80 to 14.7 per cent in 1996-98 (Table 8.1). In other words, if electoral volatility is any index of effective use of the vote in mass elections, the facts reveal that the voters are less decisive now than they were earlier.

Table 8.1 : Aggregate Volatility between Lok Sabha Elections, 1977-1998

(Percentage)

Election Years	1977-1980	1980-1984	1984-1989	1989-1991	1991-1996	1996-1999
Aggregate Volatility	23.8	21.5	16.1	11.8	12.9	14.7

Source: Yadav, Yogendra (1999), "Electoral Politics in the Time of Change", EPW, August 21-28, 2392-2399.

Secondly, voting patterns based on community, economic status and education have shown interesting results for the period 1971-98 (Table 8.2). The facts reveal that the proportion of dalit votes are much higher today than that of upper caste votes. This has been accompanied by their deep involvement in various forms of political activities. Also, the socially and the economically privileged section of society have recorded a diminishing trend in political participation while the very poor, poor and middle class have shown a surge in this regard. It is interesting to note that an educated voter is more likely to be non-participant and churlish about political matters than his counterpart among the less educated.

Thirdly, women participation in political affairs has shown an upward trend. This is corroborated by the fact that the proportion of women who vote (in percentage) and women as a proportion of total voters in Lok Sabha elections were 38.8 and 38.3 respectively in 1957 while these figures stood at 61.0 per cent and 46.9 per cent during 1998, respectively (Table 8.3).

Table 8.2 : Odds-Ratio for Voting: 1971, 1996 and 1998

	1971	1996	1998
Community			
* Hindu Upper	1.11	0.90	0.97
* Hindu OBC	0.82	1.07	0.94
* SC	1.04	1.22	1.21
* ST	0.65	0.91	0.95
* Muslim	1.59	0.92	1.12
* Sikh	1.53	0.86	1.60
* Christian	2.29	1.13	1.05
Economic Status			
* Very Poor	0.89	1 24	0.92
* Poor	0.98	1.13	1.05
* Middle	1.14	0.94	1.18
* Upper Middle	1.06	0.89	0.96
* Upper	1.38	0.75	0.75
Education			
* Illiterate	0.82	1.03	0.91
* Upto Middle	1.49	1.01	1.33
* College	1.29	1.05	0.91
* Graduate	1.07	0.70	0.66

Source: Yadav, Yogendra (1999), "Electoral Politics in the Time of Change", *EPW*, August 21-28, 2392-2399.

Table 8.3 : Women's Turnout and Women as Proportion of Total Voters, Lok Sabha Elections, 1957-98

Year	Women (Per cent Turnout)	Men (Per cent Turnout)	Women (Per cent of Total Voters)
1957	38.8	55.7	38.3
1962	46.6	62.1	39.8
1967	49.0	61.0	42.0
1971	49.2	61.2	42.4
1977	54.9	65.4	43.6
1980	51.2	62.2	43.1
1984	59.3	68.4	44.5
1989	57.5	66.4	44.1
1991	50.5	60.7	42.9
1996	53.4	62.1	44.0
1998	61.0	65.9	46.9

Source: Yadav, Yogendra (1999), "Electoral Politics in the Time of Change", *EPW*, August 21-28, 2392-2399.

Fourthly, the emergence of regional parties and region-centric politics has been salient features of the modern political structure of India. Regional politics has flourished in the periphery signifying that the Central Government has shown negligence to regional aspirations and identity. And finally, the electoral verdict, especially during the past ten years, has resulted in a coalition culture at the centre and at the state level.

Indian Polity and MVH: Empirical Evidence

In order to test the median voter hypothesis, inter-state expenditure patterns (revenue account) on Education, Medical & Public Health for nineteen major states of the country has been taken into consideration during the period 1971-1995. Median state income has been estimated through growth rate of per capita State Domestic Products (SDPs) and their overall ranking during the period (Table 8.4). Kerala and Madhya Pradesh occupied the rank of median income states when reckoned on the basis of geometric as well as exponential growth rate mechanism respectively, during the period 1971-95. Invariably, the states of Himachal Pradesh, Orissa, Assam, Uttar Pradesh, West Bengal, Rajasthan, Bihar occupied the lowest ranking in the hierarchy of median income states during the period (Table 8.4). Inter-state Human Development Indices for educational attainment (1971-95) are presented in Table 8.5. It is obvious that Kerala and M.P., both median states, have lost their relative positions in terms of educational attainment during the period. For instance, Kerala occupied 3rd rank in 1971, which deteriorated later, and it stood at 5th rank in 1995. Similarly, M.P. ranked 14th position in 1971 and dropped gradually until it stood at 17th rank in 1995. States below median income like Andhra Pradesh, Assam, Rajasthan, and West Bengal have lost their relative ranking during the period while the states of Uttar Pradesh and Bihar occupied 18th and 19th position consistently during 1971-95.

Table 8.6 depicts inter-state Human Development Indices for Medical and Public Health attainment for nineteen major states. It reveals that Kerala improved its ranking from 8th in 1971 to 4th in 1995 while M.P., another median income state lost slightly from 15th rank in 1971 to 16th in 1995. It is significant to note that states below median income like A.P., Bihar, Orissa, Rajasthan, U.P. and W. B. lost

Table 8.4 : Inter-state growth of per capita State Domestic Product (SDP)

	Per capita SDP at Factor Cost (current prices) (1970-71) (Rs.)	Per capita SDP at Factor Cost (current prices) (1994-95) (Rs.)	Geometric Growth Rate	Exponential Growth Rate
A.P.	585	7787	10.91 (7)	10.35 (7)
Assam	535	5924	10.10 (14)	9.62 (14)
Bihar	402	3678	9.26 (18)	8.854 (18)
Gujarat	809	10731	10.90 (8)	10.34 (8)
Haryana	877	12099	11.07 (5)	10.50 (5)
H.P.	651	7736	10.41 (12)	9.90 (12)
Karnataka	641	8229	10.75 (9)	10.21 (9)
Kerala	595	7194	10.48 (10)	9.94 (11)
M.P.	484	5825	10.46 (11)	9.95 (10)
Maharashtra	783	13007	11.90 (1)	11.24 (1)
Manipur	390	6433	11.86 (2)	11.21 (2)
Nagaland	489	8043	11.85 (3)	11.20 (3)
Orissa	478	5298	10.11 (13)	9.62 (13)
Punjab	1070	14594	10.02 (6)	10.45 (6)
Rajasthan	651	6311	9.51 (17)	9.09 (17)
Tamil Nadu	581	9115	11.64 (4)	11.01 (4)
Tripura	502	4295	8.97 (19)	8.59 (19)
U.P.	486	5266	10.00 (15)	9.53 (15)
W.B.	722	7345	9.72 (16)	9.28 (16)

Notes:
1. Figures for per capita SDP have been estimated by the author through SDPs and mid-year population figures. These figures have been taken from various issues of Report on Currency and Finance (Vol. II).
2. Figures in the parentheses indicate respective state-wise ranks.

their relative positions in terms of Medical and Public Health attainment during the period 1971-95.

It is evident from this analysis that poorer states like Orissa, Assam, Bihar, Rajasthan, U.P. and W.B. were deprived of basic facilities in terms of education, medical and public health during the period 1971-95. This is contrary to the basic idea of the median voter hypothesis.

Table 8.5 : Inter-state Human Development Index in India (1971-95) : Educational Attainment

	1971	1972	1973	1974	1975	1976	1977	1978	1979	1980	1981	1982	1983
A.P.	0.1278 (13)	0.1229 (14)	0.0824 (16)	0.1070 (14)	0.1238 (15)	0.0904 (15)	0.1803 (13)	0.1196 (14)	0.0575 (16)	0.1090 (14)	0.0943 (14)	0.1350 (13)	0.1217 (13)
Assam	0.1861 (9)	0.1858 (10)	0.1243 (13)	0.1289 (12)	0.2138 (9)	0.1077 (13)	0.1715 (14)	0.2405 (9)	0.0958 (13)	0.1754 (10)	0.1354 (11)	0.1096 (15)	0.0770 (14)
Bihar	0.0134 (17)	0.0000 (19)	0.0000 (19)	0.0000 (19)	0.0000 (19)	0.0000 (19)	0.0000 (19)	0.0000 (19)	0.0000 (19)	0.0183 (19)	0.0618 (17)	0.0618 (17)	0.0404 (16)
Gujarat	0.1598 (11)	0.1854 (11)	0.1535 (12)	0.1374 (11)	0.1715 (13)	0.1473 (9)	0.4193 (7)	0.2576 (8)	0.1613 (9)	0.2213 (8)	0.1747 (9)	0.2016 (9)	0.1717 (9)
Haryana	0.2123 (6)	0.2136 (8)	0.2000 (8)	0.1936 (9)	0.2403 (8)	0.1631 (8)	0.2640 (9)	0.2982 (7)	0.1231 (10)	0.1846 (9)	0.1942 (8)	0.2282 (8)	0.1655 (11)
H.P.	0.0690 (15)	0.5780 (3)	0.6000 (3)	0.5166 (4)	0.7266 (2)	0.4687 (2)	0.5995 (2)	0.5383 (2)	0.3475 (3)	0.4996 (3)	0.5818 (3)	0.6114 (3)	0.4969 (3)
Karnataka	0.2104 (7)	0.1864 (9)	0.1900 (10)	0.1598 (10)	0.1953 (11)	0.1354 (10)	0.2300 (11)	0.1765 (12)	0.1127 (11)	0.1530 (12)	0.1211 (12)	0.1460 (12)	0.1299 (12)
Kerala	0.4085 (2)	0.4299 (4)	0.4043 (5)	0.4213 (5)	0.5644 (5)	0.4557 (3)	0.5973 (3)	0.4899 (4)	0.3148 (4)	0.4803 (4)	0.4271 (4)	0.4970 (4)	0.3776 (5)
M.P.	0.0794 (14)	0.0831 (15)	0.0863 (15)	0.847 (16)	0.0982 (17)	0.0504 (17)	0.1157 (17)	0.0575 (17)	0.0278 (17)	0.0310 (17)	0.0105 (18)	0.0284 (18)	0.0058 (18)
Maharashtra	0.2326 (5)	0.2201 (7)	0.2069 (7)	0.2317 (7)	0.2828 (7)	0.1967 (7)	0.2805 (8)	0.2128 (10)	0.1718 (7)	0.2608 (7)	0.2375 (7)	0.2627 (7)	0.2014 (7)
Manipur	0.7237 (2)	0.7523 (2)	0.6834 (2)	0.6482 (2)	0.7185 (3)	0.4400 (4)	0.5666 (4)	0.5110 (3)	0.4298 (2)	0.7530 (2)	0.8063 (2)	0.8932 (2)	0.8309 (2)
Nagaland	1.0000 (1)	1.0000 (1)	1.0000 (1)	1.0000 (1)	1.0000 (1)	1.0000 (1)	1.0000 (1)	1.0000 (1)	1.0000 (1)	1.0000 (1)	1.0000 (1)	1.0000 (1)	1.0000 (1)
Orissa	0.0572 (16)	0.0698 (16)	0.0441 (17)	0.0334 (17)	0.1183 (16)	0.0894 (16)	0.1703 (15)	0.1051 (16)	0.0684 (15)	0.0849 (16)	0.0753 (16)	0.0756 (16)	0.0515 (15)
Punjab	0.2889 (4)	0.2796 (5)	0.3322 (6)	0.3548 (6)	0.3606 (6)	0.3118 (6)	0.4213 (6)	0.3619 (6)	0.2430 (6)	0.3567 (6)	0.4117 (6)	0.4117 (6)	0.3261 (6)
Rajasthan	0.1652 (10)	0.1644 (12)	0.1678 (11)	0.1283 (13)	0.1754 (12)	0.1149 (12)	0.1905 (12)	0.1485 (13)	0.0874 (14)	0.1277 (13)	0.0890 (15)	0.1230 (14)	0.0280 (17)
Tamil Nadu	0.1955 (8)	0.2361 (6)	0.1957 (9)	0.2045 (8)	0.2088 (10)	0.1220 (11)	0.2318 (10)	0.1840 (11)	0.1236 (9)	0.1659 (11)	0.1454 (10)	0.1792 (11)	0.0692 (10)
Tripura	0.0000 (19)	0.0134 (18)	0.5407 (4)	0.6277 (3)	0.5731 (4)	0.4050 (5)	0.4993 (5)	0.4770 (5)	0.3015 (5)	0.4413 (5)	0.3826 (6)	0.4587 (5)	0.4446 (4)
U.P.	0.0120 (18)	0.0380 (17)	0.0208 (18)	0.0138 (18)	0.0511 (18)	0.0444 (18)	0.0950 (18)	0.0368 (18)	0.0118 (18)	0.0020 (18)	0.0000 (19)	0.0000 (19)	0.0000 (19)
W.B.	0.1570 (12)	0.1603 (13)	0.1227 (14)	0.0876 (15)	0.1407 (14)	0.0924 (14)	0.1649 (16)	0.1145 (15)	0.0961 (12)	0.0970 (15)	0.1103 (13)	0.1959 (10)	0.1895 (8)

	1984	1985	1986	1987	1988	1989	1990	1991	1992	1993	1994	1995
A.P.	0.1712 (12)	0.1651 (10)	0.1180 (13)	0.1341 (14)	0.1638 (15)	0.0899 (15)	0.1347 (11)	0.0615 (15)	0.0976 (16)	0.1196 (14)	0.1090 (15)	0.0965 (16)
Assam	0.2465 (8)	0.1626 (12)	0.1474 (11)	0.2827 (8)	0.2016 (12)	0.1355 (12)	0.1320 (13)	0.2260 (11)	0.3075 (9)	0.3135 (88)	0.3453 (9)	0.2554 (10)
Bihar	0.0274 (7)	0.0192 (17)	0.0160 (17)	0.0000 (19)	0.0000 (19)	0.0148 (18)	0.0325 (18)	0.0101 (18)	0.0000 (19)	0.0000 (19)	0.0000 (19)	0.0000 (19)
Gujarat	0.2070 (10)	0.3099 (7)	0.2649 (7)	0.2425 (9)	0.2723 (8)	0.2410 (8)	0.2487 (8)	0.2975 (8)	0.3314 (8)	0.2858 (10)	0.3136 (9)	0.3077 (8)
Haryana	0.1870 (11)	0.2070 (9)	0.1651 (10)	0.2028 (11)	0.2697 (9)	0.2237 (9)	0.2109 (10)	0.2130 (12)	0.2548 (11)	0.2499 (11)	0.2119 (13)	0.2041 (13)
H.P.	0.5086 (3)	0.4818 (4)	0.4348 (4)	0.5084 (4)	0.6002 (4)	0.6873 (4)	0.6947 (4)	0.7833 (4)	0.9333 (2)	0.6972 (3)	0.6195 (3)	0.6610 (3)
Karnataka	0.1297 (15)	0.1494 (13)	0.1220 (12)	0.1660 (13)	0.2273 (10)	0.1543 (10)	0.1335 (12)	0.1463 (14)	0.2219 (12)	0.2182 (12)	0.2313 (11)	0.2548 (11)
Kerala	0.4041 (5)	0.3864 (5)	0.3661 (5)	0.4339 (5)	0.3746 (5)	0.3191 (6)	0.2940 (6)	0.4631 (5)	0.4113 (6)	0.3853 (5)	0.4368 (5)	0.4831 (5)
M.P.	0.0322 (18)	0.0176 (18)	0.0107 (18)	0.0435 (17)	0.0786 (17)	0.0201 (17)	0.0000 (19)	0.0000 (19)	0.0206 (17)	0.0317 (18)	0.0481 (17)	0.0537 (17)
Maharashtra	0.2230 (9)	0.2332 (8)	0.2129 (8)	0.2958 (6)	0.2848 (7)	0.2471 (7)	0.2960 (7)	0.2940 (9)	0.3799 (7)	0.3433 (7)	0.3282 (8)	0.3106 (7)
Manipur	0.7672 (2)	0.7295 (2)	0.7712 (2)	0.7973 (2)	0.7351 (2)	1.0000 (1)	1.0000 (1)	0.9938 (2)	1.0000 (1)	1.0000 (1)	0.8191 (2)	0.9405 (2)
Nagaland	1.0000 (1)	1.0000 (1)	1.0000 (1)	1.0000 (1)	1.0000 (1)	0.9591 (2)	0.9157 (2)	1.0000 (1)	0.8811 (4)	0.7871 (2)	1.0000 (1)	1.0000 (1)
Orissa	0.0564 (17)	0.0651 (16)	0.0267 (16)	0.0904 (16)	0.1087 (16)	0.0461 (16)	0.0511 (17)	0.0193 (17)	0.1135 (15)	0.1008 (16)	0.1042 (16)	0.1550 (14)
Punjab	0.3473 (6)	0.3381 (6)	0.2731 (6)	0.2873 (7)	0.3598 (6)	0.3273 (5)	0.4704 (5)	0.4117 (6)	0.5210 (5)	0.3451 (6)	0.3339 (7)	0.3431 (6)
Rajasthan	0.1187 (16)	0.1301 (15)	0.0843 (15)	0.1268 (15)	0.1662 (14)	0.0979 (14)	0.1058 (14)	0.1645 (13)	0.1978 (13)	0.1998 (13)	0.2122 (12)	0.2188 (12)
Tamil Nadu	0.1666 (13)	0.1638 (11)	0.1841 (9)	0.2090 (10)	0.2111 (11)	0.1458 (11)	0.2243 (9)	0.3320 (7)	0.2972 (10)	0.3126 (9)	0.2927 (10)	0.2905 (9)
Tripura	0.5042 (4)	0.5477 (3)	0.4560 (3)	0.6320 (3)	0.6415 (3)	0.8333 (3)	0.7558 (3)	0.8716 (3)	0.8831 (3)	0.6951 (4)	0.5947 (4)	0.5544 (4)
U.P.	0.0000 (19)	0.0000 (19)	0.0000 (19)	0.0304 (18)	0.0374 (18)	0.0000 (19)	0.0664 (16)	0.0485 (16)	0.0014 (18)	0.0645 (17)	0.0174 (18)	0.0363 (18)
W.B.	0.1470 (14)	0.1308 (14)	0.1098 (14)	0.1971 (12)	0.1690 (13)	0.1150 (13)	0.0895 (15)	0.2308 (10)	0.1759 (14)	0.1165 (15)	0.1472 (14)	0.1356 (15)

Note: Figures in the parentheses indicate respective state-wise ranks.

Table 8.6: Inter-state Human Development Index in India (1971-95) : Medical and Public Health Attainment

	1971	1972	1973	1974	1975	1976	1977	1978	1979	1980	1981	1982	1983
A.P.	0.1027 (11)	0.0971 (12)	0.0384 (16)	0.0398 (15)	0.0737 (15)	0.0784 (15)	0.1156 (14)	0.1003 (14)	0.0856 (14)	0.1197 (15)	0.1019 (11)	0.0962 (15)	0.1147 (15)
Assam	0.0722 (13)	0.0835 (13)	0.0252 (17)	0.0259 (17)	0.0568 (17)	0.0698 (16)	0.0664 (17)	0.0627 (17)	0.0000 (19)	0.0722 (17)	0.0661 (17)	0.0651 (17)	0.0831 (16)
Bihar	0.0071 (17)	0.0238 (18)	0.0000 (19)	0.0067 (18)	0.0000 (19)	0.0000 (19)	0.0000 (19)	0.0000 (19)	0.0023 (18)	0.0000 (19)	0.0000 (19)	0.0000 (19)	0.0000 (19)
Gujarat	0.1530 (5)	0.1691 (5)	0.0896 (13)	0.0809 (11)	0.1226 (10)	0.1084 (13)	0.1430 (8)	0.1336 (8)	0.1090 (9)	0.1701 (8)	0.0954 (13)	0.1268 (10)	0.1429 (10)
Haryana	0.1483 (6)	0.1688 (6)	0.1332 (6)	0.0966 (7)	0.1411 (8)	0.1195 (11)	0.1387 (12)	0.1772 (4)	0.1345 (5)	0.1964 (6)	0.1488 (5)	0.1975 (3)	0.2156 (4)
H.P.	0.0000 (19)	0.2679 (2)	0.2512 (2)	0.2287 (2)	0.2787 (2)	0.2387 (2)	0.2611 (2)	0.2134 (2)	0.2445 (2)	0.4225 (2)	0.3691 (2)	0.4352 (2)	0.4026 (2)
Karnataka	0.0875 (12)	0.0825 (14)	0.0974 (9)	0.0717 (13)	0.1155 (11)	0.1289 (9)	0.1400 (11)	0.1079 (13)	0.0865 (13)	0.1185 (16)	0.0746 (16)	0.0918 (16)	0.1222 (14)
Kerala	0.1376 (8)	0.1659 (7)	0.0939 (11)	0.0939 (8)	0.1442 (7)	0.1707 (5)	0.1943 (3)	0.1544 (5)	0.1151 (8)	0.1771 (7)	0.1251 (7)	0.1420 (8)	0.1260 (13)
M.P.	0.0652 (15)	0.0764 (16)	0.0603 (14)	0.0489 (14)	0.0772 (14)	0.0460 (17)	0.1083 (15)	0.0792 (16)	0.0898 (16)	0.1265 (13)	0.1027 (10)	0.1092 (12)	0.1279 (12)
Maharashtra	0.1568 (4)	0.1590 (8)	0.1531 (5)	0.1333 (5)	0.1600 (6)	0.1503 (6)	0.1411 (10)	0.1316 (9)	0.1271 (6)	0.2240 (4)	0.1281 (6)	0.1867 (5)	0.2292 (3)
Manipur	0.2358 (2)	0.2033 (3)	0.1388 (3)	0.1406 (4)	0.2269 (3)	0.2280 (3)	0.1230 (13)	0.1231 (12)	0.1380 (4)	0.2544 (3)	0.2582 (3)	0.1914 (4)	0.0516 (17)
Nagaland	1.0000 (1)	1.0000 (1)	1.0000 (1)	1.0000 (1)	1.0000 (1)	1.0000 (1)	1.0000 (1)	1.0000 (1)	1.0000 (1)	1.0000 (1)	1.0000 (1)	1.0000 (1)	1.0000 (1)
Orissa	0.0707 (14)	0.0821 (15)	0.0487 (15)	0.0326 (16)	0.0700 (16)	0.0817 (14)	0.0846 (16)	0.0814 (15)	0.0750 (15)	0.1233 (14)	0.0896 (14)	0.1000 (13)	0.1433 (9)
Punjab	0.1455 (7)	0.1551 (9)	0.1533 (4)	0.1703 (3)	0.2011 (4)	0.2237 (4)	0.1896 (4)	0.2016 (3)	0.1530 (3)	0.2210 (5)	0.1550 (4)	0.1717 (6)	0.1671 (7)
Rajasthan	0.1731 (3)	0.1932 (4)	0.0992 (8)	0.0667 (9)	0.1349 (9)	0.1409 (7)	0.1569 (7)	0.1540 (6)	0.1222 (7)	0.1599 (10)	0.1080 (9)	0.0980 (14)	0.1680 (6)
Tamil Nadu	0.1232 (9)	0.1537 (10)	0.0918 (12)	0.0820 (10)	0.1098 (13)	0.1146 (12)	0.1721 (5)	0.1282 (10)	0.1058 (10)	0.1310 (12)	0.0962 (12)	0.1507 (7)	0.1910 (5)
Tripura	0.0030 (18)	0.0000 (19)	0.1004 (7)	0.1185 (6)	0.1795 (5)	0.1325 (8)	0.1412 (9)	0.1250 (11)	0.0960 (12)	0.1671 (9)	0.0816 (15)	0.1256 (11)	0.1296 (11)
U.P.	0.0165 (16)	0.0236 (17)	0.0034 (18)	0.0000 (19)	0.0161 (18)	0.0184 (18)	0.0161 (18)	0.0385 (18)	0.0357 (17)	0.0611 (18)	0.0311 (18)	0.0311 (18)	0.0484 (18)
W.B.	0.1060 (10)	0.1083 (11)	0.0940 (10)	0.0756 (12)	0.1127 (12)	0.1281 (10)	0.1640 (6)	0.1385 (7)	0.1049 (11)	0.1575 (11)	0.1195 (8)	0.1310 (9)	0.1454 (8)

	1984	1985	1986	1987	1988	1989	1990	1991	1992	1993	1994	1995
A.P.	0.1166 (12)	0.1269 (15)	0.0688 (13)	0.0775 (14)	0.0870 (14)	0.1323 (11)	0.1075 (13)	0.0855 (15)	0.1133 (15)	0.1387 (13)	0.1070 (11)	0.735 (14)
Assam	0.0209 (18)	0.1343 (12)	0.0685 (14)	0.0814 (13)	0.0750 (15)	0.1012 (15)	0.0563 (18)	0.0856 (14)	0.0715 (17)	0.1162 (15)	0.0996 (12)	0.1138 (12)
Bihar	0.0000 (19)	0.0000 (19)	0.0000 (19)	0.0000 (19)	0.0000 (19)	0.0000 (19)	0.0000 (19)	0.0000 (19)	0.0571 (19)	0.0000 (19)	0.0000 (19)	0.0000 (19)
Gujarat	0.1213 (10)	0.1485 (11)	0.0702 (12)	0.1493 (8)	0.1171 (8)	0.1802 (6)	0.1645 (8)	0.1605 (9)	0.2958 (10)	0.2289 (10)	0.1427 (10)	0.1644 (11)
Haryana	0.0263 (4)	0.3042 (3)	0.1962 (9)	0.0983 (12)	0.0956 (11)	0.1298 (12)	0.1019 (14)	0.0886 (13)	0.1585 (13)	0.1511 (12)	0.0282 (18)	0.0432 (17)
H.P.	0.2921 (2)	0.4625 (2)	0.2607 (2)	0.3509 (2)	0.3281 (2)	0.5760 (2)	0.4771 (2)	0.6483 (2)	0.8540 (2)	0.9153 (2)	0.5801 (2)	1.0000 (1)
Karnataka	0.0767 (15)	0.1301 (14)	0.0821 (11)	0.1151 (10)	0.1129 (9)	0.1488 (10)	0.1236 (10)	0.1169 (12)	0.2377 (8)	0.2618 (7)	0.1489 (8)	0.2115 (9)
Kerala	0.0581 (16)	0.1500 (10)	0.1185 (8)	0.1610 (6)	0.1239 (7)	0.1759 (8)	0.1757 (6)	0.2415 (6)	0.3290 (6)	0.2569 (8)	0.1962 (6)	0.3097 (4)
M.P.	0.1114 (14)	0.1130 (16)	0.0357 (17)	0.0255 (18)	0.0622 (16)	0.0933 (16)	0.0631 (16)	0.0352 (18)	0.0738 (16)	0.0465 (18)	0.0349 (16)	0.0549 (16)
Maharashtra	0.2043 (5)	0.2355 (5)	0.2559 (3)	0.1535 (7)	0.1370 (6)	0.1763 (7)	0.1661 (7)	0.1527 (10)	0.2116 (9)	0.2419 (9)	0.1500 (7)	0.1682 (10)
Manipur	0.1879 (6)	0.2043 (6)	0.2347 (4)	0.1913 (4)	0.2594 (3)	0.5014 (3)	0.4063 (3)	0.4016 (4)	0.4678 (5)	0.6090 (3)	0.3766 (3)	0.3205 (3)
Nagaland	1.0000 (1)	1.0000 (1)	1.0000 (1)	1.0000 (1)	1.0000 (1)	1.0000 (1)	1.0000 (1)	1.0000 (1)	1.0000 (1)	0.1000 (1)	1.0000 (1)	0.8944 (2)
Orissa	0.1207 (11)	0.1326 (13)	0.0441 (16)	0.0752 (15)	0.0620 (17)	0.0786 (17)	0.0621 (17)	0.0433 (17)	0.1266 (14)	0.0713 0.0290 (16)	0.0650 (17)	(15)
Punjab	0.1729 (7)	0.2590 (4)	0.1431 (4)	0.1843 (5)	0.1699 (5)	0.2517 (5)	0.2741 (5)	0.2980 (5)	0.4757 (4)	0.3901 (4)	0.2470 (4)	0.2590 (6)
Rajasthan	0.1244 (9)	0.1621 (9)	0.0503 (15)	0.0640 (16)	0.0894 (13)	0.1160 (14)	0.1151 (11)	0.1352 (11)	0.1881 (11)	0.2207 (11)	0.1435 (9)	0.1376 (9)
Tamil Nadu	0.2217 (3)	0.1700 (7)	0.1678 (6)	0.1030 (11)	0.1065 (10)	0.1499 (9)	0.1559 (9)	0.2074 (7)	0.2880 (7)	0.3251 (6)	0.2046 (5)	0.2232 (7)
Tripura	0.1257 (8)	0.1678 (8)	0.1855 (5)	0.2426 (3)	0.2335 (4)	0.3850 (4)	0.3298 (4)	0.4143 (3)	0.5014 (3)	0.3788 0.0488 (5)	0.2987 (15)	(5)
U.P.	0.0555 (17)	0.0363 (18)	0.0314 (18)	0.0429 (17)	0.0454 (18)	0.0750 (18)	0.0696 (15)	0.0558 (16)	0.0000 (19)	0.0637 (17)	0.0595 (14)	0.0275 (18)
W.B.	0.1164 (13)	0.1082 (17)	0.0833 (10)	0.1210 (9)	0.0933 (12)	0.1270 (13)	0.1145 (12)	0.1790 (8)	0.1770 (12)	0.1353 (14)	0.0942 (13)	0.0985 (13)

Note: Figures in the parentheses indicate respective state-wise ranks.

Some other empirical studies [Guha, Biswajit (1998)] also have revealed similar results. For example, Table 8.7 reveals that median income state is Kerala and the states below this income are A.P., Assam, Rajasthan, M.P., Orissa, U.P. and Bihar. Index numbers of life expectancy, education, urbanisation and percentage of household with access to safe drinking water and electricity connection, which are vital ingredients of quality of human life are presented in Table 8.7 for the period 1988-94. The figures reveal that index numbers of these vital parameters have been invariably lower for states like Assam, Rajasthan, M.P., U.P., Orissa and Bihar than for the state having the median index number. For example, Orissa, M.P., U.P., Rajasthan and Bihar occupied 10th, 11th, 13th, 14th and 15th rank respectively when viewed in relation to educational status. Similarly, in terms of percentage of household with access to safe drinking water, the respective ranks of U.P., Bihar, M.P., Rajasthan and Orissa were 10th, 11th, 13th, 14th and 15th. Table 8.7 also contains some measures of inequality like Gini Coefficient, RMD, Theil Index etc., for the parameters of quality of human life under the present analysis. All these measures of inequality support the inference that inter-state inequality is higher especially in case of availability of electricity connection, per capita income of state, urbanization and education.

Table 8.8 presents percentage of population and seats in Lok Sabha for the bigger states and their ranks in Human Development Index (HDI).[2] The rank correlation between HDI and population is -0.4, which shows that HDI has been lower for the states with higher population and *vice versa*. Similarly, negative rank correlation in HDI and seats in Lok Sabha reveals that the states with more seats in the Lok Sabha had lower HDI. In other words, the states like Rajasthan, M.P., U.P., Bihar and Orissa who have 225 seats in the Lok Sabha were ranked 11th, 12th, 13th, 14th and 15th respectively in terms of HDI. This reflects a failure of policy makers and the political elite and has led to agitation among citizens of these states. This failure has perhaps been the major cause of the emergence of regional political parties in these states like S.P., B.S.P., J.M.M. etc. and has led to frequent assembly as well as Lok Sabha election in the past ten years.

Major Findings and Concluding Observations

The electoral landscape in the recent past has changed drastically and

Table 8.7 : Inter-state quality of Human Life in India: Major Trends

State	Index Number (1988-94) of				%age of Household (1991-94)	
	Life Expectancy	Per Capita SDP	Education	Urbanization	Safe Drinking Water	Electricity Connection
A.P.	59.17 (8)	19.33 (9)	45.38 (12)	26.9 (7)	66.3 (9)	48.3 (8)
Assam	49.83 (4)	17.81 (10)	50.72 (9)	11.1 (15)	63.6 (12)	17.5 (14)
Bihar	55.83 (11)	9.56 (15)	36.76 (15)	13.1 (14)	65.9 (11)	13.6 (15)
Gujarat	58.33 (9)	24.73 (4)	60.38 (4)	34.5 (2)	76.2 (4)	65.8 (2)
Haryana	63.58 (4)	32.13 (3)	56.12 (7)	24.6 (9)	75.1 (6)	69.7 (2)
Karnataka	61.33 (6)	22.01 (6)	57.12 (5)	30.9 (4)	78.3 (3)	52.6 (6)
Kerala	78.00 (1)	19.51 (8)	90.85 (1)	26.4 (8)	75.3 (5)	49.7 (7)
M.P.	48.33 (15)	15.67 (12)	46.19 (11)	23.2 (10)	62.6 (13)	44.0 (9)
Maharashtra	65.33 (3)	33.82 (2)	67.39 (3)	38.7 (1)	73.6 (8)	68.2 (3)
Orissa	50.83 (13)	13.32 (14)	47.6 (10)	13.4 (13)	52.0 (15)	24.2 (12)
Punjab	68.83 (2)	39.3 (1)	56.41 (6)	29.5 (5)	95.4 (1)	82.3 (1)
Rajasthan	54.83 (12)	16.98 (11)	39.48 (14)	22.9 (11)	60.6 (14)	33.2 (11)
Tamil Nadu	62.33 (5)	22.83 (5)	68.19 (2)	34.2 (3)	74.7 (7)	55.8 (5)
U.P.	57.33 (10)	13.97 (13)	41.14 (13)	19.8 (12)	66.2 (10)	22.4 (13)
W. Bengal	60.83 (7)	19.54 (7)	55.75 (8)	27.5 (6)	87.3 (2)	33.6 (10)
* Gini	0.0684	0.2015	0.1298	0.1772	0.0804	0.2548
* RMD	0.0511	0.1558	0.0983	0.1357	0.0635	0.2032
*Theil Index	0.00281	0.02417	0.01033	0.01951	0.00395	0.03897
*Kakwani Index	0.00454	0.03785	0.01626	0.03217	0.00639	0.06299

Source: Raw figures have been taken from Guha Biswajit (1998), Human Development in India—A Study of Interstate Disparity. Paper presented at IEA 2nd Amrit Jubilee Conference held at Bangalore during 26-28 December, 1998.

Note: 1. Figures in the parentheses indicate respective state-wise ranks.

2. Measures of inequality (*) like Gini, RMD, Theil and Kakwani have been calculated by the author of present paper.

Table 8.8 : Major State-wise Percentage of Population and Seats in Lok Sabha, their Ranks in Human Development in India

Rank According to H.D.I.	State	%age of total Population	Total No. of Seats in Lok Sabha
1	Kerala	3.4 (12)	20 (12)
2	Punjab	2.4 (14)	13 (14)
3	Haryana	1.9 (15)	10 (15)
4	Gujarat	4.9 (10)	26 (9)
5	Maharashtra	9.3 (3)	48 (3)
6	Andhra Pradesh	7.9 (5)	42 (4.5)
7	Tamil Nadu	6.6 (7)	39 (7)
8	West Bengal	8.0 (4)	42 (4.5)
9	Karnataka	5.3 (8)	28 (8)
10	Assam	2.6 (13)	14 (13)
11	Rajasthan	5.2 (9)	25 (10)
12	Madhya Pradesh	7.8 (6)	40 (6)
13	Uttar Pradesh	16.4 (1)	85 (1)
14	Bihar	10.2 (2)	54 (2)
15	Orissa	3.7 (11)	24 (11)

ρ (HDI, Popn.) = - 0.4

ρ (HDI, Seats in Lok Sabha) = - 0.44

Note: 1. Figures in parentheses indicate respective statewise ranks.
2. ρ stands for Spearman's rank correlation.

it may be viewed as the reflection of a fundamental transformation in the terrain of Indian politics. The choice of voters has been volatile and the structure of choices inherent in elections has changed. These changes in the electoral options are most probably an effort to search for good governance. The major ingredients of 'good governance' would be a government, which is stable and truly representative of the majority of people, accelerates economic development, ensures welfare of all section of society and provides social and economic justice quickly. The present paper attempts to test the existence of 'good governance' in Indian polity through Median Voter Hypothesis. The major findings are listed below:

1. The electoral volatility, which if taken as an index of effective use of vote in the elections, has reduced significantly during 1977-98.

2. Educated people have shown reluctance to participate in political affairs while non-educated persons have shown a keen interest.
3. The proportion of Dalit votes has risen more sharply, in the recent past, than that of upper caste.
4. Regional parties have emerged in the recent past and it has resulted in the existence of a coalition culture in the Indian polity.
5. Testing of MVH reveals that poorer states of the country like Assam, Bihar, U.P., M.P., Orissa and Rajasthan have been deprived continuously in terms of some major ingredients of quality of human life like life expectancy, education, safe drinking water facility, urbanisation etc. This is perhaps the root cause for emergence of regional parties and coalitions in the Indian polity.
6. The highly disquieting trend, evident in the present analysis is that five states: — Rajasthan, M.P., U.P., Bihar and Orissa, — which represent about half of the Lok Sabha seats, have had the worst positions in terms of Human Development Index during the period 1971-95.

Notes

1. There are two major assumptions [Mueller, Dennis C. (1989)] for the median voter theorem. The assumptions are (1) that issues are defined along a single dimensional vector X and (2) that each voter's preferences are single-peaked in one dimension. Let voters I's preferences be represented through a utility function U_i ( ) defined over X, $U_i(X)$. Let X_i^* be voters i's most preferred point along the X vector. Let us call X_i^* as i's ideal point.

Definition (1): X_i^* is i's ideal point if and only if (iff) $U_i(X_i^*) > U_i(X)$ for all $X \neq X_i^*$

Definition (2): Let Y and Z be two points along the X dimension, such that either $Y, Z \geq X_i^*$ or $Y, Z \leq Xi^*$ then voter i's preferences are single-peaked iff

$$[U_i(Y) > U_i(Z)] \leftrightarrow [|Y - X_i^*| < |Z - X_i^*|]$$

In other words, the definition of single peaked preferences says that if Y and Z are two points on the same side of X_i^*, then i prefers Y to Z if and only if y is closer to X_i^* than Z.

Definition (3): Let $\{X_i^*, X_2^*, X_3^* \ldots X_n^*\}$ be the *n* ideal points for a committee of *n* individuals. Let N_g be the number of $X_i^* \geq X_m$ and N_L be the number of $X_i^* \leq X_m$, then X_m will be the median position if $N_g \geq n/2$ and $N_L \geq n/2$.

Theorem : If *X* is a single dimensional issue, and all voters have single-peaked preferences defined over *X*, then X_m, the median position, cannot lose under majority rule.

2. The Human Development Report (1990) of the UNDP addresses the question of development not merely as an expansion of income, but development must encompass improvements in other non-income indicators as well. The report emphasises the use of Human Development Index (HDI), which is a composite of three elements of living standard: longevity, knowledge and income. The Human Development Index (HDI) has been formulated in terms of a Country's deprivation or shortfall in each of three separate dimensions: life expectancy (X_1), eduction (X_2), and adjusted income (X_3) [Sudhir Anand & Amartya K. Sen (1994)].

The 1990 report defined I_{ij} as the deprivation index for country j with respect to variable X_i as:

$$I_{ij} = \frac{\dfrac{\text{Max}\{X_{ij}\} - X_{ij}}{K}}{\dfrac{\text{Max}\{X_{ik}\}}{K} - \dfrac{\text{Min}\ \{X_i K\}}{K}}$$

By construction each deprivation index for country *j*, *i* = 1, 2, 3, lies in between 0 and 1. An average deprivation index I_j for country *j* across the three variables was defined as a simple unweighted average of the I_{ij}, i.e.

$$I_j = 1/3 \sum_{i=1}^{3} I_{ij}$$

The shortfall in the human development index for country *j* was then defined to be just this average deprivation. Thus, if H_j is the human development index for country j, we have, by definition:

$$H_j = I - I_j$$

H_j can directly be expressed in terms of attainment level X_{ij}. From the above,

$$H_j = 1 - 1/3 \sum_{i=1}^{3} I_{ij}$$

$$= 1/3 \sum_{i=1}^{3} (I - I_{ij})$$

$$= 1/3 \sum_{i=1}^{3} \left[1 - \frac{\underset{K}{\text{Max}}\{X_{ij}\} - X_{ij}}{\underset{K}{\text{Max}}\{X_{ik}\} - \underset{K}{\text{Min}}\{X_i K\}} \right]$$

$$= 1/3 \sum_{i=1}^{3} \left\{ \frac{X_{ij} - \underset{K}{\text{Min}}\{X_{ik}\}}{\underset{K}{\text{Max}}\{X_{ik}\} - \underset{K}{\text{Min}}\{X_i K\}} \right\}$$

$$= 1/3 \sum_{i=1}^{3} H_{ij}$$

$$\text{where } H_{ij} = \frac{X_{ij} - \underset{K}{\text{Min}}\{X_{ik}\}}{\underset{K}{\text{Max}}\{X_{ik}\} - \underset{K}{\text{Min}}\{X_i K\}}$$

it the *i*th variable's contribution to the human development index for country *j*.

References

Black, Duncan (1958): *The Theory of Committees and Elections*, Cambridge University Press.

Bowen, Howard R. (1943): "The interpretation of voting in the allocation of economic resources," *Quarterly Journal of Economics*, 58, 27-48.

Geoffrey K. Turnbull & Salpie S. Djoundourian (1994): "The median voter hypothesis: Evidence from general purpose local government," *Public Choice* 81: 223-240.

Guha, Biswajit (1998): "*Human Development in India-A Study of inter-state Disparity.*" Paper presented at IEA 2nd Amrit Jubilee Conference held at Bangalore during 26-28 December, 1998. Calcutta: The Indian Economic Association

Holcombe, R.G. (1980): "An empirical test of the median voter model," *Economic Inquiry* 18: 260-274.

Holcombe, R.G. (1989): "The median voter model in public choice theory," *Public Choice* 61: 115-215.

Hotelling, Harold (1929): "Stability in Competition", *Economic Journal*, 39: 41-57.

Inman, Robert P. (978): "Testing Political Economy's 'as if' proposition: Is the median income voter really decisive?" *Public Choice*, 33.

McFachern, W.A. (1978): "Collective decision rules and local debt choice: A test of the median voter hypothesis," *National Tax Journal*, 31: 129-136.

Mueller, Dennis C. (1989): *Public Choice II*, Cambridge University Press.

Plott, C.R. (1967): "A notion of equilibrium and its possibility under majority rule." *American Economic Review* 57: 787-806.

Romer, T. and Rosenthal, H. (1979a): "Bureaucrats versus voters: On the political Economy of resource allocation by direct democracy." *Quarterly Journal of Economics*, 93: 563-588.

Romer, T. and Rosenthal, H. (1979b): "The elusive median voter." *Journal of Public Economics* 12: 143-170.

Romer, T. and Rosenthal, H. (1982): "Median voters or budget maximizers: Evidence from school district referenda." *Economic Inquiry* 20: 556-578.

Sen, A.K. (1985): *Commodities and Capabilities*. Amsterdam: North Holland.

Sen, A.K. (1987): *The Standard of Living, The Tanner Lectures*. New York: Cambridge University Press.

Sen, A.K. & Dreze, J. (1995): *Indian Economic Development and Social Opportunity*, Oxford University Press.

Sen, A.K. & Dreze, J. (1998): *Indian Development—Selected Regional Perspectives*, Oxford University Press.

Anand, Sudhir & Amartya Sen (1992): 'Human Development Index: Methodology and Measurement', Background paper for Human Development Report 1993,UNDP, New York.

United Nations Development Programme (1990): Human Development Report, 1990, Oxford University Press.

Yadav, Yogendra (1999): "Electoral Politics in the Time of Change." *EPW*, August 21-28, 2393-2399.

9

Political Process of Voting and Social Change

BHASKAR MAJUMDER

Political Process of Voting and Social Change

This paper attempts to analyse the issue of whether we should be concerned about the level of voter participation based primarily on a theoretical analyis of social interaction rather than consideration of the current political situation. In order to carry out such an analysis we would like to pose two major questions in this paper. Why do people take part in the political processes of a country? As a corollary, why do people take part in the electoral processes? Before we respond to these two questions, let us look into the more fundamental aspects of human participation in activities or processes, specifically those which are called social activities or processes. I would contend that essentially, this participation of individuals is economic since it is in quest for food and other security. The economic existence of individuals requires after a certain stage a degree of consensus. Individuals form a society, form a polity, and interact, to arrive at a consensus. These formations follow the natural interdependence among individuals.

This paper has four sections. In Section I we talk about society and social change in a conceptual frame. In Section II, we analyze social interaction and domination. In Section III we talk about the electoral system and needed electoral reforms in the context of India. Finally, in Section IV we make concluding remarks.

Society and Change

A society is the formation of individuals who carry on activities that reflect the ideas and ideologies of those individuals. All the individuals may not be conscious at the beginning about the ideas and ideologies latent in the activities they perform. But in the ultimate analysis, activity initiated by a single individual in the society affects the rest of the individuals, including, of course, of that person. Society may get integrated or fragmented in accordance with the actions initiated by the individuals. An integrated society carries a common agenda, while a divided or fragmented society does not accept it. A polity is an institution that reflects the interaction of individuals involved in arriving at a consensus or at least a basis for future participation in the polity. A polity may have a number of wings, like political parties, organisations that deal with human needs through, for example, non-government organisations, action groups that may or may not be recognised by the existing government. The electoral system is a mechanism that is meant to maintain the mainstream political system. In other words, the mere existence of the electoral system does not imply a social change unless that is the goal of development in any society. The electoral system may indicate only some peripheral societal changes. Those societal changes are often reflected in the relative influence of individuals or groups in decision-making processes.

Social Interaction and Domination

We start with the basic proposition that it is social when it involves at least two individuals in the domain of social actions that affect both the individuals. I accept this proposition even if any one or both of the individuals are indifferent to the outcome of their social actions. This is because, even if the individuals remain (apparently) indifferent to the outcome (A12) of the action by A (A1) and reaction by B (A2), the very reaction by B implies that either A continues to perform activity A1 or reacts by performing another activity A3, so that either initial social outcome (A12) repeats itself, or there comes another social outcome (A21). Both A and B participate in relation to one another, that is, in the social domain. A and B, in fact, constitute the society by performing A1 and A2 yielding grand outcome (A12) or changing the outcome by performing A1 and A3, yielding A21, A21 being different from A12. Thus, social actions reflect formation of society and show scope for social change. In our example, societal changes occur always, like A12 to A21. However, social changes occur by negation of A12 and A21, if there comes a third individual C who accepts A12 by accommodating initial activity of A expressed as A1. The inclusion or exclusion of C, thus, is vital to explain if the social system persists, or, if it gives scope for change.

Often, collusive (indifferent) outcome by A and B remain anti-change, in absence of C. The presence of C by positive action alters the initial actions and reactions by initial participants A and B. At the risk of over simplification, we say that initial outcome by performance of A and B may remain private, unless C comes.

Actually it is C that alters the social combinations. Initially it was A → B, or B → A in a leader-follower relation, or simply AB (=BA) relation in an equality-based accommodative relation. Now, it may take a number of combinations like the following:

I. AB → C, AC → B, BC → A (all leader-follower relation, with implicit accommodative combination of any two individuals guiding/coercing/dictating the third individual).

II. A → BC, B → CA, C → AB (all leader-follower relation, with any one becoming leader, guiding/coercing/dictating the rest of the combinations of the two individuals).

III. A → B → C, B → A → C, C → A → B, B → C → A, C → B→ A, A → C → B (in-direct control on the third individual by the first individual via the second one).

It may also be accommodative with equality-based principle like (ABC) = (BCA) = (CAB), the brackets showing social arrangement of the three individuals in a non-hierarchic manner.

Social concern comes as soon as the above relations, accommodative, or power-centric (pseudo-accommodative) relations, are questioned/disturbed. The reason why we say pseudo-accommodation is really a reflection of disharmony/conflict (concealed/revealed) in a post-private property structure. In a broader/international context, this also leads to formation of political states that withstand the actions of the rest of the world (other states). This power to withstand reveals also the power to react in response to the acts initiated by other state(s).

Electoral System and Electoral Reforms

An electoral system, in principle, can be thought of as a choice or preference that the individuals are free to exercise. This freedom is to be understood as freedom from any personal preferences, from any authority-imposed ideas and opinions, where the authorities are understood as the state or its different wings for execution of state policies. The arithmetic of most electoral systems is one-person-one-vote, and hence, in principle, this electoral system can be thought of as rational and equitable. It is rational in the sense that all are free to choose or not to choose the peoples' representatives in a system of Parliamentary Democracy. This system is equitable in the sense of equal distribution of political power, the latter understood as power to be chosen by the people or the equal right to choose the representative. The electoral system thus envelops all the people in the process of social consensus whether they actually exercise their right to chose or not.

India is a Democratic Republic by declaration of the Constitution of India. It is a Parliamentary Democracy and thus there is natural inclusion of people above a certain age in the electoral system. The latest Parliamentary election held in India was in 1999. As high as 62.0 per cent of the eligible voters cast votes in this election (UNDP, 2000, p. 245). The previous one was held in 1998 when 62 per cent of the eligible voters *i.e.*, rational individuals above the stipulated age, cast their vote. These show an improvement over the percentage of votes polled in previous Parliamentary elections. Sometimes there comes a tendency to correlate the consciousness of people and percentage of votes polled. However, across countries there is no such correlation (see Table 9.1).

Table 9.1 : Voter Turnout at latest Elections in Selected Countries (Percentage eligible voters by age)

Country	Year of latest Elections	Voter Turnout (%)
United States	1998	36
United Kingdom	1997	72
Japan	1996	59
Germany	1998	82
France	1997	71
Italy	1996	83
Canada	1997	69
India	1998	62

Source: UNDP, 1999, Human Development Report, pp. 217, 219.

Considering countries in G-7, namely, US, UK, Japan, Germany, France, Italy, and Canada, we find a high percentage of votes polled in all non-US countries and only 36 per cent of votes polled in US in 1998 (UNDP, 1999, pp. 217, 219). In the context of imperfect voters' list in an underdeveloped country like India, the percentage of valid votes polled may conceal more than it reveals. There may be several reasons behind this. For example, agents who may not have adequate skill to include the names of all the valid voters in all the regions prepare the list. The number of absentees may not be included in the list. There may be malpractice in the process of casting votes like multiple votes cast by a single individual, booth (that is, centre of casting votes) jam, rigging etc. Rigging is to be understood as manipulation, a credible threat to the genuine voters or actual violence executed by the agents of political parties or other with an interest in the outcome of the election. The malpractice may or may not be recognised by the Election Commission, which is an autonomous body to set the rules of the game related to the holding of elections. Thus, the true figure for votes polled as percentage of eligible votes recorded may be much less than what is calculated.

Now why do people cast votes? The simple answer is that they like to elect the representative of their choice, given a chance. They choose a party or a person. While choosing a party, or the individual representing a party, the people are generally guided by the polity or the spokespersons representing the party. An individual may like to be elected as an independent, *i.e.* independent of any influence of any political party. Whatever be the case, while electing the representative of a party or an independent individual, people are guided not only by their own choice or consciousness, but also by the polity. In a macro sense thus the polity plays a significant role in the electoral process. Just as the polity influences the decisions of the individuals, so also the individuals influence the polity in two ways, first by actively participating in the electoral process and second by abstaining from it. The second one seems paradoxical, but really it is not. The initial alienation of people from the processes of decision-making also makes them abstain from the electoral processes, because they think that the electoral system only reinforces the existing power structure and the role of the individuals in it. In the context of India this section may be identified in part with the middle class. The working of the electoral system understood as a system of maintaining *status quo* or change thus comes to be influenced by both participation and non-participation in it. Non-participation in the context of a highly skewed distribution of political power shows a necessity for a change in that structure. The required change may get reflected in the polity and hence in selection of the peoples' probable representatives. In the context of non-participation in the electoral system in the US it may be a silent judgment in favour of *status quo*. Thus, the same phenomenon, namely non-participation in the electoral system may have different implications in different localities, even within one country. In the context of India, as possible in inner city areas of the United States, there may be another group of non-participants, namely the really marginalised people. This group does not know why it should participate in the electoral process. Or this group may not know if it really has the right to exercise its votes. In political principle, it is a system of one person-one vote-one value, but in the economic domain it is not really one person-one value. The economic domain both includes and excludes people. The economically deprived people may have the idea of exclusion in the political domain also.

Concluding Remarks

No social system is perfect or fool proof, whether it is a local, national, regional or global system. The basic reason is that the current social system at any one time has evolved from a past social system. Changes were required in the past system, so the agents of change initiated steps to reorient the system. The system includes the mode of production, the belief structure, the human relations, the human rights and responsibilities etc. The electoral system is one dimension of execution of the required changes in the social system. Answers to all the questions in a social system are political questions. The task is to understand those questions at the right time and act accordingly to avoid social disaster. Social disaster is man-made or non-natural. Those most affected by social disasters are those who have least capacity to influence its course or impact. The task of the ruling coalition is to include that alienated social section in the political decision-making processes and hence ensure dynamic stability in the society. The concept of dynamic stability accommodates changes in the society, *i.e.* changes that are anti-*status quo*. A solution to the problem of non-response of people in the electoral system thus rests not only on electoral reforms but also on bigger structural issues including changes in the given power structure.

References

UNDP, 1999, Human Development Report, Oxford University Press, New Delhi.
UNDP, 2000, Human Development Report, Oxford University Press, New Delhi.

10

Electoral System and the Fate of Secular Nationalism

RAJEN HARSHE

Introduction

Any electoral system invariably stimulates electoral practices that essentially aim at mobilisation of maximum support from the targeted social groups or communities. Such support, in the context of several developing countries, is more often built round politics of social identities. Social identities, in general, are conceived and shaped by individuals around perceptions of sameness and continuity. Apart from being psycho-cultural, all the larger social identities are relational and tend to constantly harp on the distinction between "self" and the "other". Politics of identities formed by larger social groups such as nationality, religion, language and ethnicity tend to have their impact on the electoral system as well as changing notions of governance. Keeping the inter-relations between social identities and electoral politics in the sight, this paper would attempt to put across the declining significance of secular nationalism in the political process in India. The sequence of our brief argument would run as follows. To begin with, we would try to define the notions of secularism and nationalism and situate them in the context of India. Subsequently, we would reflect on the practice of secular nationalism in India by underlining the political behaviour of the mainstream political parties.

Defining Secularism

Before attempting any definition of the concept of secularism, it may be worthwhile to trace the genesis of the term secular. The term secularism has evolved in the context of a triangular relationship between the church, the state and society in the west. In the western societies, as the tussle between the church and the state began to get resolved in favour of the state, the ecclesiastical institutions or organised religion in any form had to function under the shadow of the supremacy of the state as an institution. To put simply, secularisation of the western societies has been an outcome of the peoples' struggles during the past three centuries. Such struggles have led to the rise of religion neutral states in the western societies. These states allow diverse religions to exist and even flourish but the religious considerations rarely influence the political processes or the statecraft, decisively, under any secular state. And yet, relatively conservative political parties are still organised around religion in all the western societies. Naturally, it would be imprudent to visualise a separation between the spheres of activities of religion and state into watertight compartments even in the most advanced liberal and secularised societies. Irrespective of this, it could be argued that there are more clearly dividing boundaries between the religious and secular domains in the west.

In contrast to the western societies, in the oriental societies, especially in countries like India, religious and social life are inextricably intertwined. In fact, Hinduism is more often conceived as a way of life. It neither has any religious dogma nor any organisation comparable to more institutionalised religions like Christianity. In the light of the enmeshed ties between religion and social life in India, to be secular in the Indian context would be tantamount to giving equal respect to all religions. At the same time, to be secular also ought to imply conscious discouragement to politics that invokes religious sentiments to fan and consolidate communal sentiments. During the past five decades, the political process in India has witnessed three distinct attitudes towards the ties between religion and politics. Out of these, Mahatma Gandhi and his followers represented the first one. Being a deeply religious person Gandhi saw politics as religion by other means. Jawaharlal Nehru, who represented the second attitude along with the left forces, was secular democrat and a liberal socialist. He harped on the impracticability of the Hindu Raj in India as he believed that a substantial number of people belonging to the other faiths including Islam, Buddhism, Jainism, Sikhism, Zorastrianism and Christianity also have been an integral part of India. His notion of secularism separated politics from religion. Finally, the third major strand of thinking on religion and politics has been steeped in politics of communalism, primarily, representing the ideological strands of Hindu chauvinism and Muslim separatism. Indeed, communalism has also been one of the dominant ideologies with in built potentials to shape social attitudes towards religion and politics. The stance of communal forces has always been sectarian and exclusionist. In India, Sang Parivar does smack of communal orientation.

However, it may be necessary to draw a line between terms like religious and communal while the notion of secularism is being debated. For instance, leaders such as Mahatma Gandhi and Maulana Azad were deeply religious but they were not communal. Whereas Savarkar and Jinnah were not religious but they were overtly communal. To a large extent the latter two epitomized varying tendencies towards communalism among the Hindu and the Muslim populations of the Indian sub-continent. In the process, the Savarkar brand of Hindu communalism stood for Hindu India while Jinah championed the cause of Muslim separation. In the political process of post-colonial India, the communal forces, under the guises of different political parties, have often activated politics of communalism. Having placed different perceptions on religion and politics and their impact in shaping the notions of secularism in India, a few words on secular nationalism are in order.

Secular Nationalism

Independent India under Nehru's stewardship launched its emancipatory project in the spirit of secular nationalism. Although nationalism, like secularism, as a phenomenon grew in the west, it also had its oriental dimension. To put it tersely, nationalism in the context of the west displayed aggressive and even imperialist tendencies of the modern state. In contrast, nationalism in the orient was reactive and it blossomed in the form of anti-colonial nationalism. The notion of nation intrinsically is psycho-cultural. It acquired a sharp edge in the Indian psyche in the context of British imperialism. Capitalizing on the anti-colonial mass movement led by the Indian National Congress (INC) as well as emphatic electoral verdict in favour of the Congress in successive elections, the Nehru regime chose to fashion its notion of secular nationalism. Such notion obviously separated politics and religion, protected the rights of all the religious minorities and chose to be sensitive to the socially plural context of India. It harped on the geographic and socio-cultural unity of the Indian nation while celebrating social diversities. With the demise of Nehru (1964) as also the one party dominant system the project of secular nationalism has been gradually receding into the background. The decline of secular nationalism is so obvious that India, at this juncture, is in search of a secular polity. This point can be further highlighted with reference to concrete ground realities of the recent current political process in India.

Political Process and the Status of Secular Nationalism

The political process in India since the past decade is being shaped by the three dominant political groupings. They are: (a) the Bharatiya Janata Party (BJP) and its Sangh Parivar including Shiv Sena, Vishwa Hindu Parishad and the Rashtriya Swayam Sevak Sangh (RSS), (b) the Indian National Congress (I), and (c) the Janata Dal along with left parties including both Communist Parties of India *i.e.* CPI and CPI(M). We shall proceed to discuss their orientation towards secular nationalism in the same order, it must be stated, at the outset, that all the mainstream political parties, in theory, claim to be secular. But despite such claims the politics that they pursue does not necessarily offer an evidence of secularism. Let us begin our analysis with the politics of the BJP.

The BJP and Sangh Parivar, over the years, had made Hindu cultural nationalism as a major plank to garner and consolidate the support of the Hindu community. By building their social base among the numerically preponderant Hindu community, they aspire to promote majoritarian nationalism. Even though the Hindus by no means are homogenous the BJP has found ways of rallying them together. Basically, the BJP conceives that the policies of the Congress towards minorities, especially the Muslims, have been dictated by opportunist logic of appeasement. This appeasement, in BJP's perception, was being made to pamper Muslim minorities and capture their consolidated vote bank during the time of elections. That is why the BJP leaders have often been vehement in exposing an intrinsically pseudo-secular character of the Congress. To gather the support of the masses of Hindus, the BJP and Sangh Parivar chose to build the Ram Temple in Ayodhya. They also had a hand in demolishing the Babri Masjid, in 1992, which was supposed to be replaced by Ram Temple. In addition, while promoting its brand of secularism the BJP has opted to be a staunch champion of the uniform civil code in India. In substance, the BJP and the Sangh Parivar's notion of India has been built on majoritarian nationalism that does not leave adequate space for the self-expression of diverse minority communities. While building India of their dreams the Sangh Parivar would like to take full advantage of the coercive apparatuses of the modern state in its internal and external policy. Being obsessed with the security matters, in general, the Sangh Parivar believes in spending substantial amount on security related expenditure, including building of nuclear arsenal. The overall strategy of nation building of the Sangh Parivar is certainly not devoid of fascist tendencies. After having tasted the fruits of power, the Sangh Parivar might mitigate its extremist communal stances out of tactical expediency. However, in essence, the Sangh Parivar has been transparently communal.

If the Sangh Parivar is obviously communal, the Congress Party, in recent times, has shown an uncanny ability of being communal in a pragmatic manner. This point can be highlighted with a few illustrations. First, Indira Gandhi due to sheer short-term considerations of getting control over the affairs in Punjab chose to encourage the Sikh fundamentalists such as Bhidranwale in the eighties. Second, in the aftermath of Indira Gandhi's assassination on October 31, 1984 the anti-Sikh riots took place in Delhi. In those riots so many innocent Sikhs had to lose their lives. Some of the senior Congress leaders were allegedly involved in promoting the riots. Third, Rajiv Gandhi succumbed to the pressure of Muslim fundamentalists in the Shah Bano case. Finally, after the communal riots of 1993 in Mumbai, the Congress leadership could not come out unscathed. Irrespective of the above incidents, the Congress has been fairly vociferous in championing its secular credentials.

The so-called left forces, in their own ways, have been promoting communal tendencies. To start with, Samajwadi Party (SP) led by Mulayam Singh Yadav, in the context of politics in Uttar Pradesh, has mastered the art of exploiting the Muslim vote bank. For the sake of electoral expediency Mulayam Singh Yadav has seldom fought shy of promoting minority communalism. Similarly, Laloo Prasad Yadav of the Rashtriya Janata Dal (RJD) has also opted to cultivate the Muslim vote bank in Bihar. Furthermore, the electoral understanding and alliance between the Communist Party of India (Marxist)—(CPM) and the Muslim League in Kerala in the history of coalition politics of that state does not enhance the secular credentials of parties like the CPM. For, how a party such as the CPM can even conceive of an association with a religion-based party solely interested in protecting sectarian interests of a particular community? Of course, any facile rationalisation of such alliances can always be worked out after arriving at an understanding with the communal forces. Similarly, the left parties are often vehement in raising the flag of the minorities. However, the notions of minority and majority are not static. These notions are constantly shaped by the circumstances governed by time and space. For instance, the Pandits represent a Hindu minority in the state of Kashmir. With the outbreak of violence in the Kashmir valley, the minority Hindus had to leave the state of Kashmir due to enormous sense of insecurity to their lives. Since the excesses committed on the *Kashmiri Pandits* would not garner votes the so-called progressive forces on the left almost appear indifferent to the plight of the Hindus in Kashmir.

In the light of our discussion about the genuineness of the mainstream political parties in upholding the cause of secularism, it appears evident that all the existing mainstream political parties are far from secular. Being prisoners of the politics of vote bank all the political parties, in different degrees, are capable of manipulating communal sentiments. Admittedly, communalism that stems from the abuse of religion in the public sphere has been damaging the notion of secular nationalism that had come so handy in keeping India together during the initial decades after India's independence. However, apart from religion-based communalism, the strident casteist sentiments also are threatening to uproot the very foundations of secular nationalism. Especially, the upsurge of caste based politics in India, after the acceptance of the Mandal Commission Report in 1990, has only aggravated caste consciousness and caste related tensions. In fact, reflecting on the caste based social movements is well outside the purview of this paper. However, it needs to be mentioned that the caste-based communalism, indeed, is the most divisive and vicious brand of communalism. Having underlined the role of the existing parties in undermining the fabric of secular nationalism in India, we can proceed to offer some concrete solutions to revive secular nationalism.

Future Pathways

The solution to rectify the current situation certainly lies in civil society that is desperately in need of secular discourses. Such discourses, plausibly, would gain a greater credibility if the major political parties and forces and social and educational institutions strive to build an overlapping consensus on the notion of secularism. Furthermore, sustained concentration on evolving developmental agenda can as well take the attention of the people away from divisive politics. In this context, every major political party must be virtually forced by the electorate to commit itself towards the resolution of certain basic developmental problems like illiteracy, unemployment, child labour, health care and gender equality. Accountability of political parties in building and executing a time bound developmental agenda is the need of the hour. This exercise can begin by giving secular treatment to work. Indeed, if notions of work and work places are saved from the shadows of communalism through secular treatment to work, India can face the challenges of the new century, more effectively. At the moment, the places of work, especially in the public sector are getting communalised. Showing leniency to lack of work or performance on communal grounds has become very common. The political parties, in general, have succeeded in making people in the organised sector aware of their rights without sensitising them about their corresponding duties. What is more, in the context of promoting secularism the entire policy cf reservation would deserve a second look. Indeed, only secular work culture would be able to ensure development and the notion of a nation. In this context, it would be equally necessary to explore all possibilities of initiating new kind of politics that could change the electoral system to suit the times.

11

Electoral Strategies of Ethnic Conflict Management

PRIYANKAR UPADHYAYA

Electoral systems are generally seen to reflect public opinion but they also have a role in influencing public attitudes. This is demonstrably so in situation of ethnic conflict wherein they may intensify inter-ethnic tension or can help to diffuse it and create a commitment to inter-community co-operation. While an accommodative electoral system may assuage mistrust between various cultural groups by offering incentives to political parties to seek electoral support beyond their own core support, an unsuitable election system based on a "zero-sum" contest may aggravate the ethnic conflict by inciting parties to act in a hostile and exclusionary manner towards anyone outside their home group. Clearly the structures of electoral system, constituencies and ballot have direct bearings on ethnic electoral appeals, multi-ethnic coalitions and ethnic alignments.

Despite such a critical interface, the electoral ramifications of the ethnic variable are a less investigated theme in scholarly literature. While electoral studies relate to the problematic of ethnic diversity mostly with regard to the growth of a multi-party system in proportional representation (PR) as against the first-past-the-post system (FPTP); the burgeoning literature on ethnopolitics has not assigned due significance to the critical linkages between ethnic disaffection and electoral system.[1] Conversely, politicians throughout the world are ever ready to exploit the intense appeal of ethnic impulse for reaping electoral gains. The growth of ethnically based parties, electoral manipulation and gerrymandering indicate a rising drift in this direction.

The post cold war surge of ethnic conflict has highlighted the salience of ethnic groups as a political category, which can be easily mobilized in the majority of the sovereign states. This trend is, however, more visible in the post-colonial states of Asia and Africa. "In most of the less-developed countries" according to Milton J. Esman "ethnic minorities have been mobilised to defend their collective interests and promote their demands for security, status, economic opportunities and political power in competition, civil or violent, with other ethnic communities and in opposition to governmental policies and practices."[2] When state policies appear to differentiate on ethnic lines, they create a sense of grievance and ignite ethnic conflicts which can surely be retarded by an adequate democratic representation of the disaffected communities. The marked decline of ethnic violence since early 1990, at least in part, is attributed to many states abandoning strategies of assimilation and control in favour of policies of pluralism and accommodation.[3] And to ensure this, "it is necessary that special procedures, institutions and arrangements be established through which members of minorities are able to make decisions, exercise legislative and administrative powers, and develop their culture."[4]

The non-fulfillment of democratic aspirations of communities divided on ethnic lines is a common occurrence and could even be traced in democratic systems which pride themselves on free and fair elections. This has led to a growing recognition that 'so called' free and fair elections are no assurance against the exclusion of ethnic minorities from the system of governance. In fact it is possible that such electoral systems may facilitate the growth of an ethnic state whereby ethnic majorities invariably assume political power, and minorities become permanently marginalised. "It was a fearful situation," according to Donald Horowitz "in which the prospect of minority exclusion from government, underpinned by ethnic voting, was potentially permanent."[5] Indeed the electoral system based on first-past-the-post in single member constituencies has no effective mechanism to rectify such consequences of ethnic voting. Recent approaches to conflict resolution thus confirm that "the most enduring basis for interethnic conciliation in a severely divided society, where communal allegiances are politicised, lies in an electoral system that creates some incentives rewarding moderation, even though other incentives continue to reward extremism." [6]

Enhancing Minority Participation

No wonder the scholars and practitioners throughout the world are seized with the problematic of how to enhance the ethnic electoral representation. One of the most practiced methods of ensuring the representation of specific minority groups in Parliament has been by reserving seats for identifiable ethnic or religious minorities. The list includes countries as diverse as Jordan (Christians and Circassians), India (Scheduled Tribes and Castes), Pakistan (non-Muslim minorities), New Zealand (Maori), Columbia ("black communities"), Croatia (Hungarian, Italian, Czech, Slovak, Ruthenium, Ukrainian, German and Austrian minorities), Slovenia (Hungarians and Italians), Taiwan (the aboriginal community), Western Samoa (non-indigenous minorities), and Nigeria (Taurag). In some of these cases, only electorates of the designated minority community vote to elect these reserved seats.

Ethnically dominated regions are also over-represented in Parliament to enhance the representation of minority groups. Scotland and Wales have more MPs in the British House of Commons than they would be entitled to if population size alone were the only criteria. On similar lines Mauritius allocates certain number of parliamentary seats to "best losers"—the highest polling unsuccessful candidates belonging to under-represented ethnic groups.

An extreme example of ensuring ethnic participation has been to divide the entire system of Parliamentary representation on the basis of communal considerations. This usually means that each defined community has its own electoral roll, and elects only members of its "own group" to Parliament. However such communal-roll arrangements introduced in British India, and also in Pakistan, Cyprus and Zimbabwe in the past, created unsavoury consequences. It transpired that "communal electorates, while guaranteeing group representation, often had the perverse effect of undermining the path of accommodation between different groups, since there were no incentives for political intermixing between communities."[7] The issue of how to define a member of a particular group, and how to distribute electorates fairly between them, was also strewn with pitfalls. In Fiji too the separate communal role for indigenous Fijian, Indian and "general " electors, is being given up in favour of a more open electoral competition which could encourage the growth of a multi-ethnic political system.[8]

The concept of "consociational democracy" conceptualised by Arend Lijphart and others in the 1970s offers an electoral framework to defuse minority disaffection by involving their elites in consensual politics. Because the exclusive control of power by one majority group leaves little stake in the system for minority groups, an electoral system can be re-designed to encourage forging coalitions in divided societies where political parties break along ethnic lines.[9] Despite raising controversies consociationalism informed a range of electoral mechanism which were subsequently incorporated in a number of countries. Some of these measures have facilitated a meaningful participation of disaffected groups in the making of legislation and administrative decision making in accord with their specific community needs.

In recent years some stable European democracies have improvised special mechanism to ensure an effective representation of minority groups. This has been done by multi-member PR or semi-PR election systems, which use reasonably large districts of seven or more members, thus encouraging parties to nominate minorities to increase their electoral chances. A very low threshold, or the elimination of a threshold entirely for entering Parliament for minorities and privileged funding for minority parties are also being recommended to facilitate the representation of hitherto under-represented or unrepresented groups. The avoidance of gerrymandering in constituency formation, and adequate number of special, additional designated constituencies reserved for the minority electorate are other means of effective participation of minorities.[10]

However the post-colonial democracies in Asia and Africa have been far more reluctant to consider separate electoral representation for ethnic minorities. These ethnically heterogeneous states, still struggling with the problem of nation building are wary of electoral arrangements which might incite secessionist tendencies. Such apprehensions are rooted in the fortuitous circumstances of the colonial era wherein the separate electorates were blamed for giving a free rein to divisive forces.

Communal Roll in India

The contention over the electoral protection for ethnic minorities in many ways goes back to the imposition of electoral rolls for Muslims and other communities (Sikhs and Christians) in India by the British Raj. While these colonial experiments are generally held responsible for the Partition; there are also counter opinions, which see in them an attempt to represent the marginalised communities.[11] Whatever may be the case, there is no denying that during the British Raj itself the electoral arena had become an important channel of political socialisation and for the formation political categories through which a large segment of the Indian masses could be mobilised. Various experiments of electoral democracy during this period afforded significant exposure to budding politicians from different caste and ethnic groups to evolve populist home-grown political idioms.[12]

The recognition of separate communal roll by the Minto and Morley reforms of 1909 in effect provided that certain seats in the Legislative Council be reserved exclusively for Muslims elected by separate electorates consisting of Muslim electorates alone.[13] This came as a response to the nascent All-India Muslim League, and expectedly led to a polarization of the Hindus and the Muslims as distinct supra-local political communities. Although the subsequent reforms brought by Montague and Chelmsford did mention the divisive nature of the separate electorates, they preferred to retain and extend the separate electorates throughout India. Ramsay MacDonald's 1932 Communal Award also followed the trend of extending separate electorates ostensibly to provide popular representation to Muslims and other depressed communities.[14]

The separate electorates were initially welcomed as a rational and just way of meeting the fears and claims of various communities. But haunted by the spectre of political instability inbuilt in the system, the mainstream nationalistic leadership decided to oppose it on the grounds of being too unwieldy and complicated a system for illiterate Indian masses to operate. Nehru, contrary to his earlier endorsement of the demand for a separate electoral roll, came out strongly to denounce it as a betrayal of trust in the majority. However while throwing his lot with first-past-the-post system, he cautioned that it is "an act of faith above all for the majority community because they will have to show after this that they can behave to others in a generous, fair and just way."[15] The Muslim League on the other hand, rejected the proposal of universal adult franchise made in All-Parties

Conference Committee in 1928 for not ensuring adequate participation of Muslims. This was a critical divide that led to the crystallisation of two nations theory and the subsequent demand for a separate state of Pakistan.

The acrimonious circumstances leading to Partition sounded the death knell of the communal electoral system. Committed to the vision of a homogeneous secular nation, the post-Partition nationalist leadership unwaveringly clung to the first-past-the-post system (FPTP) and declared it non-negotiable. This was evident during the debates on minority rights in the Constituent Assembly in May 1949, which saw the scrapping of the reserved seats for minorities. Similarly all proposals regarding the adoption of proportional representation, for multi-member constituencies and for cumulative voting were dismissed without any serious scrutiny.[16]

Electoral Experiments in Post-Colonial States

The electoral engineering for electoral protection of under-represented ethnic groups did not remain confined to India. Many post-colonial states especially those having ethnically heterogeneous society have tried over time to put in place special electoral devices to manage their ethnic cleavages. Interestingly many such electoral experiments have their lineage in colonial times. A cursory analysis of some of these cases *viz.* Lebanon, Cyprus, Nigeria, Guyana, Malaysia, Sri Lanka and South Africa may be instructive to gain insights into the problem.

The Lebanese case is one of the earliest and most frequently referred instances of electoral innovations, keeping sectarian identities reconciled for over three decades.[17] Formally embodied in the informal and unwritten National Pact (al-Mithaq al-Watani) of 1943, this arrangement based on quasi-presidential system facilitated power sharing among a wide spectrum of ethnic communities in accordance with the 1932 census, wherein Christians exceeded non-Christians in a ratio of six to five. The Pact also known as "confessional formula" allocated political offices to major sectarian groups to ensure a balanced representation of varied communities. Accordingly, the President of Lebanon was to be a Maronite, the Prime Minister a Sunni, the Speaker of the Parliament a Shiite, the Vice Speaker a Greek. The cabinet was, of course, composed of fixed proportions of the various groups. The composition of the Parliament was also determined on the basis of plurality and a system of multi-member constituencies based on the size of the various religious communities determined earlier by the French.

The Lebanese PR system produced inter community harmony because in order to be elected, a candidate needed the votes of members of both his own and other sects. The Cabinet so formed was like "a true Parliament on a small scale".[18] Moreover the electoral arrangement replaced inter-ethnic competition with intra-ethnic competition thus undermining the prospects of ethnic conflict. However these techniques of managing ethnic tensions were never quite satisfactory and barely kept the level of violence and discontent below the surface.[19] Observers feel that instead of using political institutions to resolve conflicts, primary concern was given to preventing conflicts from destroying the institutions.[20] One of the problems that plagued these inter-ethnic arrangements was the rising discontent against the 6 to 5 formula (drawn up far back in 1932) for political representation between Christians and Muslims. With growing awareness about their subordinate political status, the Sunni and Druze elites demanded a fair and equitable distribution in accord with the altered demographic status of each community. The demand to change the *status quo* was naturally opposed by the Maronite Christians, as it would undermine their claims for the Presidency. "The inertia against change and failure to affect social reforms to eliminate sectarianism" according to Milton J. Esman "undermined the spirit of the National Pact which had otherwise innovated an effective election scheme to strike a political reconciliation among various sectarian communities."[21] The onset of civil war in 1975-76 took a toll of the political reconciliation between various sectarian communities, but this is not attributed to the failure of the electoral arrangements, which in any case had remained functional for over three decades.

In Cyprus too, the pressure of Western powers led to the adoption of Consociational governance based on an electoral system which could accommodate ethnic diversities. According to the 1960 Constitution, the Greek community comprising of three-fourths of the population would elect the President; while the Turkish community was to elect the Vice-President with almost equal powers. Similarly the Greek President was to nominate seven members of the Cabinet while three were to be nominated by the Vice-President. Further, 35 members of the legislature were elected by Greeks and 15 by Turks. The Constitution also ensured autonomy for the two ethnic segments by setting up two separately elected communal chambers and exclusive legislature. However unlike the Lebanese experiment the 1960 Constitution could not elicit adequate public support and broke down in 1963 amid a protracted civil war. While the Greek majority could never reconcile with minority Turks acquiring political power almost on par with them, the Turks spared no chance of obstructing legislation and other decisions overusing the veto.[22]

Nigeria too tried-out a unique electoral system in 1978 under British influences to accommodate ethnic diversities. Even earlier the Nigerian ethnic nationalities had evolved their own indigenous mode of representative governance that however collapsed in course of colonization and the long sweep of military rule. The Constitution of 1960 enacted soon after independence had also provided for ethnic accommodation by according veto power to delay legislation for up to six months to three ethnically dominated states (Hausas in North, Ibos in East, Yorubas in West). This experiment however did not bear the desired results. One unintended consequence of such power sharing on ethnic lines was the domination of the largest segment over smaller ethnic groups within the three states.[23] The military coup of 1966 saw the end of this arrangement.

The Nigerian Constitution of 1978 was framed against the backdrop of protracted ethnic violence in Biafra signifying the failure of the Parliamentary system to prevent ethnic exclusion. The Constitution, though in operation for five years, improvised an elaborate mechanism to accommodate ethnic diversities through a system of proportional electoral distribution. Accordingly a nationally elected Presidency was set up to act as the representative of diverse ethnic groups. In order to be elected as President, a candidate was required to win a plurality of votes nationwide, plus at least 25 per cent of the votes in no less than two-thirds of the nineteen states. This was to ensure that a president had some support across the country and did not just represent one region or ethnic group.[24] The ethnic engineering of the presidential electoral formula, however, could not create a stable multi-ethnic party system but the intense electoral competition between ethnically based parties precluded the fears of a grand divide between the North and South. Since the return to civil rule and the setting up of a Constitution Review Committee, there have been comprehensive debates through public hearings, organised in the six geopolitical zones in respect of power sharing, resource control and the political autonomy of various political identities. The recent Presidential election, held after two decades, is a testimony of Nigeria's quest to quench ethnic exclusion through a nationally elected President.

Sri Lanka too has a long history of trying out various electoral mechanisms to cope with the problem of ethnic divide. The protracted ethnic unrest underlined the weakness of the first-past-the-post (FPTP) elections to accommodate the minority interests and thus led to the drafting of the Second Republican Constitution of August 1978. While the constitution makers introduced a French-style executive presidency that could remain insulated from the vicissitudes of Parliament, a preferential or alternative vote system was used to prevent a candidate from winning the presidential election disregarding plurality. The new office of executive president was to be filled by a national figure capable of encouraging consensual politics between opposing interests. The initial plans provided for a Two-Round System (TRS) of presidential elections. However, the logistical constraints led to an innovative solution of combining the initial and run-off rounds of voting into one election through the expression of preferences. Thus if no candidate has a majority of first preferences, all candidates other than the two leaders are eliminated, and the second preferences distributed to one or the other of the top two to ensure a majority winner. Accordingly each voter was given a choice to specify his second and third preferences which will then be distributed to one or the other of the top two candidates in the event of no candidate having an absolute majority.[25] Similarly the legislative electoral system stipulated that "Every elector at an election of Members of Parliament, shall, in addition to his vote, be entitled to indicate his preferences for not more than three candidates nominated by the same recognised political party or independent group." [26]

The past three national presidential elections, have witnessed the winning candidate attaining an absolute majority in the first round itself, and thus ruling out the counting of preferences votes. However, the possibility that preferences may one day decide the result, does appear to have influenced the campaign strategies of Sri Lankan parties, and there is considerably more attention paid to minority groups in election campaigning for presidential elections than was formerly the case. Thus the preferential or alternative vote system of proportional representation did create a space for the ethnic minorities to acquire bargaining chips in relation to Singhalese political parties. As there was no practical possibility of a Tamil candidate winning the Presidential election, Tamil voters could at least ensure that winning Tamil support would remain a strong incentive for Singhalese candidates.

These new voting provisions did lead to an increase in Tamil and Muslim representation in Parliament. But *per se* these electoral provision were not enough to assuage the quest of democratic assertion for ethnic minorities and thus could not forestall the Tamil minority from getting sucked into the politics of violence.[27] No wonder amid lingering peace talks there are significant differences among various political groups on whether the system of proportional representation be given up and the first-past-the-post system reintroduced?

The PR system initiated by the British in Guyana, on the eve of its independence in 1964 is also instructive. Before leaving the island, the British replaced the first-past-the-post system with a proportional representation system ostensibly to forestall a permanent domination by the majority group and to ensure Christians, Hindus, and Muslims attained fair representation. But it transpired that this electoral engineering was affected by the cold war dynamic of the Anglo-American bloc.[28] Wary of the pro-Soviet leanings of Cheddi Jagan, the western bloc sought to create fissures within the Asian dominated Progressive Party. With the whole country delineated as a single constituency and each party putting up a single list nationwide, the PR system was meant to splinter the hitherto cohesive East Indian group between Hindus and Muslims. Interestingly the electoral consequences in Guyana did not usher in sub-group divisions between the Hindu and Muslim community. The reason was that for the East Indian community the religious divide was not as critical as the consciousness of losing their majority due to any such split. Although the PR system so introduced did obtain a discernible level of proportionality for various ethnic communities, it could not scale down the inter-ethnic tension which still plague its poor population despite

Guyana getting a new constitution in 1980 and the first completely free Parliamentary elections since independence in 1992.

Malaysia began working on inter-ethnic accommodation quite early in view of the past history of inter-ethnic violence. Ethnic Malays and other indigenous peoples, sometimes known as Bhumiputra (sons of the soil), comprise 59 per cent of Malaysia's population. While other groups include ethnic Chinese, who constitute 26 per cent of the population, and ethnic Indians, who make up about 7 per cent. Starting with the constitutional bargain of 1956-57, which established single-member multi-ethnic constituencies, in course of time, many constitutional provisions and amendments granted electoral incentives to inter-ethnic coalitions.

Single-member multi-ethnic constituencies created the avenues for coalition partners to provide marginal votes on a reciprocal basis. This arrangement thus promoted multi-ethnic coalition formation and undermined the dominance of ethnically edged parties. It is against this background that the Malaysian party system polarized around two multi-ethnic coalitions —namely, the Alliance and its successor the National Front. It is clear that the Malaysian system of plurality election in single-member constituencies brought in inter-ethnic checks and balance. Describing this calculus Donald Horowitz observes:

> In many constituencies, Chinese voters could punish Malay extremists and reward moderation. There were not always more Malay votes to be gained than Chinese votes to be lost by taking extreme positions. By the same token, Chinese and Malay parties could pool votes profitably at the constituency level and come out ahead. Where there where more Malays than Chinese in a constituency, a Chinese party could urge its supporters to vote for a friendly Malay candidate, and *vice versa* where there were more Chinese than Malays in a constituency. Parties might still evolve along wholly ethnic lines,— especially if there were more than one party per ethnic group—there would be countervailing incentives fostering inter-ethnic coalition.[29]

Nonetheless, scholars caution against exaggerating the effect of plurality election on enhancing ethnic participation in power sharing.

It is more a case of 'manufacturing' the desired outcome of elections through 'electoral management', according to Lim Hong Hai. And the plurality arrangements provide easy grounds for "a variety of manipulation in multitudinous ways of varying subtlety by and for the benefit of the dominant Malay community." [30] For instance, the provision of "rural weightage" leads to a significant enhancement of Malay electoral power at the federal level tilting the ethnic balance in favour of the largest ethnic group in Malaysia. The possibility of a non-Bhumiputra party or coalition "going it alone" and winning an election is thus ruled out. Consequently the Chinese and Indian politicians could participate in government only by allying themselves with Malays, inevitably as junior partners. In practice, only two types of government could emerge from elections: an all-Malay government or a Malay-dominated coalition.[31] It is instructive that in the last general election, the ruling coalition secured support from barely half the ethnic-Malay voters but nevertheless clinched a two-thirds Parliamentary majority.[32]

South Africa's choice of a list proportional representation system offers an interesting African model of conflict management. The first elections held in South Africa in 1994 under a national list PR wherein one nationwide constituency (with 400 members) was used for translating votes into seats, and no threshold for representation was imposed. Half the National Assembly came from a single national list and other half from the provincial list. The Droop quota was used to apportion seats, and surplus seats were awarded by an adaptation of the largest-remainder method. It was agreed not to have any "mandatory" threshold. But only those parties with 20 or more MPs, 5 per cent of the Assembly, were assured seats in the cabinet.

The choice of list PR encouraged political parties to induct ethnically diverse candidates who could elicit support transcending ethnic loyalties. This turned out to be an effective device of ethnic collaboration and for the first time in the turbulent history of South African Parliament, one could see blacks sitting with whites, Zulus with Xhosas, and Muslims with Christians under the same party banners. The resulting National Assembly was 52 per cent black, 32 per cent white, 8 per cent Indian and 7 per cent coloured. This compared to an electorate, which was estimated to be 73 per cent black, 15 per cent white, 9 per cent coloured and 3 per cent Indian.[33]

Indeed the PR system allowed more representation to Indians and whites in the new National Assembly than they would be entitled to if population size alone were the only criteria.

Summing Up

Evidently the above-analysed cases of electoral experiments are embedded in their own specific history and may not yield generalizations about the precise interface between electoral systems and ethnic conflict management. However the colonial interest in establishing separate electoral mechanism for ethnic identities emerges as a convergent feature and deserves attention. Although such colonial initiatives were ostensibly promoted in the name of plural democracy, they invariably raised the spectre of divide and rule, associated with the colonial rule. British Guyana is often referred to as a reproving case regarding colonial intent wherein the cold war considerations prompted British to employ an electoral system to fragment the majority group led by a pro-Soviet leader. Similar contentions wrap the British electoral experiments to accommodate the politicisation of religious divisions in Nigeria. The ethnic participation arrangements embodied in the 1960 Constitution led to the domination of the largest segment over smaller ethnic groups within the states.

In the case of India too, the policy of divide and rule was blamed for creating the communal roll and was seen as the main reason for partition. Superficially pluralistic in scope, it reflected a primarily two-fold division of the sub-continental electorate. Independent India thus ruled out a PR system and electoral benefits based on religion. The linguistic post-independence reorganisation of the Indian states has, arguably, made it easier for New Delhi to decentralise conflict and, with varying degrees of success, to insulate the politics of the periphery from those of the centre. Over time the mainstream political opinion has been rather disparaging to any basic review of the FPTP system. However the persistent under-representation of religious minorities, especially Muslims in legislatures has been attributed among other factors to the unfair operation of the FPTP system. The Constitution Review Commission (2000-02) was also seized of the problematic of exploring electoral devices that can ensure due representation of dispersed minorities like Muslims. To rectify this anomaly, a range of suggestions are being offered which include:

making all political parties nominate a fair share of minority candidates; excluding minorities from meeting the threshold of a minimum percentage of votes, say 5 per cent; a fixed number of seats, say 75 to 100, earmarked for allocation to under-represented communities; effecting reverse gerrymander by redrawing constituencies; clubbing certain constituencies to return three or four members—one of whom must be from an under-represented minority; PR with single transferable vote (STV); and multi-member constituency without minimum threshold requirement.[34]

It is evident that despite an increased premium on ethnic political participation in the western liberal democracies and also in some of the post-colonial states, the nascent democracies in Asia and Africa are still apprehensive about separate electoral measures which may disrupt national unity and lead to secessionist demands. In Sri Lanka the electoral provision to accommodate minorities did not satisfy the Tamil minority, which found them inadequate, and the Singhalese on the other hand feel that the system of proportional representation should be given up and the first-past-the-post system reintroduced. The Malaysian system too is often construed as a case of 'manufacturing' the desired outcome of elections through 'electoral management'. In fact of all the cases of electoral arrangements, it is the South African electoral system, which stands out as making significant progress and has the support of civil society in the process of conflict transformation.

Indeed it becomes apparent time and again that no system can be imposed against the wishes of one or more segments in a plural society and in particular against the resistance of a majority segment. There is a strong political under-current in many societies which disfavours minority empowerment and advocates a system based on 'Control' as against 'Consociationalism'[35] The argument is that ethnic identity is too evanescent to be relied upon as a viable and self-contained political category and thus unworthy of assigning separate political space. Moreover unlike other cleavages, ethnicity is not manageable through political bargaining by group representatives and the recognition of ethnicity, which is predicated on intense primordial affinities, defies rational solutions and invariably spirals into a secessionist track.[36] This is a typical dilemma confronting the post-colonial states where the exigency of state-formation has taken precedence over nation building. The problem according to a critical view is that—

> The fiction of homogeneity or the homogenising impulse that underlies post-colonial nationalism is a recipe of partition that produces nothing but endless sectarian violence. A possible way out of post-colonial aporia is to re-envision the nation not as a space for the realisation of a unified sense of identity but one with a plural ethos where alterity is respected rather than disciplined, suppressed, or assimilated.[37]

Moreover it is prudent not to overestimate the political consequences of electoral systems as "the effects of electoral systems are limited with respect to their scope, relative (that is, not deterministic) with respect to casual relations, and variable according to place and time." [38] Indeed the electoral systems on its own cannot offer a universal remedy to rectify the ethnic imbalance in democratic governance. As admits the International IDEA Handbook of Electoral System, "(T)he overall effects of other variables, particularly a nation's political culture, usually have a much greater impact upon democratic prospects than institutional factors such as electoral systems. Moreover, the positive effects of a well-crafted electoral system can be all too easily submerged by an inappropriate constitutional dispensation, the domestic dominance of forces of discord, or the weight of external threats to the sovereignty of the state." [39]

But, even though the electoral systems *per se* cannot do much to reduce protracted societal tensions, the bottom line is that they should, at the very least, not exacerbate existing majoritarian and exclusionary policies. It is in this context that a case is made in favour of a PR system, which takes special care to facilitate constitutional power-sharing mechanisms; encourage the formation of multi-ethnic coalitions; reduce the disparity between votes won and seats won and thus create the atmosphere of reconciliation. Indeed electoral incentives can serve as a technique of conflict resolution by avoiding a winner takes-all outcome. A preferential representation of marginalised ethnic community in the democratic process diminishes the fear of minority groups thus paving the way for inter-community reconciliation and harmony.

Notes

1. However, there are some outstanding studies focusing on the interface between ethnic conflict and electoral systems. See Rae, D.W., *The Political Consequences of Electoral Laws*, Yale University Press, New Haven: 1971; Horowitz Donald L, *Ethnic Groups in Conflict*, University of California Press, Berkley, 1985; Grofman, B. and Lijphart, A., *Electoral Laws and Their Political Consequences*, Agathon Press, New York: 1986
2. Esman Milton J, "Public Administration, Ethnic Conflict and Economic Development", *Public Administration Review*, November/December 1997.
3. See findings of a recent study by Gurr Ted R., "People versus states: minorities at risk in the New Century", Herdon, VA: USIP, 2000 cited in *Peace Research Abstract Journal*, Sage Publications, Vol.39, no 6, Dec. 2002, p. 770.
4. Ghai Yash, Public Participation and Minorities, Minority Rights Group International, London, 2001, pp. 4-5.
5. Horowitz, n.1, p. 629.
6. Horowitz Donald L. (1990): Community Conflict: Policy and Possibilities, Occasional Paper No 1, Centre for the Study of Conflict, University of Ulster, Coleraine, p.13.
7. Reynolds A. & Reilly B., *The International IDEA Handbook of Electoral Systems*, International Institute for Democracy and Electoral Assistance, Stockholm, 2002, p.99.
8. *Ibid*, p.10.
9. See Lijphart, Arend, Democracy in Plural Societies: A Comparative Exploration, Yale University Press, New Heavens, CT 1977; Timothy Sisk, *Power Sharing and International Mediation in Ethnic Conflict*, US Institute of Peace, Wash. DC 1996.
10. Frowein J.A. and R. Bank, The Participation of Minorities in Decision Making for Council of Europe in November 2000 E/CN.4/Sub.2/AC.5/2001/CRP. 6
11. Ansari Iqbal A. (2001): "Minority Representation" *Seminar*, October, pp. 406-9
12. Chiriyankandath J. (2001): "Democracy under the Raj: Elections and Separate Representation in British India" in Jayal N.G., (ed): *Democracy in India*, Oxford, 2001.
13. See Rama Devi & S.K. Mendiratta (2000): *How India Votes: Election Laws, Practice and Procedure*, Butterworth, New Delhi, p.5.
14. n. 12.
15. See Jawaharlal Nehru, 'Note on Minority', *Young India*, 15 May 1930 cited in Ansari, n. 11.
16. See Ansari, n.11, p. 407-09.
17. Lijphart, n.9, pp. 48-52
18. Lijphart, *ibid*, p. 49. Also see Jacob M Landau *et al* (1980): *Electoral Politics in the Middle East: Issues, Voters & Elites*, Croom Helm, London.
19. Kerr M., Political Decision Making in a Confessional Democracy" in L. Binder (ed) (1966): *Politics in Lebanon*, Wiley, New York, p. 291.

20. Lijphart, n 9, p 49. Also see Horowitz, n.6, pp. 7-8.
21. Esman, n .2, p. 532.
22. Lijphart, n 9, pp 158-59. Also see Ra'nan Gavriel D., "Cyprus, 1974 to 1978: Problems of Conflict Resolution in a Multi-ethnic Country" in Uri Ra'nan (ed) (1980): *Ethnic Resurgence in Modern Democratic States: A Multidisciplinary Approach to Human Resources and Conflict*, Pergamon Press, New York.
23. Lijphart, n 9, p.163
24. http://news.bbc.co.uk/1/hi/world/africa/country_profiles/1064557.stm
25. Reynolds, A. & Reilly, n. 7, pp.108-09 .
26. http://www.priu.gov.lk/Cons/1978Constitution/Chapter_14_Amd.html
27. See Warnapala N.A.Wiswa & Hewagama L. Dias (1983): *Recent Politics in Sri Lanka: A Study of Electoral Practice and Behaviour in Asian Democracy*, Navrang, New Delhi, pp. 54-112
28. Horowitz, n.1, p. 644. Also see Peter N (1964): *British Guyana: Problems of Cohesion in an Immigrant Society*, Oxford.
29. Horowitz, n 5, p 12.
30. Lim Hong Hai Electoral Politics in Malaysia 'Managing' Elections in a Plural Society, in Aurel C., Gabriele B and Marei J. (eds) (2002): *Elections in South Asia*, Friedrich Ebert Stiftung, Singapore, pp. 141-02.
31. *Ibid.*
32. Asia Times Online, www.atimes.com, (Hong Kong) Aug 24, 2002.
33. Reynolds A., "South Africa: Electoral System Design and Conflict Management in Africa", in Reynolds & Reilly, n.7, p 70.
34. Ansari, n 10, pp.108-09.
35. Barry Brian, "Political Accommodation and Consociational Democracy" *British Journal of Political Science*, October, 1975, pp. 502-4. Also see Ian Lustick "Stability in Deeply Divided Societies: Consociationalism *versus* Control", *World Politics*, Vol.31, no.2,1978-79 pp. 325-44.
36. Kasfir Nelson, "Explaining Ethnic Political Participation", *World Politics*, Vol. 31, 1978-9, pp. 387-88; Also see Sankaran Krishna (1999): Post-colonial *Insecurities: India, Sri Lanka and the Question of Nationhood*, Oxford University Press.
37. Sankaran Krishna (1999): *Post-colonial Insecurities: India, Sri Lanka, and the Question of Nationhood*, Oxford University Press, p.242.
38. Nohlen Dieter, Elections and the Electoral Systems, Friedrich Ebert Stiftung, Bonn, p.137
39. Reynolds A. & Reilly, n.7.

12

Lack of Political Will and Electoral Reforms

RAKA ARYA

People's democracy is the ultimate dream of the civil society. Free and fair elections are the backbone of a perfect democracy. In an ideal democracy, the people govern themselves through their elected representatives. In a Parliamentary democracy, the executive is formed from the legislature and remains part of it and also responsible to it. The members of the two Houses of the Parliament are elected through an electoral process, which is the foundation of a Parliamentary democracy. They have major influence over the improvement and distortions of the political culture of the country. Indian democracy is a unique example of democracy in the world because of its size. With six hundred million voters, it is not easy to conduct elections in this country. Nevertheless one does not find many faults and lacunas with the basic structures of the electoral system when one compares it with the functioning of other democracies elsewhere. In 1952, when the first general elections were held in India, it achieved an impossible task of conducting free and fair election with 176 million voters of whom about 85 per cent could not read and write. The Election Commissioner Sukumar Sen was faced with a tremendous task, from preparing voters list, ballot papers, party symbols, to building polling stations, and recruiting presiding officers, a task that he completed successfully.[1]

The electoral scenario in India has deteriorated dismally. Indian democracy is suffering from different maladies such as the three MPs *i.e.* money power, muscle power and mafia power along with four Cs *i.e.* criminalisation, corruption, communalism, and casteism. The majority of Indian political representatives are elected by a minority of votes cast, thereby making the credentials of these representatives doubtful. Therefore the legitimacy of the Indian political process is seriously compromised. While reflecting on the state of the electoral system in India, Atal Behari Vajpayee said, "Elections are not entirely free and fair, they are not reflecting the true will and aspiration of the people...The electoral system has been almost totally subverted by the money power, muscle power and vote bank consideration of castes and communities. As a result casteism and communalism are being aided and abetted by the electoral process. With a few exceptions, those who get elected are neither trained in law-making nor do they seem to have the inclination to develop the necessary knowledge and competence in their profession.... The natural inclination of today's M.P.s and M.L.As is to get influence and that too without accountability and much capability. The exceedingly high premium placed on capturing power by fair or foul means is because of the conviction that power is the passport to personal prosperity. Corruption in the governing structure has, therefore, corroded the very core of elective democracy."[2]

This paper looks into the different problems faced by the electoral system of India during these past years and adds some more suggestions to existing suggestions given by several eminent politicians, jurists, writers, and scholars. It points out the failure of the government and parliamentarians to implement most of the ideas, which have been put forward to improve the system. For the last thirty odd years several endeavours have been made to stop these political malpractices in the electoral process of the country. The explanation for the lack of progress would seem to be that there is no political will to reform the system and strong vested interests block changes which would make elections more fair. It must be noted that those who have the responsibility to implement reforms are themselves elected under the present system and this may explain why they are not willing to take steps which would improve the system. To demonstrate the failures of reform the paper assesses the experience of the many committees established to review the electoral system and what happened to their recommendations. Though elections are held for different types of institutions—*i.e.* Parliament, State Assemblies and local bodies like Pancahyats and Nagar Palikas etc—the paper focuses on reforms related to stopping malpractices in the process of electing representatives of the Union and the State legislatures. Different governments at times took many steps. Many committees were formed to clean up the electoral process in the last decade. These committees are:

(i) The Goswami Committee on Electoral Reforms (1990),
(ii) The Indrajit Gupta Committee on State Funding of Elections (1998),
(iii) The Law Commission Report on Reform of the Electoral Laws (1999),
(iv) The Election Commission has also documented its own thoughts based on the recommendations of these three committees as well as their own experience of ground realities.

Some of the major problems confronting the election process are as follows:

(i) The high cost of election attracts unethical, illegal and even mafia electoral funding;
(ii) Majority of candidates are being elected by a minority of votes, thus, representative character of the representatives itself becomes doubtful;
(iii) The question of defection from one party to another and the provisions in the Tenth Schedule of the Constitution to control political defections has proved ineffective;
(iv) Inaccurate and flawed electoral rolls and voters' identities lead to rigging and denial of voting right to a large number of citizens;
(v) Criminalisation of electoral process—increasing number of contestants with serious criminal antecedents play havoc with the electoral process and adversely affect the political system of the country;
(vi) Booth capturing, fraudulent voting by rigging and impersonation; use of muscle power in the form of intimidating voters; partisan behaviour of officials and local administration; engineered mistakes in counting of votes all adversely affects election results and consequently freedom of choice;

(vii) Divisive and disruptive tendencies including the misuse of religion and caste in the process of political mobilisation of group identities on non-ideological lines;

(viii) Slow judicial process in disposing of pending election petitions;

(ix) Incongruities in de-limitations of constituencies resulting in inequalities in representation;

(x) Participation of too many candidates and too many political parties;

(xi) Unequal participation of women; and

(xii) Illiterate and poor electorate.

To seek solution to these problems different approaches have been proposed by the politicians, jurists and others involved in this endeavour. There are various approaches put forward by different organisations to make necessary reforms in the electoral process– one such approach is to tackle the problem within the boundaries of the current, electoral process without altering the basic framework of the system. The other major approach is to strike at the root of the problem.

Electoral Roll and Voter Identity

The inaccuracies in the electoral rolls may be the result of inefficiency and a flawed system but certainly, as pointed out by the Goswami Committee, some of it is also the result of purposeful tampering which may happen due to partisan attitude of local officials who may have their own local affinities or may be bought over by vested interests. The rules and laws to punish erring officials in this respect have been totally ineffective. The Dinesh Goswami Committee recommended a more stringent punishment for breach of official duty in connection with preparation of electoral rolls.[3] This recommendation has since been implemented with the enactment of Representation of People's (Amendment) Act, 1996. [4]

To establish a fair and impartial democratic process several suggestions were made by various governmental and non-governmental organisations. One such suggestion was based on the idea that the electoral roll and voters' identity should be related to each other because, an authentic and revised voters' list would serve the objective of curbing impersonation and rigging. In the long-run, such list would create widespread faith in the fairness of Indian electoral process thereby providing it with a high degree of institutional legitimacy.

At national level the Election Commission is responsible for preparing the electoral rolls for the state and union legislative constituencies. The State Election Commissioners (SEC) are responsible for the electoral roll for local bodies. To avoid duplication of voters' list, a single joint exercise by the EC at national as well as state level should be enough for preparing electoral rolls covering the lowest to the highest constituency that a voter belongs to.

A suggestion was made by the National Commission to Review the Working of the Constitution that these electoral rolls should be updated constantly and not just at the time of election. This information should be given on the web site of the Election Commission and CD ROMs should be available to all political parties or any one interested at a reasonable price. Prior to elections these rolls should be printed and publicly displayed at the post offices in each constituency as well as at the panchayats or relevant constituency HQs.[5]

Secondly the Goswami Committee had recommended a scheme for a multipurpose photo identity card in coordination with other ministries and government departments so that the possession of this card would become compulsory for adult citizens. This identity card should be used as an ID for many benefits that are provided by various government agencies. Such as the issuance of ration card, a passport, driving license, telephone for individual, application for a government or private sector job, admission of children to school or college, for opening bank accounts, for transfer of one's property etc. Each ID card should have a number that would make fraudulent duplication impossible.

Booth Capturing

In the Representation of People's (Amendment) Act, 1996, in addition to returning officers, observers appointed by the Election Commission of India have also been empowered to send reports to the Election Commission in respect of booth capturing etc. and the Election Commission is authorized to issue appropriate directions for countermanding the elections or to order the repolling in certain polling stations where booth capturing has taken place on the basis of such reports (Section 20B of R.P. Act 1951).[6]

To further discourage booth capturing, the EC might consider having some form of tamper-proof video cameras or surveillance equipment as a deterrent in sensitive areas. The punishment to offenders should be swift and heavy.

Inciting Communal and Caste Hatred

The offences committed under Section125 of R.P. Act 1951, should be punishable with mandatory imprisonment for three years and not discretionary as the section says. As far as political will to deal with the problem of communalism and casteism is concerned one can see their reluctance in passing a comprehensive constitutional amendment bill (80th Amendment Bill) and Representation of the People's Act (Amendment) Bill 1993 which were introduced to de-link politics from communalism, casteism and linguism etc.[7]

It is an open secret in India that criminals are becoming political leaders. In 1998 Lok Sabha elections a record number of candidates with criminal credentials contested the election. Out of 13952 candidates about 1500 were under prosecution for crimes like murder, dacoity, rape, theft and extortion. Out of 1500 candidates under prosecution 820 were from Bihar and UP.[8]

In 1997 the Election Commission issued an order that candidates contesting election for the State Assembly and Parliament have to submit an affidavit about their convictions in cases covered under Section 8 of R.P. Act, 1951; The Election Commission held that if the trial court had convicted the candidate this was enough to attract disqualification. The Election Commission wrote a letter to the prime minister in September 1997 that there were incongruities in the existing provisions of sub-sections (1), (2) and (3) of the said Section 8 of the R.P. Act, 1951, illustrating the case of a rapist, convicted and sentenced to ten years imprisonment, being disqualified only for six years under sub-section (1) and being free to contest elections, even while in prison serving the last four years of his sentence. The Commission suggested that the law may be simplified by amending Section 8 to provide that whoever is convicted of any offence by a court of law and sentenced to imprisonment for six months or more should be debarred from contesting elections, for a period totalling the sentence imposed plus an additional six years. If an elected representative is convicted on charges related to specific crimes, he should be required to withdraw until he is cleared of the charges. Among other proposals made by the Election Commission there was a suggestion to make a provision for the person who is convicted of a non-cognizable offence and undergoes five years' rigorous imprisonment should be debarred from contesting any election.[9] It is also worth considering that when political parties are seen to abet criminalisation by fielding criminals, there should be some provisions to enable action against them including their derecognition. The other way to restrict criminals entering into politics suggested by Justice Kuldeep Singh Panel is that "if we cannot bar criminals from contesting elections until they are convicted by the courts, then the next best course would be to get speedy verdicts in their cases. Special courts and benches to try cases against legislators and other high profile people should be set up for speedy trials."[10]

Misuse of Money

The unscrupulous use of money in the elections to ensure protection from criminals and buy votes have not only vitiated the whole electoral process but political system as well. The sources of some of the election funds are believed to be unaccounted criminal money in return for protection, unaccounted funds from business groups who expect a high return on their investments, kickbacks or commissions on contracts etc. which lay foundation of a compromised government, and the huge amount of money that is spent on elections adversely affects economy of the nation and weakens it's financial structure. It also breeds uncontrolled corruption. The consequences of widespread corruption are even more serious. Political patronage in return for unaccounted and uncontrolled use of money makes any reform in electoral process virtually impossible. In the Goswami Committee, leaving the question of the existing ban on donations by companies and corporate bodies for political purpose to the collective wisdom of "the government and parliament", a continuance of the ban on donations by the government companies was sought. The logic behind this was that if trade unions and other organisations had been allowed to contribute to political parties, there was no reason that companies should be banned from making political contributions. M.S. Gill, former Election Commissioner said that in a democratic set-up, companies should be allowed to contribute for political causes.

However, he said, these contributions should be limited to reasonable level and all transactions in this regard must be made above board. To solve problems related to political funding during the time of election some proposals were made by an advisory panel consisting of eminent constitutional experts. One such proposal was to form "a comprehensive legislation regarding the regulation of political contributions to political parties and towards election expenses. Legislation should provide for compulsory auditing of the accounts of all political parties registered with the Election Commission by an independent authority specified under the new law regulating the functioning of political parties, publishing of audited party account, and immediate de-recognition and enforcement of penalties for filing false or incorrect election returns. Accounts should be made available for public inspection."[11] The Indrajit Gupta Committee on State Funding of Elections suggested that there should be at least a partial though non- cash state funding of elections. Whatever levels of permissible expenditure may be fixed, unless there is (a) a reasonably foolproof method of enforcing these and (b) to take action when these are violated, these exercises may turn out to be meaningless. There is an effective systemic acceptance of full audit of campaign funds, deletion of explanation 1 to Section 77(1) of the RP Act, 1951, a foolproof mechanism to deter expenditure violations, and until the government is convinced that these improvements have been institutionalised and are no longer being breached, the question of state funding should not even arise.

Defections

Since late sixties Indian democracy is suffering from *Aya Ram Gaya Ram* syndrome. The political defections made by elected members, to the Union Legislature and State Legislature, have not only made mockery of Indian democratic system but have also weakened the very foundation of it. To deal with the malady of the defection some effective remedy should be found. It was thought that defections encourage corruption to the highest level, the disqualification of defectors from one party to another should be automatic and immediate, their votes should be annulled. Because if their votes are not annulled the defectors may bring down the government before they are disqualified.[12] Defectors should not be eligible for any public office until re-elected."[13] The defectors should also be debarred to hold any public office of a minister or any other remunerative political post for at least the duration of the remaining term of the existing legislature or until, the next fresh elections which ever is shorter.

Multiplicity of Candidates and Instability

Too many candidates contesting election from the same constituency have a nuisance value and make selection of a candidate with clear-cut majority difficult. To discourage too many candidates from contesting the election certain recommendations were made by the Law Commission in which it was held that independent candidates should be discouraged from contesting elections to the Lok Sabha and legislative assemblies. Even Goswami Committee report made the suggestions on similar lines permitting only those candidates who have a track record of having won any local election *i.e.* at Panchayat and Municipal level primarily. In the Representation of People's (Amendment) Act, 1996, security deposit for independent candidate was enhanced to twenty times of the earlier limit. Under the act if any independent candidate fails to get at least 5 per cent of the total number of votes caste in his constituency, he/she should not be allowed to contest as independent candidate for the same office again at least for six years. The RP Act has many other suggestions to check the proliferation of independent candidates. No candidate should be allowed to contest election from more than one constituency at the same time.[14]

Political Morality

The very purpose of democracy is to educate people about political life, fundamental rights and duties. It is rightly said that elections are complex events involving individual and collective decisions, which directly affect and are affected by the total political and social process. Elections are intended to open up channels between society and the polity, between the masses and the elites and between the individual and government. They are major source of political socialisation and participation. Dr. S. Radhakrishnan said,

> "Our Constitution has adopted adult suffrage. It is the most powerful instrument devised by man for breaking down social and economic injustice and destroying the walls that imprison men's minds. This can be achieved only if our people are aware of their rights and responsibilities and this is the task of dedicated

leaders to teach the people."[15]

Some other Observations

In 1993 the V.R. Krishna Iyer Committee made a suggestion to add a provision in R.P. Act, 1951, to the effect that unless at least 30 per cent of the votes in a constituency are cast, the election shall not be regarded as valid. C. Subramaniam was in favour of prescribing minimum qualification for legislators.

Also a provision needs to be made in the constitution to facilitate the inclusion of renowned experts into the cabinet to handle portfolios such as finance, planning, education, medicine, science and technology. When a government system requires every person working in it has to posses minimum qualification, the political leaders seemed to be exempted from it. To make laws and policies on the issues that require expertise in the related area the ministers in charge of the ministry have no clue on the subject. As it was rightly observed by the Advisory Panel on Electoral Reforms: Standards in Political Life which says, "Today, a person can be a Law Minister without even a nodding familiarity with law and an Education Minister without any formal education...should we not lay down some qualifications: Impeccable integrity, Proven ability, Academic standards in consonance with the requirements of the job, otherwise leaders can be a liability. And surely, rule of the majority does not mean rule by the illiterate."[16]

Lack of Political Will—The Crux of the Problem

Leaders have suggestions, they have laws but they do not have the will to implement them. Without having political will no suggestion, no law could be effective. There is no dearth of rules and laws for conducting free and fair elections but as far as implementation of these laws is concerned political as well as administrative will is hardly visible. As T.U. Mehta rightly observed, "Should we allow this process to continue or should we start thinking of taking necessary remedial steps to stem the rot? There is no dearth of remedial steps. The question is only of earnestness. Those who have a vested interest in the increasing deterioration of values will, of course, resist any proposal for reform. Similar views were expressed by N. K. Trikha. When commenting on electoral reforms, he stressed the lack of political will in the context of political defection. According to him, "...there was no dearth of serious and rational thought given to the problem, no paucity of material to formulate reforms, no lack of public opinion to lend popular legitimacy to an enactment in this regard. Ban on defection has always remained on top of the agenda for electoral reforms and there were no two opinions about the desirability or feasibility of banning defections. But it was not done. Why? Clearly, it was lack of political will on the part of rulers that was responsible for the sad spectacle of horse trading witnessed during the past two decades, and the ever increasing malpractices seriously vitiating the outcome of election. But when the new government at the centre willed to do it, it was done in no time."[17]

This discussion shows that what is required is not new laws but the will to implement these laws. The views expressed by Madhu Dandvate fifteen years ago, substantiate this idea. In 1987 he said that there is no need of any new committee to formulate the scheme of electoral reforms, since already available are the reports of the committee on defections, the report on proposed amendments to election laws, the recommendations of the Tarkunde Committee set up by Late Loknayak Jayaprakash Narayan, and the suggestions made by the former Chief Election Commissioner, S.L. Shakdher. What is needed is not only further study or scrutiny of proposals for electoral reforms but also expeditious implementation of the reforms recommended.

Notes

1. In 1952, fifty six thousand presiding officers were recruited; two lakh twenty four thousand policemen were on duty to control poll violence and intimidations. In year 2002, the number of voters has increased to six hundred million and the number of polling booths has gone up to nine lakhs which is the equivalent of an average of six hundred sixty seven voters for each booth. Five persons are needed for each polling booth making a total of 4.5 million to 5 million electoral personnel and 2 million security personnel to maintain law and order on polling day. See, A Consultation Paper prepared by National Commission to Review the Working of the Constitution, on 'Review of Election Law, Processes and Reform Options' presented in a national seminar on 'Reforms for a Resurgent Republic', jointly organised by Department of Culture, Ministry of Tourism and Culture, Govt. of India, and Lok Bharati, Uttar Pradesh on 3-4 March 2001, at Allahabad University.
2. Shri Atal Bihari Vajpayee's speech before assuming Prime Ministership, quoted in, Rao, P.P. (2002): 'Elections sans reforms' *The Hindu*, February 9.

3. ..... (1990), Committee on Electoral Reforms (Dinesh Goswami Committee), Report of the Committee on Electoral Reforms, Legislative Department, Ministry of Law and Justice, New Delhi.
4. n 3; and T.N. Seshan (1996): 'Election in India: The Magnitude of the Task and Challenges Ahead', *Politics India*, New Delhi, June.
5. n.1.
6. *Ibid.*
7. n.1 & also see, Kothari, Rajni (2001): *Politics in India*, Orient and Longman, New Delhi and Hegde, Ramakrishna (1984): *Electoral Reforms: Lack of Political Will, Karnataka State Janata Party*, Banglore.
8. Seshan, T. N & n 4.
9. n.1& also see The Vohra Committee Report; Ministry of Home Affairs, New Delhi; The Notification of Election Commission of India, 6th January 1998 and 28th August 1998; Express News Service, 'EC Focus on Crime- Politics Ties', 1997, *Indian Express*, 1997.; Newsletter-Foundation for Democratic Reforms in India, 'Major Achievements in the Battle for Disclosure of Information by Candidates for Public Office', 31st October 2002; The Consultation Paper on ' Review of the Working of Political Parties Specially the Relation to Election and Reform Options', prepared by The Advisory Panel on Electoral Reforms: Standards in Political Life, headed by Shri R. K. Trivedi; V. Venkatesan, ' Crime and Politics', *Frontline*, July 2002.
10. n.9 & Express News Service.
11. V. A. Pai Panandikar and Navnita Chadha Behera (2000): *Perspectives on South Asia,* Konark, New Delhi; Advani, L. K. and others (eds.) (1987): *Electoral System in India: Need for Reforms*, Panchnad Research Institute, Chandigarh; and Trikha, N. K. (1996): 'Electoral Reforms: State Funding as First Step', *Indian Express*; ——— (1998): Committee on State Funding of Elections (Headed by Indrajit Gupta), Government of India, Ministry of Law, Justice and Company Affairs, New Delhi.
12. Though a committee on defection was set-up in Dec. 1967, its report was laid before Parliament only in Feb. 1969, and many recommendations made by the committee have still remained unimplemented. Another effort regarding electoral reform was made by a 21-member 'Joint Parliamentary Committee on electoral reforms', which produced a two volume report in Feb. 1971 but met the same fate. Kashyap, S. C. (ed) (1995): *Anti-Defection Law and Parliamentary Privileges*, N.M. Tripathi Pvt. Ltd., Mumbai.
13. n.1.
14. May 1999, One Hundred Seventieth Report on Reform of the Electoral Laws, Law Commission of India, New Delhi; .... (1995): Tarakunde Committee, Report of the Committee on Electoral Reforms; Citizens for Democracy, New Delhi.
15. Quoted in Advani, L.K. and others & n.11.
16. n 9.
17. Trikha, N. K. & n.11.

13

Electoral Reforms in India

An Overview

D.K. SANKARAN

A lot of heat has been generated over Electoral Reforms in India. Indeed, in many democratic countries around the world Electoral Reforms is the flavour of the day. The row about Chinese Government funding of President Clinton's electoral efforts in 1996 and the recent controversy about ex-Chancellor Helmut Kohl of Germany regarding electoral fund malpractices highlight the fact that weaknesses in the election system is in the fore-front of even mature western democracies. Indeed, Election Reforms are required on a continuous basis. It is difficult to say that an ideal election system has been reached and there is never a need to review the system.

I would highlight about 3-4 areas where Electoral Reforms are urgently needed in India. These are (a) Funding/Maintenance of accounts by political parties and candidates; (b) Measures to check criminalisation of politics; (c) Ban on defection; and (d) Check on corrupt electoral practices.

These views of mine are shaped by my experience of nearly 7 years as Chief Electoral Officer, Maharashtra. Maharashtra has no incidence of electoral malpractice, like booth capturing, ballot-paper stuffing, etc., unlike many other states. In fact, since elections were introduced in 1952, there has been only one incidence of a ballot box being snatched away during 1991 Lok Sabha elections in the naxalite infested Gadchiroli District where the ultras decamped with a ballot box containing 28 ballots. This led to the only incidence of repolling ever in General Elections in Maharashtra.

Funding/Maintenance of Accounts by Political Parties and Candidates

This is an area requiring urgent attention. There is a strong need for transparency in the matter of fund collection by the political parties and their accounting and auditing. The accounts must be audited by agencies registered with the Election Commission of India. While the blanket ban on donations by companies to political parties is not recommended, such donations should be transparent and subject to reasonable limit. One is reminded here about the controversy in the United States of America where the funding of political parties by the corporate sector has skewed the taxation structure to the detriment of the individual tax payers and the benefit of corporate sector.

In the Indian context, the election expenditure of the candidates and the political parties has been a perennial subject attracting the reformers' attention. There is an urgent need to annul the amendments made in 1976 and bring the expenditure of the political parties on behalf of candidates within the limits prescribed for the candidate. This needs to be done urgently by amending Sections 77 and 78 of the Representation of Peoples' Act, 1951.

Another area of interest when one talks about election finances is that of public funding of political parties/candidates. A committee, set up recently, has submitted its report on this issue and it is under consideration by the Government of India. The Election Commission has also introduced public funding in the form of free time on radio and the electronic media. It is doubtful if public funding to candidates and parties will lead to cleaner elections. It is like arguing that increasing salaries of public servants will reduce, if not eliminate corruption. However, two crucial changes in this area will be welcomed. The first one is to make the election expenditure limit more realistic. This can be done by relating it to the total number of voters in a constituency. For example, the Thane Lok Sabha Constituency in Maharashtra has nearly 28 Lac voters, but the expenditure limit for a candidate is Rs.15 Lacs. The same is the limit for candidates in Mumbai South Lok Sabha Constituency, where the total number of voters is about 7 Lacs.

Secondly, there is an urgent need to abolish this constituency specific fund of Rs.1 crore allotted to each M.P. by the Government for special development work in their constituency. On a similar basis, the State Governments have allotted constituency specific grants to the members of the State Legislature. It is also extended to Municipal Corporation and Local Bodies. This has given an unfair advantage to the incumbent M.P./M.L.A. over the others and it needs to be changed forthwith giving a level playing field for all candidates.

Measures to Check Criminalisation of Politics

After financing of political parties and candidates one area which has immense importance in the context of Indian elections is criminalisation. Notwithstanding, the Election Commission's recent action to effectively bar those who are convicted of various criminal acts mentioned in Section 8 of Representation of People's Act, 1951 from contesting elections, criminal and anti-social elements still enter the legislature. This is because people under trails, especially when they are facing serious charges like murder, dacoity or rape, etc. are perceived as criminals. There is continuous chorus for debarring such people from contesting elections and holding elective offices. The present provision of the act, as implemented by the Election Commission of India, puts no restrictions on such people. Urgent reforms are needed in this area and various recommendations of the Election Commission as well as Law Commission of India have underlined the need to ban a person who is accused of any offence punishable with imprisonment of say 4 or 5 years or more from standing for elections, even if he is under trial, if the Judicial Court concerned has framed charges against him.

This will be a very major Electoral Reform and will go a long way in checking the entry of criminals into the legislature. These amendments need to be introduced forthwith.

Ban on Defection

Defection of elected legislators is another crucial area, which requires immediate attention. No act of a legislator negates the will of the people more than that of defections. At present, the Election Commission has no role to play in this area. The present Anti-Defection Law recognises splits of political parties and there is an urgent need to change this. Once a person is elected to a legislature, he or she should be prevented from changing party affiliation before resigning his or her seat. The Election Commission should be empowered to decide issues relating to the defection and to advice the State Governor or the President, as the case may be. The Election Commission is now a multi-member Commission and has been widely recognized to be a neutral and an impartial body. Such a move will completely change the electoral system in the country and make elections truly representative of the will of the people.

Check on Corrupt Electoral Practices

Finally, the present Indian election law relating to corrupt electoral practices needs a serious re-think. Until 1976, once an elected person was unseated by the courts for corrupt electoral practices, he or she was debarred from standing for elections for six years. And such an individual had his or her name struck off from the Electoral Roll for six years. The present law maintains that on such conviction the President shall obtain the opinion of the Election Commission and shall act according to such opinion. There is an urgent need to restore the law prior to the present amendment.

Conclusion

These measures suggested above will make Indian Electoral System more fruitful and cleansed of corrupt practices. Hopefully, it will, to a certain extent, increase voter participation, which is now low. One other area, which will require attention of all, including the political parties, is selection of candidates for various elections. The Election Commission or law has no role to play here except fixing minimum age requirements and some other criteria. The political parties must urgently make vast improvements in the selection of candidates. One reason for low voter participation is disenchantment with candidates. In United States of America, they have primary elections for deciding candidates for various election posts. Notwithstanding some deficiencies, this is a model worth considering. Ultimately, for greater voter participation, candidates with considerable voter appeal will act as a catalyst.

14

Reforms for a Better Representation of the People

DAVID ANNOUSSAMY

Percentage of Votes to Get Elected

The ideal would be that elected bodies are exact miniaturized replicas of the social bodies. This is not practically feasible. However, we should endeavour to come as near as possible to that ideal. Otherwise decisions of elected bodies will not command respect. How far in the present system those who are proclaimed elected are representative of their constituencies and how to improve their representativeness are questions of vital importance. This query has two aspects, one quantitative *viz.* how many people the winner represents, another qualitative *viz.* how much of the aspirations of the various segments of the people is carried by the persons elected.

One is stunned by the scant percentage of votes with the help of which our representatives get elected in the prevailing system. One may even come across people declared elected with 15 per cent of votes polled *viz.* 9 per cent of electors on the rolls. It has also been found that the majority to form a government was achieved by a party securing only the support of 30 per cent of votes polled *viz.* 18 per cent of the electors on the rolls. In some cases a party, which obtained a lesser number of votes, gets a larger number of seats. Small parties do not get any seat even if they have secured 10 per cent of votes polled. They do not have the opportunity to ventilate their views inside the House; and they are thus driven to resort to demonstrations or agitations. No wonder that the government is weak. Having a controvertible legitimacy it is not able to assert itself *vis-a-vis* the other limbs of power like the judiciary or even the civil service; it yields easily to pressure groups of all brands.

Some measure has to be devised to improve the representativeness of those elected. Two solutions may be thought of, the first one is re-poll if no candidate gets 50 per cent of votes polled. Only the two candidates who have obtained the highest number of votes will then be in the fray. This is the practice in some countries. It is not without some very serious drawbacks. There is greater abstention rate in the second round so that no party may get votes from 50 per cent of persons on the rolls. There are sordid transactions in order to purchase the support of eliminated candidates by the surviving ones.

The second solution would be the list system with allocation of seats to parties in proportion to the votes polled. It will give representation to all hues of the political world. It will rather project the image of the party to the detriment of that of the candidate. It may reduce the ferocity of election battles and election expenditure. It may take care of scheduled castes as well, if constituencies are properly and carefully carved out. It will not be conducive to the stability of the government in the parliamentary system. The present system is no better in this regard in Indian conditions.

Abstentions

An important factor, which keeps down the number of votes obtained by candidates, is large-scale abstention, which is to the tune of 40 per cent. Compared to international standards this is not catastrophic. But that is no solace. Something has to be done to improve the civic performance. In some countries voting has been made compulsory with some punishment or other meted out to abstentionists, including fine. To start with, an abstentionist may be given the opportunity of sending a letter of apology to the presiding officer of the polling station as early as possible on the polling day. This will have the additional benefit of reducing cases of impersonation. On the other side those who are handicapped should be given adequate opportunity to vote by correspondence, and equally those who live far away from the polling booth, in hilly or sparsely populated areas.

Before moving to take any compelling action in this regard, it is essential to study the phenomenon in depth. Who are those who do not go to the polling booth and why? If abstentionists represent a cross-section of the population similar to those who vote, we may presume that the result of the poll would be the same if all people had voted, and then we may ignore the abstentions. If not, the problem is serious, because the result of the poll is altered by abstentions. Then we have to continue the probe and determine the ratio of abstentionists by sex, age group, education, wealth, social status. The other questions to be addressed are: how many of them are chronic abstentionists? Why do they prefer abstaining and what according to them should be done to draw them to the polling station ? Such a survey can be undertaken by university departments of politics all over the country and any other research institutions at the behest of the Election Commission or any other apex body.

Pending such a study the lawmaker may prescribe that abstentions would be considered as rejection votes. People would hardly go to the polling station to cast a blank vote rejecting all candidates. That happens, but in a very small way. If abstentionists added to blank votes exceed 50 per cent of persons on the electoral rolls there should be a re-poll. In that way those who do not want their abstention to be construed as rejection of all candidates may decide to exercise their franchise. On the other side candidates who most probably would like to avoid re-polling would make efforts to draw more people to the polling station.

Readjustment of Constituencies

In principle all citizens in the country should have the same voting power wherever they are located. Accordingly Article 82 of the Constitution provides that after each census the allocation of seats in the House of the People and the division of each state into territorial constituencies shall be readjusted. This arrangement was tampered with by the Forty-second Amendment, freezing the constituencies to the pre-1977 position. This was done at the behest of States that have made significant advances in family planning. Their plea was that they would get punished for their earnest implementation of the policy of the Union Government and get a lesser number of seats.

First, for this purpose it was not necessary to freeze the constituencies within each state. During these last 25 years there has been a large-scale migration of population from villages to towns. Urban population has grown from 20 per cent to 30 per cent. In some places it is found that the population in the most populated constituency is three times the least populated one. This has to be remedied by altering the constituencies to make them more or less equal in population, or at least by correcting the most glaring discrepancies.

Secondly, freezing the number of seats irrespective of the population violates the basic principles of equal representation. States that have registered success in family planning should not have any feeling of regret, they have ensured better conditions of life to their youth for which they may be proud. Their performance may be acknowledged by granting other advantages to enable them to improve the skills of their meagre youth population. Further if states are vested with more autonomy, they may not have the same feeling of frustration in respect of their share in the House of the People.

The initial constitutional arrangements for periodical readjustment of constituencies, which are in conformity with fundamental principles of people's representation, have to be restored in respect of the House of the People. However, advanced states have a good case for a representation not proportionate to population in the Council of States. In this body it is not the citizen who is represented, but the State with an identity of its own. Normally all States of a federation would have the same number of seats. Since in India there are States having less than a million of inhabitants and others having more than 50 millions, they could be classified into three groups: small, medium and large and a fixed number of seats allotted to the States in each group. The powers of the Council of States could also be reinforced to prevent important decisions being rushed through by the strength of sheer number in the House of the People in disregard of the diversity of the country.

Election of the Leader

Now the leader of the House, though he wields immense powers, is first elected in a constituency by a small segment of population. On account of the uncertainty attached to the election process, party leaders stand for election in more than one constituency. If elected in both, they vacate immediately one seat leaving those who voted for them disappointed and creating the need for a fresh poll. This is not fair to the electorate; it deserves a better treatment. There is also a complaint that the constituency, which elected the leader, receives more grants than the others in violation of the principle of equal distribution of public funds.

There is now no legal bar to being a candidate in more than one constituency. But since a person can occupy only one seat it goes without saying that he should stand only in one constituency. Further if many persons start competing in more than one constituency that will create chaos. Therefore, this curious practice, which has crept in, has to be brought to an end. It is to be borne in mind that one becomes leader of the House or leader of the Opposition only after his election by his fellow representatives. Under these circumstances the solution in vogue is rather crude and inadequate. Something statelier has to be found for the leader of the party.

It is enough for that purpose to look at the realities. In the present system the vote cast by a citizen in each constituency is at the same time for the party, the leader and the candidate. The respective importance of the three may vary from case to case. But all the three are present in the mind of the voter. Why not institutionalize the reality? The name of the leader, which is present in watermark in the ballot paper, should be made to appear in printed form. He will be thus present in all constituencies; no need for him to sit as a simple candidate of one constituency. Under such circumstances the requirement of being a member of the Parliament may be dispensed with.

Qualifications of Candidates

Now there is only a condition of age and the age prescribed is so low that practically no person is debarred from standing for election on that count. There is a general feeling that the representatives should have a good educational background. This is a delicate problem. On one side every citizen is entitled to be an elected representative. At the same time he should be able to discharge his function to his own satisfaction, which he will find difficult to do once elected, if he is not adequately equipped.

A happy solution may be found in combining age, educational qualification and previous political experience. For instance, the condition of age may be fixed rather high for a person possessing neither education nor previous political experience but only his experience in life. The age can be brought down according to educational qualification and previous political experience *viz.* membership of a State Assembly for election to the State Assembly.

So the qualifications required will not be the same for the three tiers of elected bodies. In that way even a person without any instruction may be able to get elected on the basis of his long experience in life. A young man, talented and attracted by public life, will be able to enter the fray if he is highly qualified.

Reservation of Seats

This practice was started by the British in 1909. Under the Government of India Act, 1935 reservation was provided in a large scale for the following categories: Women, Scheduled Castes, Sikhs, Anglo-Indians, Europeans, Indian Christians and representatives of commerce, industry, land owners and labour.

At present Scheduled Castes and Tribes are given the benefit of reservation of seats corresponding to their demographic strength. This gives rise to an important question of principle. Reservation of a single member constituency to a particular class of citizen deprives citizens of other classes in the constituency of two of their essential civic rights. They cannot stand as candidates in their own constituency. Secondly if they do not want to cast their votes to a person belonging to the reserved category they are deprived of their right of franchise.

Such restrictions are repugnant to democratic canons. The British who were respectful of these fundamental principles have solved the problem in two ways. For Scheduled Castes they made reservations in general category seats but in multi-member constituencies; for the other categories they opted for separate electorates.

The Constitution makers, who wanted to erase any distinction between citizens, were averse to separate electorates and were also not in favour of reservation in elected bodies. They however reluctantly agreed to reservation of seats, as a very temporary arrangement for ten years, knowing well the flaws of such an arrangement in the single member constituency system for which they had opted. Unfortunately this faulty arrangement is renewed every ten years without any debate on whether the concerned categories are still politically immature and unorganised, or whether reservation in a single member constituency violates democratic principles. No party is willing to take the initiative to reconsider the issue, fearing loss of popularity among the beneficiaries of reservation. On the contrary each party would like to outshine the others in bringing in more reservations. If reservation as contemplated for backward classes and women is effected, only 33 per cent of seats would be free from reservation. Can we boost universal, unfettered adult suffrage in this predicament? Is not the unity of the country in jeopardy?

It is therefore necessary to pause a while and ponder whether reservation is still necessary in the political field. Do not Scheduled Castes have strong political parties, which would enable them to have a more genuine representation with the help of appropriate alliances? Is not the position of backward classes the same? If after deliberation it appears that reservation is still necessary it should be realised without affecting any citizen's right and without impairing the unity of the country. The only way out is multi-member constituencies, each party filing a list containing as many names as there are seats with at least one name belonging to the category whose representation is to be ensured in the constituency. The list having scored the highest percentage of votes will be declared elected.

This way of proceeding will have the tremendous advantage of bringing the communities together instead of creating rivalry and animosity between them. It is also worth noting that in European countries where such a system is prevalent there are more women who get elected than in countries with single member constituencies. This is quite understandable because more women are forthcoming to campaign along with men. They are apprehensive of facing alone an electorate consisting of men and women out of which more men than women turn out to hear electoral speeches.

Separation of Elections for Parliament and States

The responsibilities of a state and those of the union are different; their role is distinct. Candidates who wish to monitor the political activity of the one or the other are expected to shape their programmes accordingly. Citizens should be enlightened separately on the problems pertaining to the union and those falling on the shoulder of the state. They need to be told separately the programme advocated and the corresponding fiscal implications for the union and for the state.

When elections are held simultaneously for both, issues are blurred. Candidates get elected for the Parliament on the strength of their commitment to state ideals. Similarly others find their way to the State Assembly merely for their allegiance to a central leader. It looks like posting of officers. National parties miss the opportunity of considering in depth the problems of each state and do not allow the state units to grow to their full stature, stifling thereby the democratic process at that vital level. Regional parties are not given the opportunity of developing a national mindset. While concluding alliances they go even to the extent of trading parliamentary seats against assembly seats, unmindful of what happens at the national level.

Regarding past failures it is not rare to hear one party attributing them to the union government and the rival party putting the blame on the state government. It may be sometimes the mistake of both, in which case the respective role of each should be made known. It can obviously not be the mistake of the one or of the other, as candidates would like us to believe alternatively. On account of the confusion created by concomitant elections, problems relating to a state are raised in Parliament and problems within the sphere of the union are agitated in the state assembly with the sole purpose of embarrassing the relevant government and with the net result of waste of time of elected bodies.

When elections are held simultaneously, candidates belonging to the same alliance appear in the same booth with different symbols for their elections to the Parliament and to the State Assembly, creating perplexity in the mind of voters.

The drawbacks arising out of combination of elections to the two tiers of the federation are becoming more and more patent. Is there any legal reason for doing so? Clearly no. Instead, the Representation of the People Act contemplates two separate elections, one for the election to the House of the People by notification of the President and other for the State Assembly by notification of the Governor. The obnoxious practice of combining both the elections cropped up in the first years of the working of the Constitution without any thought being given to the implications. Further at that time it was a single party show all over the country. It was the same programme throughout and there was no previous performance to be assessed. The states were in a nebulous stage without clear identity. But the accidental has become routine.

Now that states have been reorganised with strong identities, now that solid regional parties have come into existence, it is imperative to hold elections separately. Otherwise the essential aim of having proper representatives for each is misused. Economy is no consideration in a matter so vital for good governance. The change over may be ushered in by the Election Commission. If necessary; separate elections for the union and the state may be made mandatory by a necessary provision to that effect in the Representation of the People Act.

Alliances

With the proliferation of parties all of them have come to the conclusion that they cannot reach a majority with their exclusive strength. Parties, which have lost ground, and those who have not yet garnered a proper following combine their force with the hope of emerging victorious. The result of elections now depend much on alliances. So alliance has become a key word. Parties vie with each other to have the best alliance. There is a pre-nuptial atmosphere before elections. Nothing wrong. But parties should commit themselves to a common programme, which would make the system workable. Alliances should not be reduced to a mere device to get elected without accepting the responsibilities arising there from.

Opportunistic alliances make a mockery of democracy. For instance two parties make an alliance sharing the seats in the ration of 2/3 and 1/3 with the understanding that if the first party gets the majority of seats it will form the government by itself. The other one takes the decision to sit in the opposition even before election. Relations turn sour when they are actually on each side of the fence. Parties, which posed as allies before the electorate, are pitted one against the other, leaving the voters bewildered. Sometimes an allied party after getting its members elected with the help of the alliance goes even to the extent of pulling down the government run by the alliance for no apparent rhyme or reason. Such sorts of alliances amount to taking voters for a ride and should be banned.

For this purpose it will be necessary to prescribe that parties, which want to fight elections for the Parliament, should file candidates in all the constituencies in the country. Then candidates and parties with a national outlook only and aware of national problems will be in the fray. Similarly, parties fighting State Assembly elections should be compelled to file candidates in all the constituencies of the state. In this way the number of competitors for election will be lower than at present.

If a single party is not able to file candidates in all the constituencies it may forge an alliance with others to achieve the purpose. Such an alliance should be deep rooted, not a bogus one, just an electoral strategy to capture more seats. All allied parties will have to fight under the same name, the same programme, the same leader, the same symbol, if any. The alliance will have to be considered as a party for the purpose of anti-defection law. Parties may not have major objection to this condition if elections to the Union and the State are held separately.

Symbols

Electoral symbols served some purpose when adult franchise was introduced for the first time. Now after fifty years of experience one wonders whether they are still necessary. It is also worth probing whether they are innocuous or distorting the decision of the voter. Symbols are not always indicative of the philosophy of the parties. The latter have no free choice. The symbol is meant to be a mere distinctive sign of the party for the purpose of identification at the time of casting vote. But there are symbols that are more to the liking of people than others, for superstitious, aesthetic or any other reason. Or a symbol may be reminiscent of a departed charismatic leader. So the symbol is not neutral, it is likely to influence the votes of some citizens and to divert them from the present programmes and assessment of past achievements of the party or of the candidate. More so, if one remembers that in the course of election campaign people are called loudly again and again to vote for this or that symbol!

Thus symbols are not innocuous; in fact there are terrible fights for vote catching symbols. So it is advisable to get rid of them. People are now accustomed to the electoral process. The name of the candidate with his initial in bold character and his photo would be sufficient. For further identification, the serial number will come to the rescue. The list of candidates as they appear in the ballot paper may be exhibited two or three days in advance in conspicuous places so that people may form an idea as to how to express their choice. Candidates will also have a vested interest in educating citizens in this respect.

There is no ready-made solution for perfect representation. Well-recognised guiding principles have to be respected. Actual practice has to be adapted to the need of the country at present. Our problems are of great magnitude because the architects of the newborn republic in their over enthusiasm at one stroke ushered in adult franchise in an immense and half literate country. At that time the average citizen could hardly grasp the concept of a party and hardly assimilate the device of representation. He has learnt a bit to his cost in the course of years.

The greatest obstacle is the enormous size of constituencies for the House of the People. They are too big for the mutual access of citizens and candidates, so essential for healthy democratic life. The system needs to be entirely revamped. Pending such an exercise, it would be possible to improve substantially the existing system. There are areas where clearly better solutions are in sight. In others, though the alternatives are not ideal, they are worth trying wherever the existing ones have become too bad. They will yield results till such time they are corrupted by users. There is nothing to be gained in waiting.

15

Making the Electoral System Work
Promoting a Democratic Culture through Political Engagement

CLEM MCCARTNEY

In discussing the state of democracy in India or elsewhere, it is common to focus on the electoral system and the structures and mechanisms to regulate elections. For example if there are problems of corruption and violence, they limit the candidates' capacity to seek votes in a fair and free manner and the voters are less likely to make a free choice between candidates. The natural response is to look for ways to tighten up electoral procedures and rightly so. If there is voter apathy we again look to the election process to provide ways, which will encourage the individual to exercise the right to vote.

However many of these problems point us to a deeper malaise within the body politic and they cannot be dealt with solely by tighter laws and regulations. We cannot expect the electoral commissioner to be able to make the democratic system work effectively, even if we provide him or her with the most comprehensive powers, if at the same time we do not ensure that the political parties and the electorate have an awareness of the political process and an understanding of the importance of developing a democratic culture based on free and fair participation in the political process.

If we look at standard descriptions of democracy, four essential elements are normally included:

- The capacity to change the government through the expression of the will of the people.
- Government openness and accountability to the people

through systems of free and open public debate.

- Government responsiveness to the expressed wishes of the people.
- Opportunities for meaningful participation by the people in the political process without threat or coercion.

It is understandable that public discussion on the protection of democracy tends to focus on the tangible structural questions about the electoral process or the protection of the freedom of the press. But if we think seriously about the key elements it is clear that the health of democracy depends as much, if not more, on the existence of an informed, aware and interested public and a political elite committed to these ideals. The means to achieve such a goal are more difficult to identify because they are more diffuse and wide ranging and relate to the underlying political culture and the broader environment. But there is little value in having a sophisticated and streamlined voting system if the public are uninterested in using their democratic rights or have no informed basis on which to make a judgement about the candidates. In these circumstances the electorate will be easily managed and corruption will be possible. Equally a free press only has an impact if the public is interested, can understand the issues, has access to the media, and in the case of print media, can read. If politicians do not know how to function effectively in the political system then it is not surprising that they will use threats and/or bribes to gain electoral support.

Therefore we have also to consider ways to develop an informed and aware public, and examine experience in other places. An informed and aware public contains a number of features. Literacy is sometime considered to be a necessary condition for a functioning democracy, but India shows that the democratic system can work in populations where a sizeable number of the electorate are illiterate. It is perhaps more useful to consider what capacities the community requires to exercise the franchise effectively. At the most basic level they need to understand the electoral process. In some societies there may be no tradition of democracy and the people are not familiar with the voting process. They may be very keen to exercise their new found right but they do not know the practical procedures for voting. Other communities are proud of the democratic traditions in their country but they may have limited understanding of why it is important and the responsibilities which democracy places on the individual voter. So they may not cast their vote or sell it to the highest bidder. We can think of the 1994 elections to the transitional authority in South Africa when there was a systematic process of education for those who never had the chance to vote before and during the election itself there were the moving sights of long lines of voters of all ages queuing patiently in the sun to cast their ballots for the first time. For them the denial of their right to vote had made the election very precious and contrasted with the apathy which exists in societies where many take the right to vote for granted and do not use it, as in many developed countries of the west.

In yet other societies the public may have strong opinions and support particular politicians and political movements but this may not indicate a well thought through analysis of the issues and may reflect family traditions and habits or peer influence, and in such circumstances there is a temptation for candidates to lapse into crude populism and perhaps an appeal to anti-minority sentiments.

Even when the electorate are motivated and informed those who seek their votes may need assistance in understanding how to gain popular support by constructive and legal means. They too may need help to understand the nature of the political process. They may also need to develop their skills in the mechanisms and systems for canvassing, identifying voters and monitoring elections. The politicians themselves may need help to develop their skills in representing the public, increasing their sensitivity to the concerns of the public and understanding the need for appropriate ethical standards for those in public life.

Background to Political Development in Northern Ireland

This paper looks at one example of trying to promote such awareness in Northern Ireland. In terms of form, the democratic process has been long established in Northern Ireland as in the rest of the United Kingdom. The stages through which the United Kingdom advanced towards universal suffrage beginning with the Great Reform Act of 1832, all applied equally to Northern Ireland and in addition there was the campaign for Catholic emancipation that led to the Catholic Emancipation Act of 1829. But while the form of democratic elections were well entrenched the democratic culture which developed was stultified by sectional voting, especially after partition. Protestants were by and large unionist, which meant they supported the union with Britain and therefore they voted for the Ulster Unionist Party. Catholics were mainly nationalist or supporters of the unification of the nation of Ireland and voted for the Nationalist Party even though for long periods it boycotted Parliament. On occasions there was some support for Sinn Fein though it too was an abstentionist party. It was only with the outbreak of the recent Troubles in 1969 that there was a break up of the monolithic parties on each side of the community but there was still almost no voting across the religious divide.

Most voters decided their electoral preferences on the basis of where the party stood on the constitutional status of Northern Ireland and other social and economic policies were not significant in voting decisions. As a result there was little discussion of wider issues and parties' policies and manifestos on these matters was often scanty or non-existent. Political parties did little to make their message relevant to those who did not normally vote for them and try to win them over. They were however extremely efficient at identifying their supporters and organising their vote on election day, so much so that the dead were often said to vote! There was a popular phrase "Vote early. Vote often."

The Marketing Approach to Political Development

At various points during the course of the troubles and particularly as a political settlement began to seem possible in the 1990s, analysts identified a political vacuum in the society, and programmes for political development were offered to the mainstream political parties mainly by organisations based in the United States. Political parties were not ready to accept that they were not competent and experienced since they had managed successful election campaigns in their own way for many years. But like all politicians they were ready to consider any ideas that might ensure continued electoral success. They were willing to take part in workshops and meetings, but were reluctant to accept criticism of their existing approaches and often did not think the orientation of the organisers fitted with their needs.

The programmes promoted the approach to politics adopted by the American political parties and their use of marketing techniques.

They showed the parties ways to assess the interests of the electorate, with the underlying assumption that the parties could and should adjust their policies to satisfy the interests of the voters. However the local political parties are conviction parties in the sense that they exist to promote certain ideas. One may not agree with those ideas and it is true that they have a populist appeal, but it is also true that the party members are in politics firstly to promote those ideas and only secondly for personal advantage. Therefore they have not been willing in the past to compromise on their positions. Parties did not want to modify their message to satisfy the electorate and they certainly did not want to lead their communities in new directions. They found it distasteful to discuss the idea of trimming positions and policies to fit more closely with the interests of the electorate even if they were already doing this in an intuitive way. They took what they found useful from these programmes in terms of polling and organisation but were not really swayed by the idea of becoming US-style parties.

What was needed was a way to help the political parties to look at the limitations of the existing political culture and develop, in association with their supporters and the wider electorate, a political culture that would be more appropriate and effective for the local circumstances. A small grant scheme for emerging political groups provided some indication of how such processes could be facilitated and encouraged.

Encouraging Political Engagement

The scheme began almost by accident. In the mid-1990s a donor wanted to give support to emerging political parties, which were a response to the changing political environment. Some movements wanted to develop their own political organisation because they felt that their supporters had been marginalised and inadequately represented by existing political parties. Some of them had been supporters of armed groups and there was a vicious circle which mutually reinforced the connection between their marginalisation and their support for militant action. In contrast there was also the emergence of small groups supporting moderate and inclusive politics and they also could take advantage of this scheme though they were not marginalised in the same way and found it easier to get other support including political scientists in universities.

The donor recognised the importance of bringing militant groups into the mainstream political process and wished to help them financially to make that transformation. The scheme lasted for three years until the new Northern Ireland Assembly was functioning and some of the parties had become sufficiently established to have members in the Assembly. The donor placed no restrictions on how the scheme would work and different approaches could have been used, including an open annual grant to each group for general expenditure. He wished to remain anonymous and some of the groups for their part were likely to be questioned about the source of donations, both by their supporters and opponents. So it was decided to set up a small organisation that would channel funds to the groups. The committee decided to use an approach, which it judged, would best encourage developmental processes.

Groups and parties had to make specific requests and small grants were awarded on the merits of the application. It was intended that the groups and parties would have to think about what they needed and it was hoped that the funds would encourage the parties to think about what would best aid their development. In order to help groups develop their requests a consultant supported the groups in developing their proposals and advised the committee on its decisions.

The committee decided that some things would not be financed including general office expenditure and staffing. They were willing to support some infrastructure costs including improvement to premises and the purchase of equipment. But they preferred to support organisational and policy development and gave grants for activities such as internal training courses, including training for electioneering, participation by members in external training, strategy reviews, member consultation, annual conferences, which were a tangible sign that the group was becoming a properly constituted party which involved its members. The committee wanted to be careful that it was not contributing directly to election activities and be seen to be supporting one party over its opponents and therefore it was more oriented to helping parties to develop their capacities. This meant it was more open to support efforts to engage more effectively with its members and in general it preferred to give grants that encouraged interaction, debate and engagement both with members and outsiders. An interesting decision was the refusal to support an application by one party for video equipment to enable it to carry out its own training in interview techniques for television appearances. The request might have been seen as an opportunity for the party to become self-reliant, which is normally the aim of grant schemes, but the committee felt it was important to have the input of external people who were knowledgeable about the subject and therefore preferred to support the engagement of media consultants by the party.

The committee was also doubtful of the value for giving support for personnel costs. Such support could be divisive and create resentment from those party members who did not have such opportunities. However being able to pay individuals to take responsibility for specific areas of party organisation would free the individual to concentrate on the work and they could more legitimately be called to account if they did not meet expectations. It was also argued that it was pointless to propose schemes for party development without people in place to implement them. While the arguments have force it was noticeable that the parties which were most committed to development were least likely to look for assistance with personnel costs.

In practice the approach worked better for some parties than others. Some parties found it difficult to think beyond tangible needs such as equipment and staff, even with the help of the available consultant. They were very burdened by their limitations in these areas and argued that they needed to get the infrastructure in place before they could think about development. The committee felt that the core costs of a party still had to be found by the party itself and in any case they could only make a very small contribution and never underwrite the practical administrative needs of the parties.

Perhaps a more important factor was that some parties were more committed to building an effective party which could engage with the electorate while others were mainly a vehicle for specific pressure groups and allowed them to have a public presence. Key people may have wanted to maintain control of the group and were not willing that the party should have a life of its own. Some groups may not have believed that they could ever make a break-through in electoral terms and were less interested in building a broad-based party and engaging with the electorate, but more interested in maintaining their core group as a platform for expressing their ideas. In early meetings with each group, they were asked for their vision of their development: did they want to be a ginger group or pressure group or did they hope to become a fully functioning party? All said that they wanted to become a significant electoral force but it was clear that some were more committed to that path than others and the former were more aware of the value of the types of activities which the scheme was most willing to support.

Lessons Learnt

The scheme tried not to challenge directly the underlying political philosophy of the parties with which it worked. But at the same time it had its own assumptions about the nature of the political process. These were never fully articulated but they included the idea that the political process requires dialogue and engagement around the issues that confront the society: dialogue within the party and dialogue with the wider electorate. In this way the ideas that emerge are more rooted in the needs of the society and there is a greater understanding and commitment to the resultant policies among party workers and the electorate. In the long run this strengthens the society's political structures and makes them better able to support informed discussion and debate at times of tension and change. During the scheme it was evident that when a party engaged with its own members that then translated into a more meaningful engagement with the wider electorate. In the end these parties have survived better and maintained some level of electorate support even though fragile. While it is possible to help a party with a limited vision of how it can reach its goal of widening its support, if a group prefers to remain a small pressure group, perhaps the only role for external support is to help it recognise the nature and consequences of its choice.

The scheme also demonstrated the importance of offering a consultant to help a party think through its options. Otherwise the range of requests for help would have been much narrower. A member of one party noted that the consultant was able to raise questions and challenge members, which was more effective than if the same questions had been raised by someone from within the party.

This scheme was only directed to small emerging parties. But there is still a need for developmental support for all parties and through that for the political process. Larger parties are less likely to acknowledge their need for growth and development, other than in electoral terms, but this scheme was rather unique in that it did start with the party's own assessment of itself. It was based on a collaborative approach to help the party to articulate its requirements and that process was itself a model for how the party could work collaboratively with its members and with the wider electorate. Therefore it will be important to develop mechanisms in every country to help to consolidate the political process

16

Enhancing Women's Representation in Legislatures

An Alternative to the Government Bill for Women's Reservation*

MADHU KISHWAR, JAYAPRAKASH NARAYAN,
DHIRUBHAI SHETH and YOGENDRA YADAV

The ugly scenes and stalemate over tabling the Women's Reservation Bill in Parliament have had a very beneficial effect. They have finally brought the grim truth into sharper focus that politics has proven to be very inhospitable for women in independent India. What we are witnessing today is a worrisome phenomenon of future decline in the participation of women, not only in our legislatures, but in many other of our political and public spaces.

Most countries in the world have failed to give due space and representation to women in their political life. Women are moving in the direction of near equal participation in only a handful of countries, such as Germany, Sweden, Norway, Denmark and Finland. In these societies women have begun to seriously alter the very nature of politics, making enduring, and substantial gains in every field. However, in all other countries, including the supposedly advanced democracies of western Europe and North America, where women exercise certain freedoms and have acquired the wherewithal for economic independence, female presence in legislatures remains small and relatively insignificant.

In India the problem for women is more serious for several reasons:

* MANUSHI began this Campaign in 1996 and this document is a part of this campaign.

- While in many other countries women are inching forward, in India the participation of women in politics has actually declined since the days of the freedom movement, both in quantity and quality.
- Government and politics are more important factors in the economic, social and power structures in India than in most other countries with stronger civil societies, and so, the effect of women's marginalisation in politics is even more detrimental here.
- The increasing violence, sexual harassment and victimisation of women at the ground level in many of our political parties has made their participation extremely hazardous now.

There were many more outstanding women leaders and workers in the Congress Party at all levels during the freedom movement than there are at present in all parties put together. In states like Maharashtra and Gujarat, virtually every neighbourhood and most villages could boast of at least one effective woman leader, even into the 1950s. But as politics became more centralized as well as criminalised, thus undermining all other institutions of civil society, women were pushed out of leadership positions to function on the margins, at best relegated to the domain of social work at the local level. Even that tradition has eroded from the 1970s onward.

The setback to women's participation is even more severe at the state level than in the Lok Sabha (see Tables 16.1 & 16.2). This is clearly evident in Bihar, which had 14 women elected to the Vidhan Sabha in 1952, 31 women in 1957, and 26 women in 1962. But in the 1967 elections, women won only 11 seats. Their number declined to 4 in 1969. Thereafter, it reached a plateau, levelling at a mere 13 during the last state assembly elections.

The representation of women in the Lok Sabha has basically remained stagnant. It reached a "high" of 8 percent in 1984. This figure has not been crossed since then. Thereafter, it has showed some decline rather that register an increase. This despite the fact that all major national parties in recent years have declared through their manifestos that they would implement a 33 per cent reservation for women in all legislatures.

Table 16.1 : Women's Representation in Parliament 1952 - 1999

Year	Lok Sabha			Rajya Sabha		
	Seats	Women MPs	% of Women MPs	Seats	Women MPs	% of Women MPs
1952	499	22	4.41	219	16	7.31
1957	500	27	5.40	237	18	7.59
1962	503	34	6.76	238	18	7.56
1967	523	31	5.93	240	20	8.33
1971	521	22	4.22	243	17	7.00
1977	544	19	3.49	244	25	10.25
1980	544	28	5.15	244	24	9.84
1984	544	44	8.09	244	28	11.48
1989	517	27	5.22	245	24	9.80
1991	544	39	7.17	245	38	15.51
1996	543	39	7.18	223	19	8.52
1998	543	43	7.92	245	15	6.12
1999	543	49	9.02	245	19	7.76
Average	528	33	6.15	238	22	9.00

Source: CSDS, Data Unit.

One of the most puzzling features of this depressed level of women's political representation in our legislative bodies is that it seems to have no direct correlation with literacy and other apparently related indicators. A comparison between the states of Kerala and Rajasthan, whose literacy rates are at opposite ends of the spectrum, demonstrates this clearly. In Kerala, the overall literacy rate is reportedly 90 per cent, with 86 per cent female literacy. By contrast, in Rajasthan, female literacy is a mere 20 per cent and only 12 per cent of females are literate in rural areas. Kerala has a matrilineal tradition in which women have a much larger measure of autonomy and freedom of movement. Kerala's women also tend to marry at a much later age compared to women in other states. Most women in Rajasthan live far more restricted lives in aggressively patriarchal communities that still practise purdah and perform child marriages. But the cultural and educational advantage that women in Kerala have, does not translate into higher political participation as compared to Rajasthan. The percentage of women in the legislative assemblies of

Table 16.2 : Declining Representation of Women in State Legislatures 1952 - 1999 (% of Women MLAs)

State	1952	1957	1960-65	1967-69	1970-75	1977-78	1979-83	1984-88	1989-92	1993-97	1998-99	State Avg.
Andhra Pradesh	2.9	3.7	3.3	3.8	9.1	3.4	4.1	3.4	3.7	2.7	9.5	4.6
Arunachal Pradesh	****	****	****	****	****	0.0	3.3	6.7	3.3	3.3	1.7	3.0
Assam	0.5	4.6	3.8	4.0	7.0	0.8	0.8	4.0	4.0	4.8	****	3.2
Bihar	3.6	9.4	7.9	2.2	3.8	4.0	3.7	4.6	2.8	3.4	****	4.3
Goa	****	****	****	6.7	3.3	3.3	0.0	0.0	5.0	10.0	5.0	4.4
Gujarat	****	****	8.4	4.8	3.2	****	2.7	8.8	2.2	1.1	2.2	4.0
Haryana	****	****	****	7.4*	6.2	4.4	7.8	5.6	6.7	4.4	****	6.2
Himachal Pradesh	0.0	****	****	0.0	5.9	1.5	4.4	4.4	5.9	4.4	8.8	4.2
Jammu & Kashmir	****	****	0.0	0.0	5.3	1.3	0.0	1.3	****	2.3	****	1.5
Kamataka	2.0	8.7	8.7	3.2	5.1	4.0	0.9	3.6	4.5	3.1	2.3	4.3
Kerala	0.0	4.8	3.9	0.8	1.5	0.7	3.2	5.7	5.7	9.3	****	3.6
Madhya Pradesh	2.1	10.8	4.9	3.4	5.4	3.1	5.6	9.7	3.4	3.8	8.1	5.4
Maharashtra	1.9	6.3	4.9	3.3	9.3	2.8	6.6	5.6	2.1	3.8	4.2	4.6
Manipur	****	****	****	****	0.0*	****	0.0	0.0	1.7	0.0	****	0.3
Meghalaya	****	****	****	****	1.7	1.7	0.0	3.3	****	1.7	5.0	2.2
Mizoram	****	****	****	****	0.0	3.3	3.3	2.5	0.0	0.0	0.0	1.2
Nagaland	****	****	****	0.0	****	****	0.0	1.7	****	0.0	****	0.5
Orissa	9.6	3.6	1.4	3.6	1.4*	4.8	3.4	6.1	4.8	5.4	****	4.0
Punjab	2.2	5.8	5.2	1.0*	5.8	2.6	5.1	3.4	5.1	6.0	****	4.0
Rajasthan	0.0	5.1	4.5	3.3	7.1	4.0	5.0	8.0	5.5	4.5	7.0	5.0
Sikkim	****	****	****	****	****	****	0.0	0.0	6.3	3.1	3.1	2.5

(Contd.)

Table 16.2 (*Contd.*)

Tamil Nadu	0.3	5.9	3.9	1.7	2.1	0.9	2.1	3.4	9.0	3.8	****	3.6
Tripura	****	****	****	0.0	3.3	1.7	6.7	3.3	****	1.7	****	3.0
Uttar Pradesh	1.2	5.8	4.4	2.8*	5.9	2.6	5.6	7.3	3.3*	4.0*	****	4.1
West Bengal	0.8	3.6	4.8	2.9*	1.6*	1.4	2.4	4.4	7.1	6.8	****	3.4
Delhi	4.2	****	****	****	7.1	7.1	7.1	****	****	4.3	12.9	7.3
Pondichery	****	****	6.7	3.3	0.0	0.0	3.3	3.3	1.7	3.3	****	2.6
Period Average	1.8	6.3	4.9	2.9	4.4	2.8	3.8	5.3	4.5	4.0	6.0	4.1

Source: CSDS Data Unit.

Notes: Table entry stands for % of women MLAs elected to state legislature in the relevant election.
(****) States did not exist/ no elections held in that year/period.
(*) Two elections held during this period. The figure given here is an average of the two.
The figures given here are based on name recognition and hence liable to under-reporting of women representatives.

both states is low. In Kerala it rose from less than one percent in 1967 to six per cent in 1991. However, in Rajasthan, the representation of women was four per cent in 1967 and reached eight percent in 1985-90, slightly more than in Kerala, but not significantly greater. Since then it has been going down.

Similarly, the state of Manipur, with its tradition of women playing the dominant role in both the family and the community (again due to a matrilineal heritage), has elected its first legislator only as late as 1990. Nagaland and other North-eastern states which have less repressive cultures for women have similarly low levels of women's representation. By contrast is the proportion of women in politics in Uttar Pradesh, Bihar, and Madhya Pradesh. Though these states are known for their low education levels and repressive cultural norms for women, they have not only sent a relatively larger proportion of women to the Lok Sabha than those from the North-East, but have also elected relatively more women MLAs.

In independent India, pervasive gender discrimination has resulted in sidelining even veteran women politicians. It is difficult for women to establish a foothold without patronage from powerful men in the party—that too through close personal relations, as wives, daughters and sisters. This is indeed a matter for serious concern because the level of political participation among women in any society acts as a reliable barometer of the health of its democracy.

It is significant that stagnation and/or decline in the rate of women's political participation runs contrary to trends in many other fields.

Women in India have made major inroads in various male-dominated professions, including the governmental bureaucracy. In the fields of business, medicine, engineering, law, art, and culture, women who were given opportunities to acquire the necessary skills and education have proven themselves capable of holding their own, without availing of any special measures to facilitate their entry. But they have failed to gain ground in the field of politics. Moreover, the agenda of women's empowerment seems to have lost the kind of moral and political legitimacy it enjoyed during the freedom movement, as was evident from the ugly scenes in the aftermath of tabling the Women's Reservation Bill in Parliament. Such a response would have been inconceivable in India of the 1920s to the 1940s.

All these trends indicate that women's representation in politics requires special consideration, and cannot be left to the forces that presently dominate our parties and government. Today, even the best of our female parliamentarians feel sidelined and powerless within their respective parties. The few women in leadership positions have not been able to encourage the entry of greater numbers of women in electoral and party politics, and are an ineffective minority within their own respective political groupings.

The very same male party leaders who compete with each other in announcing their support of special reservations for women have shown little willingness to include women in party decision-making, or even to help create a conducive atmosphere for women's participation in their own organisations. In fact, women's marginalisation is even more pronounced in the day-to-day functioning of almost all political parties than in the Lok Sabha. Therefore, it is urgently required that we take special measures to enhance women's political participation in ways that help them influence decision-making at all levels of our society and polity. Our democracy will remain seriously flawed if it fails to yield adequate space to women.

Given this worrisome scenario, the national debate and efforts to provide constitutional and legal mechanisms to enhance women's participation in legislatures are welcome and long-overdue.

Problems with the Government Bill

The 85th Constitutional Amendment Bill, introduced in Lok Sabha in December 1999, includes the following key provisions:

- One-third of all seats in the Lok Sabha and the Vidhan Sabhas shall be reserved for women.
- Such reservation shall also apply in case of seats reserved for Scheduled Castes (SCs) and Scheduled Tribes (STs).
- There shall be rotation of seats so reserved for women.
- Such rotation shall be determined by draw of lots, in such a manner that a seat shall be reserved only once in a block of three general elections.

This Bill is seriously flawed, insofar as it mechanically provides for entry of women members to fill one-third of vacancies in Lok

Sabha and Vidhan Sabhas. Such mechanical reservation and rotation suffers from serious defects:

1. One-third seats are reserved, and such reserved seats are rotated in every general election. This rotation will automatically result in two-thirds of incumbent members being forcibly unseated in every general election. The remaining one-third will be left in limbo until the last moment, not knowing if their constituency will form part of the one-third randomly reserved seats. This will require them to scramble at short notice to find another seat from which to contest.
2. There is already resentment about reserved seats for SCs and STs being frozen in the same constituencies over a long period of time. Inevitably, there will be vociferous and justified demands for rotation of seats reserved for Scheduled Castes, and in some cases Scheduled Tribes, where their population may not be very large. This will trigger off further instability in our polity.
3. The population of Scheduled Castes and Scheduled Tribes is now estimated to be around 16 per cent and 8 per cent respectively, on an all India basis. In certain states their combined population is much higher, reaching 35 per cent or more. In the event of rotation of all reserved seats (women plus SCs, STs) with one-third seats reserved for women, every single seat will be rotated in every general election. This will result in practically every member of a legislature being unseated in every single general election (see Table 16.3 and Pie Chart).
4. Such compulsory unseating violates the very basic principles of democratic representation. It jeopardizes the possibility of sensible planning to contest and nurture a political constituency for both male and female candidates.
5. As legislators do not have the incentive to seek re-election from the same constituency, politics will be even more predatory and unaccountable. This will contribute to a more unstable political process, and make it difficult for women to build their long-term credibility as effective representatives, since they will not be able to contest twice from the same constituency.

6. If seats are reserved exclusively for women in every election through territorial constituencies, voters in such reserved constituencies would have no choice but to elect women only, violating the basic principles of democratic representation.
7. In such a situation, there is likely to be greater resentment against women, undermining the very objective of the Bill. Those men who get pushed out of their constituencies or who see their allies sidelined will either sabotage female contenders in revenge, or spend much of their political capital helping their own female relatives in cornering these reserved seats. Such proxies would be expected to keep the seat "safe" for the men until the next election, when they would again try to reclaim their seats. Such women would lack legitimacy in the eyes of the voters.
8. Women elected in reserved constituencies will have their legitimacy questioned and will be contesting against other women only, and will lack the legitimacy and opportunity needed to prove) their ability and acceptability. Leadership acquired in such a manner will be seen as unnatural, artificial and foisted.
9. Women legislators, when elected, will not able to nurse their constituencies on a long-term basis, and thus will be deprived of a strong political base and will forever be regarded as lightweight politicians. This in effect will make their presence in legislatures ornamental, and will not lead to a more effective participation in politics.
10. This Bill does not address the more fundamental issue of inadequate participation of women in politics and their much greater marginalisation within the political parties.
11. The experience of fixed quotas in a few countries where it has been tried, such as Nepal, the Philippines, and the erstwhile Soviet Union, has not produced very successful results for women's political participation.
12. While this Bill provides for election of SC and ST women as legislators, it does not adequately address the issue of participation of backward castes (BCs) and minorities. As parties have no choice about the seats reserved for women, they will be unable to nominate women candidates from these

under represented sections in constituencies where they stand a reasonable chance of success.

13. Even though there will be no legal bar on women standing from general constituencies, it is highly unlikely that any women will obtain party tickets to run for office outside the reserved constituencies. This same pattern is evident with SCs and STs who have been permanently ghettoized to fixed reserved constituencies.
14. This Bill is completely silent about women's representation in the Rajya Sabha and the Legislative Councils.

Given these serious infirmities, it is necessary to design better models for enhancing women's representation in legislatures, Therefore, we present an alternative which will address many of the flaws listed above.

Table 16.3 : Rotation of Seats

	Now %	From 2001 (%)
Reservation for SCs	15.0	16.0
Reservation for STs	07.5	08.0
	22.5	**24.0**
Balance Seats	77.5	76.0
Reservation for Women 33.3%	26.0	25.4
Open for Men	51.5	50.6

Source: Lok Satta Data Unit.

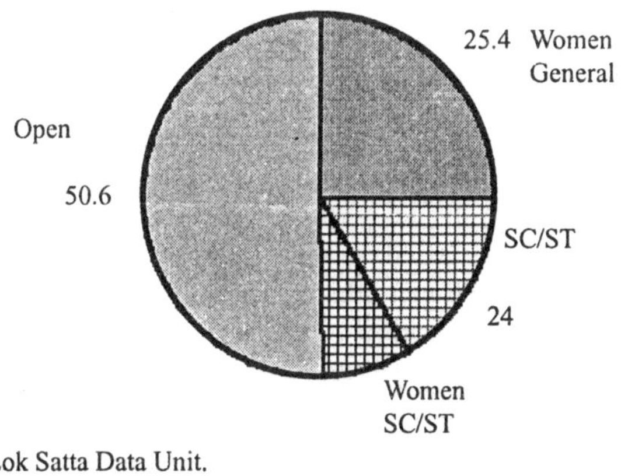

Source: Lok Satta Data Unit.

The Proposed Alternative Women's Reservation Bill

The important provisions of the proposed Alternative Bills are as follows. The text of the Bills are given in Appendix II.

1. A law should be enacted amending the Representation of the People Act, 1951, to make mandatory for every recognised political party to nominate women candidates for election in one-third of the constituencies.

2. Among seats reserved for SCs and STs also, one-third of the candidates nominated by recognised parties shall be women.

3. Each party can choose where it wishes to nominate women candidates, duly taking local political and social factors into account.

4. To prevent a party from nominating women candidates only in states or constituencies where the party's chances of winning election are weak, and to ensure an even spread of women candidates, the unit for consideration (the unit in which at least one out of three party candidates shall be a woman) for the Lok Sabha shall be a state or union territory; for the State Legislative Assembly, the unit shall be a cluster of three contiguous Lok Sabha constituencies.

5. In the event of any recognised party failing to nominate one-third women candidates, for the shortfall of every single woman candidate, two male candidates of the party shall lose the party symbol and affiliation and all the recognition related advantages.

6. A law amending Articles 80 and 171 of the Constitution should be enacted providing for women's reservation of one-third of the seats, elected or nominated, to Rajya Sabha or Legislative Councils. Corresponding amendments need to be made in the Fourth Schedule of the Constitution and the Representation of the People Act, 1950.

Advantages of this Model

1. Parties will be free to choose their female candidates and constituencies depending on local political and social factors. Parties will nurture women candidates where they can offer a good fight rather than in pre-fixed lottery based constituencies, where they may or may not have viable women candidates. Thus there is flexibility and promotion of natural leadership.

2. Though seats are not reserved, there will be a large pool of credible and serious women candidates in the fray. This is so because the real contest in elections is only among candidates nominated by

recognised parties. Table 16.4 clearly shows that the role of Independents in our elections is marginal and declining. In Lok Sabha elections, as many as 99.7 per cent of Independents are in fact losing their caution deposits.

3. A woman candidate will be contesting both against female and/ or male candidates of rival parties. Therefore, the democratic choice of voters is not restricted to compulsorily electing only women candidates.

4. As women members are elected in competition with other candidates—without reserving seats—they will be seen as legitimate representatives in the eyes of the public and not just beneficiaries of charitable measures.

5. A winning woman candidate will have been elected on her own strength, backed by party support. She will not be a mere proxy or political lightweight.

6. There will be no need for rotation of reservation. Therefore the elected women and men can nurture their constituencies and emerge as major political figures in their own right, with an independent power base.

7. At the same time, in the absence of reserved seats, there will be healthy competition for nomination for a particular seat between men and women politicians.

Table 16.4 : Independents Elected to Lok Sabha in Successive General Elections

Year	No. of Seats Filled	No. of Independents Elected	Percentage of Independents Who Lost Deposit
1952	489	38	66.6
1957	494	42	60.1
1962	494	20	79.0
1967	520	35	86.2
1971	518	14	94.0
1977	542	9	97.2
1980	529	9	98.9
1984	542	5	99.7
1989	529	12	98.9
1991	534	1	99.5
1996	542	9	99.7
1998	542	6	99:1

Source: Lok Satta Data Unit.

8. Parties will be able to nominate women from BCs, minorities and other communities for elective office in areas where there is electoral advantage to them. This obviates the need for a quota within quotas—an issue which has blocked the existing bill. Those who are concerned about BC representation need not settle merely for one-third quota for BC women within the 33 per cent women's quota as they are demanding now. They can field as many BC or minority women as they think appropriate.

9. This method is mostly likely to find favour with political parties and incumbent legislators, as there will be no fear of being uprooted at short notice by drawing of lots. Both compulsory reservation and regular rotation are avoided.

10. Unlike the lottery system of reserved constituencies, in which women's presence is likely to get ossified at 33 per cent since there would be resistance to letting women contest from non-reserved constituencies, this model allows for far greater flexibility in the number and proportion of women being elected to legislatures. If women are candidates for one-third of all seats contested by each party, theoretically they could even win the vast majority of seats—all on merit.

11. This model also provides for reservation of seats for women in the upper houses.

However, given the present state of affairs, it is likely that, to begin with, about one-third of the contested seats will be won by women. But this percentage is likely to grow over time as women gain more confidence and strength. It also ensures that their presence in legislatures more nearly reflects their actual electoral strength so that they are not seen as mere recipients of charitable measures.

Plugging Possible Loopholes

A party may be tempted to nominate women for constituencies where it is weak. However, by making the unit of consideration the state or union territory for Lok Sabha, and a cluster of three Lok Sabha constituencies for the Legislative Assembly, this risk is avoided. Parties will be compelled to nominate women in all states and regions. No serious party seeking power can afford to deliberately undermine its own chances of election on such a large scale. It is also mandatory

Table 16.5 : The Gender Advantage Though the number of women elected to Lok Sabha has not been very impressive, their success rate (% of contestants getting elected) has always been higher than the male aspirants.

Year	No. of Seats Available	Total No. of Contestants	Male			Female		
			Contested	Elected	% Winning	Contested	Elected	% Winning
1952	489	1,874	—	—	—	—	—	—
1957	494	1,518	1,473	467	31.7	45	27	60.0
1962	494	1,985	1,915	459	24.0	70	35	50.0
1967	520	2,369	2,302	490	21.3	67	30	44.8
1971	520	2,784	2,698	499	18.5	86	21	24.4
1977	542	2,439	2,369	523	22.1	70	19	27.1
1980	542	4,620	4,478	514	11.5	142	28	19.7
1984	542	5,570	5,406	500	9.2	164	42	25.6
1989	529	6,160	5,962	502	8.5	198	27	13.6
1991	521	8,699	8,374	492	5.9	325	39	12.0
1996	543	13,952	13,353	504	3.8	599	39	6.7
1998	543	4,750	4,476	500	11.2	274	43	15.7
Total			52,806	5,450	10.32	2,040	350	17.16

* Gender-wise data for 1952 not Available

Source: September 14, 1999, Times of India, New Delhi.

to nominate women in one-third of constituencies because otherwise twice the number of male candidates of the party will lose party nomination.

In the absence of actual reservation of seats, there could be fears that women may not be elected in one-third of constituencies, as the voters may prefer a male candidate over a female candidate on account of gender bias. However, evidence so far suggests that women candidates of parties have not suffered any gender discrimination at the hands of voters. In fact, very often, the percentage of success of woman candidates is higher than that of male candidates. Table 16.5 shows that the success rate of women candidates in Lok Sabha elections has been uniformly higher than that of their male counterparts in every general election. It is possible to argue that the few women who contest are more often party candidates, and therefore, their success rate is exaggerated. However, Table 16.6 clearly shows that even among candidates of recognised political parties, the success rate of women candidates is higher than that of men. While 32.53 per cent of women candidates of recognised parties have been elected to Lok Sabha since 1984, the success rate of male candidates is only 26.50 per cent. This trend is seen in all general elections since 1984, except in 1989. Therefore, it is reasonable to assume that women will be elected in large numbers, and that, in fact, their presence in Lok Sabha will exceed one-third in many cases. In any case, past evidence suggests that in at least a quarter of the constituencies, women are likely to get elected if recognised parties nominate them in at least one-third of constituencies.

It is noteworthy that women's participation has increased dramatically, to near equal or even higher than equal participation, only in countries like Sweden, Denmark, Finland, Germany and the Netherlands which have implemented party-based quotas of the kind we are proposing.

Other Necessary Measures for Enhancing Women's Participation

While it is necessary to institute a system of reservation for women as spelt out above, this or any other system of ensuring women's presence in legislatures is not by itself sufficient if our objective is to make women equal partners in democratic politics. The problem is not just

Table 16.6 : Comparative Performance of Men and Women Candidates of Recognised Parties in Lok Sabha Elections

Year	Total Party Contested	Elected	%	Male			Female		
				Contested	Elected	% Winning	Contested	Elected	% Winning
1984	1,394	510	36.59	1,327	469	35.34	67	41	61.19
1989	1,523	498	32.70	1,437	474	32.99	86	24	27.91
1991	2,319	516	22.25	2,180	479	21.97	139	37	26.62
1996	2,269	530	23.36	2,153	493	22.90	116	37	31.90
1998	1,964	488	24.85	1,831	451	24.63	133	37	27.82
Total	9,469	2,542	26.85	8,928	2,366	26.50	541	176	32.53

Source: Complied by Lok Satta Data Unit from Statistical Reports on General Election, Election Commission of India, New Delhi.

that women in the political arena are denied tickets by political parties. The fundamental problem is that given the nature of electoral politics today, women are discouraged from playing their full part in the political process. Proposals for reservation for women must therefore be a part of a larger package of general reforms in electoral politics.

The following general measures of electoral reform would go a long way towards making politics less intimidating for women.

1. Measures to check criminalisation of politics:

(a) The list of offences where a conviction leads to disqualification from contesting elections should be expanded as per the recommendations of the Law Commission.

(b) Disqualification should not be conditional upon final conviction. It should come into operation as soon as the judge has framed charges with references to offences specified above.

(c) At the time of filing nominations, a candidate should be required to make a declaration of all the cases pending against him or her, involving charges of criminal conduct or corruption. This declaration should be made public. False declaration should be a ground for disqualification.

2. To bring about internal democracy within political parties, all the recognised (national or state) political parties should be required to include in their respective constitutions:

(a) Rules governing the membership of party and a Register of Current Members that is open for inspection by any member or the representatives of the Election Commission of India.

(b) Provisions for a periodic and democratic election of all the office bearers and the highest executive body by the members of the party.

(c) Procedures for selection of party's candidates for elections to legislatures.

(d) Procedures for deciding upon various policy documents including the party's election manifesto.

(e) Internal mechanism for adjudicating any dispute, including those concerning the interpretation of the party constitution.

(f) Provisions for the Election Commission to review the party constitutions for their compliance with the above mentioned requirements, and also to serve as a court of final appeal against any decision of the internal adjudicating authority in every party. The failure to comply with the Election Commission's instructions or decisions will invite de-recognition of the party.

3. Measures to curb the influence of black money in politics:

(a) Every candidate shall make a declaration of his/her income and property at the time of nomination. False or incomplete declaration shall invite disqualification.

(b) All citizens and corporations shall be exempted, upto a certain limit, from paying income tax on donations made to registered political parties.

(c) The candidates and political parties shall be required, after the completion of election, to file a detailed statement of account. Non-disclosure or false declaration should result in disqualification for candidate and de-registration for political parties.

(d) While the current ceiling on electoral expenses needs to be revised, certain items of expenditure (direct inducements in cash or kind to the voter, or expenditure to bribe officials or hire hoodlums) shall be considered illegal.

(e) Every candidate who secures 2 per cent or more of the valid votes polled in a constituency shall be reimbursed a reasonable sum of, say Rs. 10 for each vote secured.

(f) It shall be compulsory for all registered political parties to get a statement of income and expenditure audited annually. The statement shall be a public document.

4. Measures to curb electoral malpractices:

(a) The local post-office shall be in charge of maintaining and revising electoral rolls on a regular basis. At present most citizens have no access to electoral rolls, and the procedure for additions, deletions and corrections are ineffective in reality, though the law is eminently sensible. There is evidence to suggest that in urban areas the electoral rolls are flawed by upto 40 per cent.

(b) It should be mandatory for the Election Commission to provide voter Identity Cards to every citizen who figures on the electoral rolls. Once this process is completed, the voter identity card or other means of identification should be made compulsory for voting.

(c) If the proportion of "tendered" votes in a polling booth is greater than one percent of the total electorate, a re-poll shall be ordered in the booth. A tendered ballot is given to a voter in whose name a false vote was already cast, and who establishes identity. Therefore, a tendered vote is indisputable proof of personation and rigging. At present a tendered ballot is kept in a separate cover and is not counted, while the false vote cast is counted! If this re-poll provision is incorporated and publicized, people will then avail the facility of tendered vote, and rigging will be self-limiting for fear of a re-poll.

17

Some Useful Sites and References on Election and Electoral Reforms

RACHANA NARAYAN

Electronic Information Resources

http://www.eris.org.uk/default.htm

Electoral Reforms International Services: This site gives information about Electoral Reforms International Services (ERIS). ERIS is a leading European provider of electoral and democratisation assistance. Programmes are conducted to consolidate and monitor the electoral process, to strengthen democratic institutions and to promote civic awareness. ERIS works in partnership with national electoral commissions and civil society organisations, on behalf of international donors.

http://www.article19.org

This site deals with Article 19 of the Universal Declaration of Human Rights. It works worldwide to combat censorship by promoting freedom of expression and access to official information. It has partners in over 30 countries and works to strengthen local capacity to monitor and protest institutional and informal censorship. It monitors, researches, publishes, lobbies, campaigns and litigates on behalf of freedom of expression wherever it is threatened.

http://www.ifes.org/afrassoc1/afrassoc/index.htm:

Association of African Election Authorities: The site gives information about Association of African Election Authorities (AAEA). AAEA is a membership organisation dedicated to the professionalisation of election administration through information exchange and regional networking. The Association was conceived at the Colloquium of African Election Authorities held in Victoria Falls,

Zimbabwe in November 1994 and since then has developed into an Association with sixteen full members and six associate members. The site contains Newsletter, Bulletin, News and Information published by the AAEA.

http://www.ifes.org/AsiaAssocSite/a_asia_ea/s_gray.htm

Association of Asian Election Authorities: This site describes a paper Conducting a Non-Partisan Civic Education Program by Bill Gray, Australian Electoral Commissioner. It explains to the Australian electorates about the principles underlying the electoral and parliamentary systems and institutions in Australia. The Australian Electoral Commission (AEC) is a full-time, independent statutory authority responsible for the conduct of federal elections and referendums in Australia. The AEC undertakes both continuous long-term and election specific civic education activities to promote a better understanding of Australia's electoral system in the community. In particular, young people are a major focus of these activities.

http://www.aec.gov.au

Australian Electoral Commission: This sites explains the Australian Electoral Commission and gives answer of several question such as, What you need to know and do, Who represents you, Why we operate the way we do, When have elections been held, How elections work.

http://www.calvoter.org/links.html

California Voters Foundation: This site has many links to election and democracy websites. People can easily collect information on Polls, Surveys & Research Journalism, Resources, Voting Technology & Money in Politics etc., through this site.

http://www.electionline.org/index.jsp:

This site is a clearinghouse for election reform information, election reform legislation updates and all happenings regarding election reforms, electionline.org, produced by the Election Reform Information Project, is a non-partisan, non-advocacy website providing up-to-the-minute news and analysis on election reform. Among the site's features: (a). A Press Centre to help reporters gather information quickly and reliably; (b). Sign-up capabilities for the press, the election community and the general public to receive newsletters and e-mail alerts; (c). All the most recent data on election administration procedures and legislation around the country; (d). The latest news, on the What's Happening and electionlinetoday pages; and (e). Analysis and reports, on the What's Interesting page.

http://www.civiced.org/lesson-plans.html

Centre for Civic Education: It runs a Campaign to Promote Civic Education and helps the next generation preserve and improve constitutional democracy.

http://www.elections.ca

Elections Canada - discusses about the elections and electoral institutions in Canada. Chief Electoral Officer of Canada, Elections Canada's Official Reports, questions related to elections.....

http://www.eci.gov.in

Electoral Commission of India: Site contains factual information, policy guidelines and handbooks for the Indian Elections.

http://www.elections.govt.nz

Electoral Commission of New Zealand: Site contains factual information, policy guidelines and handbooks for the New Zealand Elections.

http://www.fec.gov/pages/fecfeca.htm#Enforcing

Federal Elections Commission (U.S.): The site deals with The FEC and the Federal Campaign Finance Law, 1996.

http://www.ife.org.mx:

Federal Electoral Institute of Mexico (IFE): The site entails the activities and programs of the Institute.

http://election.dos.state.fl.us/index.html:

The site gives information about the Division of Elections, Department of State, Florida, USA.

http://www.ft.dk/baggrund/00000048/00232623.htm

The site informs about the Parliamentary Elections and Elections Administration in Denmark.

http://www.idea.int/publications/conduct/admin/intro.htm:

International Institute for Democracy and Electoral Assistance: The site contains Code of Conduct for the Ethical and Professional Administration of Elections.

http://www.nass.org/

The site describes the activities of the organisation of National Association of Secretaries of State Resolution to Congress Urging Passage of Election Reform Bill

http://www.elections.org.za/Legislation.asp?KId=1

This site gives detail information about the Electoral Act 73 of 1999 of South Africa.

http://www.eisa.org.za

It site describes the activities and programme of the South Africa Electoral Institute.

http://www.fairvote.org/

Centre for Voting and Democracy: The Centre for Voting and Democracy is a 501(c)(3) non-profit organisation located in Maryland, USA. The Centre is dedicated to fair elections. As a catalyst for reform, it conducts research, analysis, education and advocacy to build understanding of and support for more democratic voting systems. It promotes full representation as an alternative to winner-take-all elections and instant runoff voting as an alternative to plurality elections and traditional runoff elections. The Centre is a non-profit organisation. The site has an Online library.

http://www.fairvote.net/washington/

The Washington Citizens for Proportional Representation: This site is citizens initiative for Proportional Representation in the USA.

http://students.washington.edu/tpahl/election/

US Presidential Election Reform: This site discusses three reforms that are needed in the election process of the US president. These three reforms would encourage more ideas to be discussed, more voters actually voting, and a more progressive country.

http://www.mich.com/~donald/first.html

This site deals with Vote - Voting - Elections - Proportional Representation - True Representation and New Democracy Candidate Election Methods.

http://www.wtp.org/

WTP is a membership organisation in Oakland dedicated to political reform and social justice through study, citizen action and local organising.

http://www.ifes.org/

International Foundation for Election Systems: This site explains International Foundation for Election Systems (IFES) work and activities, projects and programmes. IFES works to encourage national and international democracy. Since 1987, IFES has supplied world governments with election observation and analysis and has developed into one of the world's leading centres of election information and resources. In addition to election monitoring, IFES seeks to bolster democracy by developing programmes that strengthen rule of law, good governance and civil society. IFES is dedicated to the success of democracy worldwide and the prospect that each person in every corner of the world is entitled to have a free and informed say in how he or she is governed.

Documents:

"Representation of the Peoples Act, 1951", in *Handbook for Candidates*, Appendix – XIV Election Commission of India (Can also see on ECI website).

(1975): *Tarkunde Committee: Report of the Committee on Electoral Reforms*, Citizens for Democracy, New Delhi.

(1976): *The Report of the Commission on Electoral Reform*, The Hansard Society, London.

(1983): *Election Commission of India (EC), 1984, First Annual Report*, Election Commission of India, New Delhi.

Hegde, Ramakrishna (1984): *Electoral Reforms: Lack of Political Will*, Karnataka State Janata Party, Bangalore.

(1986): *Towards a Better Democracy, Report of the Royal Commission on the Electoral System,* Government Printer, Wellington, New Zealand.

(1990): *Committee on Electoral Reforms (Dinesh Goswami Committee), Report of the Committee on Electoral Reforms*, Legislative Department, Ministry of Law and Justice, New Delhi.

(1991): *India, Election Commission of India, Model Code to Conduct for the Guidance of Political Parties and Candidates and Related Recent Instructions of the Election Commission of India*, Election Commission of India, New Delhi.

(1992): *India, Election Commission of India, Proposals of the Election Commission for Electoral Reforms*, Election Commission of India, New Delhi.

(1993): *Electoral Politics in Pakistan: National Assembly Elections, Report of SAARC-NGO observers*, Vikas, New Delhi.

(1995): *Ministry of Law, Justice and Company Affairs, Manual of Election Law (A Compilation of the Statutory Provisions Governing Elections to Parliament and State Legislatures,. 2 Vols*, Delhi Controller of Publications, Govt. of India.

(1996): *Election Commission of India, Statistical Report on General Elections, 1996 to the Eleventh Lok Sabha*, Election Commission of India, New Delhi.

(1998): *Committee on State Funding of Elections, (headed by Indrajit Gupta), Government of India*, Ministry of Law, Justice and Company Affairs, New Delhi.

(1998): *The Report of the Independent Commission on the Voting System*, Home Department, UK.

(1999): *Election Commission of India, Political Parties and Election Symbols*, Election Commission of India, New Delhi.

(1999): *Law Commission of India, One Hundred Seventieth Report on Reform of the Electoral Laws*, Law Commission of India, New Delhi.

(2000): "Review of the Working of Political Parties Specially in Relation to Elections and Reform Options", A Consultation Paper (for Generating Debate and Eliciting Public Reactions and Opinion), National Commission to Review the Working of the Constitution, Vigyan Bhawan Annexe, New Delhi.

Election in India – Major Events and New Initiatives 1996-2000, Election Commission of India, New Delhi.

Books

Advani, L K & others (eds.) (1987): *Electoral System in India: Need for Reforms*, Panchnad Research Institute, Chandigarh.

Aggarwal J. C. & N. K. Chowdhary (1999): *Elections in India—1998*, Shipra, New Delhi.

Aggarwal J. C. & N. K. Chowdhary (2000): *Elections in India—1999*, Shipra, New Delhi.

Alexander, Herbert E. & Rei Shiratori (eds.) (1994): *Comparative Political Finance Among the Democracies*, Westview, Oxford.

Alexander, P.C. (1995): *The Perils of Democracy*, Somaiya, Bombay.

Al-Marayati, A.A. (1968): *Middle Eastern Constitutions and Electoral Laws,* Praeger, New York.

Ali, Raisa (1996): *Representative Democracy and Concept of Free and Fair Election*, Deep and Deep, New Delhi.

Amy, Douglas J.(2000): *Behind the Ballot Box: A Citizen's Guide to Voting Systems,* Praeger Publishing, New York.

Amy, Douglas J. (1993): *Real Choices/New Voices: The Case for*

Proportional Representation Elections in the United States, Columbia University Press.

Asthana, Pushpa (1988): *Party System in India: Development or Decay?,* Criterion Publications, New Delhi.

Austin, Granville (1999): *Working a Democratic Constitution: The Indian Experience*, OUP, New Delhi.

Banerjee, Kishalay (1984): *Regional Political Parties in India*, B.R. Publishing, Delhi.

Barber, Kathleen (2000): *A Right to Representation: Proportional Election Systems for the Twenty-first Century,* Ohio State University Press.

Barkan, Joel D. & Robert E. Henderson (1997): *Toward Credible and Legitimate Elections in Kenya,* International Foundation for Election Systems, Washington.

Baxi, Upendra & Bhikhu Parekh (1995): *Crisis and Change in Contemporary India*, Sage, New Delhi.

Baxter, Craig (1969): *The Jan Sangh: A Biography of an Indian Political Party*, University of Pennsylvania Press, Philadelphia.

Betelle, Andre (1993): *Society and Politics in India: Essays in a Comparative Perspective*, Oxford, New Delhi .

Bhagat Anjana Kaw (1996): *Elections and Electoral Reforms in India*, Vikas, Delhi.

Bhambhri, C.P. (1999): *BJP-led Government and Elections,* Shipra, Delhi.

Bhandari, Ashish & Samar Sen (1997): *Politics and Development: Theory and Strategy*, Kanishka, New Delhi.

Bhargava, G.S. & Umashanker Phadnis (ed.) (1995): *To whom does the State Belong: Emerging Issues in Indian politics*, Har-Anand, New Delhi.

Bhatt, S. & V.S. Mani (ed.) (1999): *Indian on the Threshold of the 21st Century: Shape of Things to Come*, Lancers, New Delhi.

Biju, M.R. (1999): *Parliamentary Democracy and Political Change in India*, Kanishka, New Delhi.

Bogdanor, V. & D. Butler (eds.) (1983): *Democracy and Election; Electoral System and their Political Consequences,* Cambridge University Press, Cambridge.

Bott, Alexander J. (1990): *Handbook of United States Election Laws and Practices: Political Rights,* Westport, Greenwood Press, Connecticut.

Butler David, Ashok Lahiri & Prannoy Roy (1991): *India Decides: Elections 1952-1991*, Living Media India Ltd., Delhi.

Butler, D. & A. Ranney (ed.) (1978): *Referendums: A Comparative Study of Practice and Theory*, AEI (American Enterprises Institute for Public Policy Research), Washington.

Carl W. Dundas (ed.) (1997): *Let's Talk About Elections*, Commonwealth Secretariat, London.

Carstairs, A.M. (1980): *A Short History of Electoral System in Western Europe,* George Allen & Unwin, London.

Chandra Deo & V. Kishore (1993): *Changing India's Political Mould: A Fair Franchise and a Federal Framework*, Konark, Delhi.

Chakravarty S. R. (1988): *Bangladesh: The Nineteen Seventy-Nine Elections*, South Asian Publishers, Jaipur.

Chaube, S. K. & Susheela Kaushik (ed.) (1999): *Indian Democracy at the Turn of Century*, Kanishka, New Delhi.

Chhibber, Pradeep K. (1999): *Democracy without Associations: Transformation of the Party System and Social Cleavages in India*, Vistaar, New Delhi.

Claude, Richard (1970): *The Supreme Court and the Electoral Process*, Johns Hopkins Press, Baltimore.

Cole, Alastair & Peter Campbell (ed) (1989): *French Electoral Systems and Elections since 1789*, Gower.

Corrado, A. & C. M. Firestone (eds.) (1997): *Elections in Cyberspace: Toward a New Era in American Politic*s, Aspen Institute for Humanistic Studies, Queenstown.

Couick, Michael N. (1993): *Where to Start: An Annotated Bibliography of Public Election Law Research Resources*, 25 URB. LAW. 915.

Craig, F.W.S. (1989): *British Electoral Facts; 1982-1987*, Parliamentary Research Services, London.

Dighe, Sharad & R. B. Sundriyal (1997): *Electoral Reforms*, Shree Publishers House, New Delhi.

Dietz, H. A., G. Shidlo, W. H. Beezley, & J. Ewell, (eds.)(1998): *Urban Elections in Democratic Latin Americ*a, Scholarly Resources Incorporated, Wilmington.

Dominguez, J. I., & A. Poire (eds.) (1999): *Toward Mexico's Democratization: Parties, Campaigns, Elections and Public Opinion,* Routledge, New York.

Dummett, M. (1997): *Principles of Electoral Reform*, Oxford University Press, New York.

Dundas, Carl W. (1994): *Dimensions of Free and Fair Elections: Frameworks, Integrity, Transparency, Attributes and Monitoring*, Commonwealth Secretariat, London.

Field, John Osgood (1980): *Consolidating Democracy: Politicisation and Partisanship in India*, Manohar, Delhi.

Gehlot, N.S. (1998): *Current Trends in Indian Politics*, Deep & Deep, New Delhi.

Ghosh, S.K. (1997): *Indian Democracy Derailed: Politics and Politicians*, APH Publishers, New Delhi.

Goidel, R. K., D. A. Gross & T. G. Shields (1998): *Money Matters: Consequences of Campaign Finance Reform in House Elections*, Rowman and Littlefield, Lanham.

Gould, Harold A. & Sumit Gangualy (ed.) (1993): *India Votes: Alliance Politics and Minority Governments in the Ninth and Tenth General Elections*, Westview, Oxford.

Goodwin-Gill, Guy S. (1994): *Free and Fair Election: International Law and Practice,* Inter-Parliamentary Union, Geneva.

Graham, B.D. (1993): *Representation and Party Politics: A Comparative Perspective*, Blackwell, Cambridge.

Grofman. B, Lijphart, A.(ed.) (1986): *Electoral Laws and their Political Consequences*, Agathon Press, Inc., New York.

Grofman, B., S. C. Lee, E. Winckler & B. Woodall, (eds.) (1998): *Elections in Japan, Korea, and Taiwan under the Single Non-Transferable Vote: The Comparative Study of an Embedded Institution*, University of Michigan Press, Ann Arbor.

Guinier, Lani (1998): *Lift Every Voice, Turning a Civil Rights Setback Into a New Vision of Social Justice,* Simon & Schuster.

Guinier, Lani (1994): *The Tyranny of the Majority: Fundamental Fairness in Representative Democracy,* Free Press.

Hand, G., G. Georgel & Ch. Sasse (1979): *European Electoral System,* Handbook, London.

Harvey, A. L. (1998): *Votes Without Leverage: Women in American Electoral Politics, 1920-1970*, Cambridge University Press, New York.

Hassall, G., & C. Saunders (eds.) (1997): *The People's Representatives: Electoral Systems in the Asia-Pacific Region*, Allen & Unwin, Sydney.

Hermens, F.A. (1941): *Democracy or Anarchy?,* University of Notre Dame, Indiana.

Herment, G., R. Rose & A. Rouqie (eds.) (1978): *Elections without Choice*, Macmillan, New York.

Hogan, J. (1945): *Elections and Representation*, Cork University Press, Oxford.

Institute of Electoral Research (1962): *Parliaments and Electoral Systems; A World Handbook,* London.

Inter-Parliamentary Union (ed.) (1993): *Electoral Systems: A World-Wide Comparative Study,* Inter-Parliamentary Union, Geneva.

Jedruch, J. (1998): *Constitutions, Elections and Legislatures of Poland, 1493-1993: A Guide to their History*, Hippocrene Books, New York.

Jones, Mark P. (1997): *Electoral Laws and the Survival of Presidential Democracies,* University of Notre Dame Press.

Karnik, V.B. (ed.) (1967): *4th General Election: Problem and Policies*, Lalvani, Bombay.

Kemp, R. L. (1998): *Local Government Election Practices: A Handbook for Public Officials and Citizens*, McFarland and Company, Jefferson.

Keyssar, Alexander (2000): *The Right to Vote: The Contested History of Democracy in the United States,* Basic Books, USA.

Khanna, D.D. *etal.* (ed.) (1999): *Principles, Power and Politics,* McMillan, New Delhi.

Klein, Keith *et al.* (1996): *Toward Credible and Legitimate Elections in Kenya: Recommendations for Action,* IFES, Washington.

Kothari, Rajni, *et al.* (1967): *Party System and Election Studies*, Allied, Bombay.

Kulapati, Mekhala (1999): *Political Disputes and Controversies: Conflict Resolution in India*, Kanishka, New Delhi.

Kumar, Krishna (ed.) (1998): *Post Conflict Elections, Democratization and International Assistance,* Lynne Rienner Publishers, Boulder.

Lakeman, E. (1970): *How Democracies Vote*, Faber and Faber, London.

Leonard, Dick *et al.*(1987): *The Economist World Atlas of Elections: Voting Patterns in 39 Democracies*, Hodder & Stoughton.

Lewis, W.A. (1965): *Politics in West Africa*, Allen and Unwin, London.

Lijphart, Arend (1999): *Patterns of Democracy: Government Forms and Performance in Thirty-Six Countries,* Yale University Press.

Lijphart, A. (1994): *Electoral Systems and Party Systems: A Study of Twenty-Seven Democracies, 1945-1990,* Oxford University Press, Oxford.

Lijphart, A. & B. Grofman (eds.) (1984): *Choosing an Electoral System: Issues and Alternatives*, Praeger, New York.

Lyons, T. (1998): *Voting for Peace: Post-Conflict Elections in Liberia*, Brookings Institution Press, Washington.

Mackenzie, W.J.M. (1958): *Free Elections,* George Allen and Unwin, London.

Mackie, Thomas T. & Richard Rose (1982): *The International Almanac of Electoral History*, Macmillan Reference Books.

McDonald R. (1971): *Party System and Elections in Latin America.* Markham, Publishers, Chicago.

Mehta, Jashwant, B. (1995): *Quest for a Better Democratic Alternative*, N. M. Publishers, Bombay.

Merloe, Patrick (n.d.): *Democratic Elections: Human Rights, Public Confidence and the Level Playing Field,* National Democratic Institute for International Affairs, Washington.

Meyns, P. & D.W. Nabudere (1989): *Democracy and the One-Party State in Africa, Institut für Afrika-Kunde*, Hamburg.

Milner, Henry (ed.) (1999): *Making Every Vote Count: Reassessing Canada's Electoral System,* Broadview Press.

Mitra, Subrata K. (1999): *Democracy and Social Change in India: A Cross-Sectional Analysis of the National Electorate*, Sage, New Delhi.

Monmonier, Mark S. (2001): *Bushmanders & Bullwinkles: How Politicians Manipulate Electronic Maps and Census Data to Win Elections,* University of Chicago Press.

Narain, Iqbal (1994): *Politics in Changing India*, Rawat, Jaipur.

Newland, Robert A. (1982): *Comparative Electoral Systems*, Arthur McDougall Fund.

Nohlen, Dieter (1996): *Elections and Electoral Systems,* Friedrich-Ebert-Stiftung, Division of International Development Cooperation, Bonn.

Nohlen Dieter & *et al.* (eds.) (2001): *Elections in Asia and the Pacific: A Data Handbook: The Middle East, Central Asia and South Asia:* (Elections in Asia and the Pacific Vol. 1).

Noiret, S. (ed) (1990): *Political Strategies and Electoral Reforms: Origins of Voting Systems in Europe in the 19th and 20th Centuries*, Baden-Baden, Noomos.

O'Leary, C. (1962): *The Elimination of Corrupt Practices in British Elections 1868-1911,* Clarendon Press.

Pai Panandikar V. A. (ed.) (2000): *Problems of Governance in South Asia*, Konark Publishers, New Delhi.

Pai Panandikar V. A. & Navnita Chadha Behera (eds) (2000): *Perspectives on South Asia,* Konark Publishers, New Delhi.

Pai, Panandikar & Subhas C. Kashyap (eds) (2001): *Political Reforms: Asserting Civic Sovereignty,* Konark Publication, New Delhi.

Pai Panandiker, V.A. & Ramashray Roy (1994): *Financing of Elections,* Centre for Policy Research, New Delhi.

Palanithurai, G. (1993): *Indian Polity: Myth and Reality*, Kanishka, Delhi.

Pattabhiram M. (ed.) (1967): *General Elections in India,* Allied Publishers, Bombay.

Paul Sharda (1977): *(1977) General Elections in India*, Associated Publishing House, New Delhi.

Peacock, A. A. (ed.) (1997): *Affirmative Action and Representation: Shaw* vs. *Reno and the Future of Voting Rights*, Carolina Academic Press, Durham.

Powell, G. Bingham, Jr. (2000): *Elections as Instruments of Democracy,* Yale University Press.

Rae, D.W. (1971): *The Political Consequences of Electoral Laws*, Yale University Press, New Haven.

Reeves, K. (1997): *Voting Hopes or Fears? White Voters, Black Candidates and Racial Politics in America*, Oxford University Press, New York.

Reynolds, A. (1999): *Electoral Systems and Democratization in Southern Africa*, Oxford University Press, New York.

Reynolds, Andrew & Ben Reilly (1997): *The International IDEA Handbook of Electoral System Design,* Broderna Carlssons Boktryckeri AB.

Reilly, Benjamin (2001): *Democracy in Divided Societies: Electoral Engineering for Conflict Management*, Cambridge University Press, Cambridge.

Richie Robert & Steven Hill (2001): *Whose Vote Counts?,* Beacon Press.

Roy, Meenu (1999): *Elections 1998: A Continuity in Coalition*, National Publishing House, Jaipur.

Roy, Ramashray & Paul Wallace (1999): *Indian Politics and the 1998 Election: Regionalism, Hindutva and State Politics*, Sage, New Delhi.

Rueschemeyer, D., E. Huber Stephens & J.D. Stephens (1992): *Capitalist Development and Democracy,* University of Chicago, Chicago.

Rule, W., J.F. Zimmerman (eds.) (1994): *Electoral Systems in Comparative Perspective: Their Impact on Women and Minorities,* Greenwood Press, Westport/CT.

Rule, Wilma & Joseph F. Zimmerman (eds.) (1993): *United States Electoral Systems: Their Impact on Women and Minorities,* Praeger.

Rush, M. E., R. D. Ritchie & B. E. Cain (eds.) (1998): *Fair and Effective Representation? Debating Voting Reforms and Minority Rights*, Rowman and Littlefield, Lanham.

Rush, Mark E. & Richard L. Engstrom (2001): *Fair and Effective Representation,* Rowman & Littlefield, Lanham.

Saggar, S. (1998), *Race and British Electoral Politics*, Taylor and Francis, Bristol.

Sartori, G. (1994): *Comparative Constitutional Engineering: An Inquiry into Structures, Incentives and Outcomes,* Macmillan, Basingstoke, London.

Sasse, Ch. *et al.* (1981): *The European Parliament; Towards a Uniform Procedure for Direct Elections,* Badia Fiesolana, Florence.

Seshan, T.N. (1995): *The Degeneration of India*, Viking, New Delhi.

Shakdher, S.L. (1980): *Electoral Reforms for India*, The Voters' Council and Citizens for Democracy, Delhi.

Shaun Bowler and Bernard Grofman (eds.) (2000): *Elections in Australia, Ireland and Malta Under the Single Transferable Vote: Reflections on an Embedded Institution,* University of Michigan Press, Washington.

Sharma, S. P. (1991): *Political Promises and Performance: Some Reflections of the Socio-Political Scenario of India Across the Eighties*, Ashish, Delhi.

Sharma, Shalendra D. (1999): *Development and Democracy in India*, Lynne Rienner, Boulder.

Shourie, Arun (1993): *Indian Controversies: Essays on Religion in Politics*, ASA Publications, New Delhi.

Singh, L.P. (1986): *Electoral Reform: Problems and Suggested Solutions*, Uppal, New Delhi.

Singh, M.P. (ed) (1998): *Ideologies and Institutions in Indian Politics*, Deep and Deep, New Delhi.

Sisk, T. D., & A. Reynolds, (eds.) (1998): *Elections and Conflict Management in Africa*, United States Institute of Peace Press, Washington.

Skillen, James W. (1994): *Recharging the American Experiment: Principled Pluralism for Genuine Civic Community,* Baker Books.

Smith, Sam (1997): *Sam Smith's Great American Political Repair Manual : How to Rebuild Our Country so the Politics Aren't Broken and Politicians Aren't Fixed,* W.W. Norton, New York.

Stoddard, Michael D. (1994), *Evaluating Elections: Basic Principles and Issues and Selected Case Studies: South African Election Studies Project, March 8, 1994.* National Democratic Institute for International Affairs, Washington.

Taagepera, R. & M.S. Shugart (1989): *Seats and Votes; The Effects and Determinants of Electoral Systems,* Yale University Press, New Haven.

Thisgarajah Jeevan (ed.) (1998): *Governance and the Electoral Process in Pakistan*, ICES, Colombo.

Weiner Myron & Rajni Kothari (eds) (1965): *Indian Voting Behaviour*, Firma K. L. Mukhopadhyay, Calcutta.

Wilder, Andrew R. (1999): *The Pakistan Voter: Electoral Politics and Voting Behaviour in the Punjab*, Oxford University Press, Oxford.

Zaidi, A. M. (ed.) (1994): *The Annual Register of Indian Political Parties 1991,* Indian Inst. of Applied Pol. Res., New Delhi.

Zimmerman, Joseph F. & Wilma Rule (eds.) (2000): *The U.S. House of Representatives: Reform or Rebuild?,* Praeger Press.

Articles

Advani, L.K. (1970): 'Indian Electoral System – A Plea for Reform', *Journal of Constitutional and Parliamentary Studies, IV (4),* October-December.

Advani, L.K., (1984): 'Electoral Reforms: Imperative and Urgent', *Journal of Constitutional and Parliamentary Studies, XVIII (1-2),* January-June.

Alexander, Herbert (1999): 'Cornerstones of Political Finance Regulation', *Elections Today*, International Foundation for Election Systems, Vol. 8.3.

Anand Y.P. (1993): 'Political Funding: Gandhiji's Guidline Best', *Business Standard*, 29 July, p.7.

Ansari, Iqbal, 'Minority Representation', *Seminar*, October 2001, pp. 37-41.

Arora, S. C. & R. Prabhakar (1997): 'Local Body Elections: A Study of Rohtak [India] Municipal Council', *Administrative Change* 24(2), pp. 149-64.

Bahuguna, Sunderlal (1996): 'India Corrupted: Case for all Party Rule', *Indian Express*, 11 April, p.8.

Bailey, M. & D. W. Brady (1998): 'Heterogeneity and Representation: The Senate and Free Trade.' *American Journal of Political Science* 42(2), pp. 524-44.

Bean, C. S. & M. P. Wattenberg, (1998): 'Attitudes Towards Divided Government and Ticket-Splitting in Australia and the United States'. *Australian Journal of Political Science* 33(1), pp. 25-36.

Bendourou, O. (1996): 'Power and Opposition in Morocco', *Journal of Democracy* 7(3), pp. 108-22.

Beyme, Klaus Von (1997): 'Party Leadership and Change in Party System: Towards a Post Modern Party State', *Hindustan Times*, 31 July, p. 13.

Bhambhri, C.P. (1970): 'Electoral Reform and Party System in India – A Plea for Proportional Representation', *Journal of Constitutional and Parliamentary Studies, IV(4)*, October-December.

Bhambhri, C.P. (1998): 'Party without Ideology', *Hindustan Times*, 31 March, p. 13.

Bhargava, G.S. (1995): 'Party Polls: The Inner Contradictions', *Hindustan Times*, 29 July, p.11.

Bhargava, G.S. (1997): 'Party System and Democracy', *Janata, 52 (14)*, 29 June, p. 11-12.

Bickel, Alexander (1979): 'Is Electoral Reform the Answer?', 46 COMMENTARY 41 (1968), in U.S. Senate. Judiciary, *Direct Popular Election...* 1979, pp. KF26 - J8359

Boston, J., S. Levine, E. McLeay, N. S. Roberts & H. Schmidt (1998): 'The Impact of Electoral Reform on the Public Service: The New Zealand Case', *Australian Journal of Public Administration* 57(3), pp. 64-78.

Brahmananda, P.R.(1999): 'Stabilising the Political System', *The Hindu*, 1 May, p. 12.

Burlet, S. & H. Reid (1998): 'A Gendered Uprising: Political

Representation and Minority Ethnic Communities', *Ethnic and Racial Studies* 21(2), pp. 270-287.

Chakravarty, Nikhil (1996): 'The Role of Regional Parties', *Tribune*, 24 May, p. 8.

Chakravarty, Nitish (1999): 'Changing Concept of Political Stability: One-Party Rule a Mirage', *The Deccan Herald*, 10 May, p. 10.

Charlot, Jean (1989): 'Political Parties: Towards a New Theoretical Synthesis', *Political Studies, 37(3)*, September, pp. 352-61.

Chatterjee, P.K. (1998): 'Analysing the Electoral Promises in Party Manifestoes', *Mainstream, 36(10)*, 28 February, pp. 13-14.

Chaturvedi, Santosh Kumar (1997): 'Dalits in Indian Politics: Rise of BSP', *Politics India, 2(4)*, October, p. 40.

Chhibber, Pradeep & Ken Kollman (1998): 'Party Aggregation and the Number of Parties in India and the United States', *American Political Science Review, 92(2)*, June, pp. 329-42.

Chhiber, Pradeep K. & John R. Petrocik (1989): 'The puzzle of Indian Politics: Social Cleavages and the Indian Party System', *British Journal of political Science, 19 (2)*, April, pp.191-210

Chhiber, Pradeep (1995): 'Political Parties, Electoral Competition, Government Expenditures and Economic Reform in India', *Journal of Development Studies, 32(1)*, October, pp. 74-96.

Copley Antony (1996) 'Pre-election India: An Historian's Report', *Contemporary South Asia*, 5(1), pp. 85-101.

Cowen, Michael & Liisa Laakso (1997): 'An Overview of Election Studies in Africa' *The Journal of Modern African Studies,* Vol. 35, p. 4.

———— (2002): 'Elections and After: Opportunity to Restore Stability', *Economic and Political Weekly,* Vol. XXXVII. No. 9, pp. 838-843.

Dahl, Bob (1999): "Diminishing the Influence of 'Money Politics' ", *Elections Today,* Vol. 8, p. 3.

Dandavate, Pramila (1997): 'Participation of Women in Political Power—Provision of 33 per cent Reservation', *Janata, 52(1)*, Annual. November, pp. 1-33.

Denemark, D. (1996): 'Political Accountability and Electoral Reform in New Zealand', *Australian Quarterly* 68(4), pp. 96-114.

Deshmukh B.D. (1993): 'Role of Regional Parties', *Hindu*, 30 December, p. 8.

DeSouza, Peter Ronald, 'Whose Representation?', October 2001, pp. 57-65.

Di Virgilio, A. (1996): 'The Regional and Administrative Elections: Bipolarization with Reserve', *Italian Politics: A Review* 11, pp. 41-68.

Donovan, T. & S. Bowler (1998): 'Direct Democracy and Minority Rights: An Extension' *American Journal of Political Science* 42(3), pp. 1020-1024.

Duncan, Ian, (1999) 'Interpreting the Uttar Pradesh Result', *Workshop on the 1999 General Election*, Institute of Commonwealth Studies, London

Dunleavy, Patrick & Helen Margetts (1995): 'Understanding the Dynamics of Electoral Reform', *International Political Science Review 16(1),* January.

——— (1989): 'Electoral Reform Belie Expectations' *The Hindu*, 9 July, New Delhi, p. 8.

Elklit, Jorgen & Palle Svensson (1997): 'What Makes Elections Free and Fair?' *Journal of Democracy,* Vol. 8, p.3.

Fischer, Jeff. (1997): 'The Role of NGOs in the Election Process', *Elections Today*, Winter, p. 18.

Fisher, Justin (1997): 'Donation to Political Parties', *Parliamentary Affairs, 50(2)*, April, pp. 235-45.

Fox, R. L. & E. R. A. N. Smith (1998), 'The Role of Candidate Sex in Voter Decision-Making' *Political Psychology* 19(2), pp. 405-19.

Gadgil, V.N. (1999): 'Politics of Alliance', *Hindustan Times*, 18 May, p. 13.

Gerber, E. R. & R. B. Morton (1998): 'Primary Election Systems and Representation' *Journal of Law, Economics & Organization* 14(2), pp. 304-24.

Gopakumar, G. (1998): 'Fragmented Party System and Indian Federalism', *Politics India, 2(12)*, June, pp. 28-31.

Gray, Bill (1999): 'Providing Information to the Electorate', *Elections Today,* Vol. 8.3.

Gupta, Suranjan (1999): 'Stable Government: Economic Growth Needs Political Vision', *Statesman,* 18 March, p. 6.

Haspel, M., T. F. Remington & S. S. Smith (1998): 'Electoral Institutions and Party Cohesion in the Russian Duma', *Journal of Politics* 60(2), pp. 417-39.

Heath, Oliver (1999): 'The Fractionalisation of Indian Parties', *Seminar, (480)*, August, pp. 66-71

Ilonszki, G. (1998): 'Representation Deficit in a New Democracy: Theoretical Considerations and the Hungarian Case', *Communist and Post-Communist Studies* 31(2), pp. 157-70.

Issacharoff, S. & P. S. Karlan (1998): 'Standing and Misunderstanding in Voting Rights Law, Commentary' *Harvard Law Review,* 111(8), pp. 2276-92.

Inderjit (1989): 'Poll Expense Ceiling Now a Farce', *Economic Times,* New Delhi, 11 July, p. 8.

Indiresan, P.V. (1991): 'Electing Representatives, Responsible and Responsive Legislation', *Indian Journal of Public Administration,* New Delhi, pp. 294-301.

Jagmohan (1994): 'De-registration of Political Parties', *Hindustan Times*, 8 Aug, p. 13

Jain, R. B., 'Regulating Political Finance in India', *Indian Journal of Public Administration,* Vol. XLI, October-December, No. 4, pp. 702-717.

Jaisingh, Hari (1999): 'Electoral Reforms: Two Party System only Way Out', *Tribune*, 29 January, p. 10.

Jayaramu, P.S. (1999): 'Political Parties and Lok Sabha Elections', *Mainstream, 37(38)*, 28 August, pp. 7-8, 23.

Jardim, Torquato (1999): 'Equality of Opportunities Essential', *Elections Today*, IFES, Vol. 8.3, September.

Jeffery, C. (1998): 'Electoral Reform: Learning from Germany' *Political Quarterly* 69(3), pp. 241-51.

Kant, Krishna (1992): 'Consensual Nationalism', *Mainstream,* Annual, pp. 27-36.

Kapur, Devesh & Bhanu Pratap Mehta (1999): 'India in 1998: The Travails of Political Fragmentation', *Asian Survey, 39(1)*, Jan-Feb, pp. 163-76.

Kashyap, Subhash C. (1999): 'Elections and Constitutional Reforms', *Nav Bharat Times*, 29 August.

_______ (1999): 'President's Rule During Elections – A Perilous Suggestion', *The Deccan Herald*, 31 July.

_______ (1999): 'Polls in Times of War', *The Hindustan Times*, 6 July.

_______ (1999): 'War, Elections and Constitution', *Rashtriya Sahara*, 3 July.

_______ (1999): 'Elections and Responsibilities of Citizens', in A Vision of Values, *Citizenship Development Society*, New Delhi.

_______ (1998): 'Gag on Opinion Polls Assault on Fundamental Rights', *The Times of India*, 23 February.

_______ (1998): 'Elections and Electoral Processes – Responsibilities of Citizenship', *Politics India*, February.

_______ (1997): 'Electoral Reforms, Power to People: Fact or Farce', *The Observer of Business and Politics*, 15 August.

_______ (1997): 'Presidential Elections (Need for Review and Reform of the Law)', *The Indian Express*, 5 June.

_______ (1996): 'Blueprint for Reforms', *The Hindu*, 31 August.

_______ (1995): 'Ensuring Stability (Election of Leader by the House, constructive vote of No-Confidence)', *The Hindustan Times*, 6 October.

_______ (1995): 'More than Stability is Needed', *The Hindustan Times*, 22 May.

_______ (1994): 'Electoral Reforms – Challenge and Response', *The Hindustan Times*, 5 August.

_______ (1994): 'Electoral Reforms', *The Observer of Business and Politics*, 31 May and 1 June.

_______ (1992): 'Urgent Need for Electoral Reforms', *The Times of India*, 6 July.

_______ (1992): 'Presidential Poll Law Needs Reform', *The Hindu*, 23 June.

Khare, Harish (1992): 'Regional Parties: Reduced Efficacy', *Seminar*, November, pp. 33-35.

Kingsley, Jean-Pierre (1999): 'Campaign Finance Reform an On-going Task', *Elections Today*, IFES Vol. 8, 3, September.

Kohno, M. (1997), 'Voter Turnout and Strategic Ticket-Splitting under Japan's New Electoral Rules', *Asian Survey* 37(5), pp. 429-40.

Kolsto, P. & B. Tsilevich (1997), 'Patterns of Nation-Building and Political Integration in a Bifurcated Postcommunist State: Ethnic Aspects of Parliamentary Elections in Latvia', *East European Politics and Societies* 11(2), pp. 366-91.

Komarov, Erik (1985): 'Political Parties in India: Change in Electoral Propaganda', *Journal of Political Studies, 5(1&2),* Calcutta, pp. 1-51.

Lanza, O. & R. Motta (1997): 'Majoritarian and Proportional Electoral Systems [in Italy]: The Sicilian Case', *Italian Politics: A Review* 12, pp. 103-24. [48-587]

Li, P. K. & D. Newman, (1997): 'Give and Take: Electoral Politics in Transitional Hong Kong', *Asian Perspective* 21(1), pp. 213-32.

McCann, J. A. & J. I. Dominguez (1998): 'Mexicans React to Electoral Fraud and Political Corruption: An Assessment of Public Opinion and Voting Behaviour', *Electoral Studies* 17(4), pp. 483-503.

Mehta, Pratap Bhanu, 'Is Electoral and Institutional Reforms the Answer?', *Seminar*, October 2001, pp. 66-69.

Merchant, A.K. (1999): 'Value Based Politics: The Crying Need of Indian Democracy', *Politics India, 4(1)*, July, pp. 29-30

Meyer Ralph C. & David S. Malcolm (1993): 'Voting in India: Effects of Economic Change and New Party Formation', *Asian Survey, 33(5)*, May, pp. 507-19.

Miller, A. H., W. M. Reisinger & V. L. Hesli (1998): 'Establishing Representation in Post-Soviet Societies: Change in Mass and Elite Attitudes Toward Democracy and the Market, 1992-1995', *Electoral Studies* 17(3), pp. 327-49.

Mishra, S. N. & Mishra, Sweta (1994): 'Political Process and Political Parties in India: Retrospect and Prospect', *Indian Journal of Public Administration, 40(3)*, Jul-Sep, pp. 443-53.

Moon, E. P. (1997): 'Single Non-Transferable Vote Methods in Taiwan in 1996: Effects of an Electoral System', *Asian Survey* 37(7), pp. 652-68.

Morlino, L (1997): 'Is There an Impact? And Where Is It? Electoral Reform and the Party System in Italy', *South European Society and Politics* 2(3), pp. 103-30.

Mulgan, A. G. (1997): 'Electoral Determinants of Agrarian Power: Measuring Rural Decline in Japan', *Political Studies* 45(5), pp. 875-99.

Mulroy, S. J. (1998): 'The Way Out: A Legal Standard for Imposing Alternative Electoral Systems as Voting Rights Remedies', *Harvard Civil Rights - Civil Liberties Law Review* 33(2), pp. 333-80.

Murray, D. (1998): 'Thailand's Recent Electoral Reforms', *Electoral Studies* 17(4), pp. 525-36.

Narain, Iqbal (1993): 'Political Parties, Electronics and Panchayatiraj Institutions', *Administrator, 38(4)*, Oct-Dec, pp. 31-37.

Neou, Kassie & Jeffrey C. Gallup (1999): 'Conducting Cambodia's Elections', *Journal of Democracy,* Vol. 10.2.

Pai, Sudha (1998): 'New Political Trends in Uttar Pradesh: The BJP and the Lok Sabha Elections, 1998', *Economic and Political Weekly, 33(28)*, 11 July, pp.1841-845.

_______(1996): 'Transformation of the Indian Party System', *Asian Survey*, Vol. 36, No. 12, December, pp. 1170-1181.

Pastor, Robert A. (1998): 'Mediating Elections', *Journal of Democracy*, Vol. 9.1.

Pendse, D. R. (1993): 'Polls and Reforms', *The Hindustan Times*, 7 October, p. 11.

Pinto-Duschinsky, Michael (1999): 'Effective Reform in Campaign Financing', *Elections Today*, IFES, Vol. 8.3. September.

———— (1993): 'Press and Fair Poll', Editorial, *The Hindustan Times,* 5 February.

Rahat, G., and M. Sznajder (1998): 'Electoral Engineering in Chile: The Electoral System and Limited Democracy', *Electoral Studies* 17(4), pp. 429-42.

Ramachandran, Raju (1991), 'Mythe of Parliamentary Democracy', *Indian Express,* 6 August.

Reddy, Agarala Easwara & Ram, D. Sundar (1990): 'Democracy and Indian Electoral System: Need for Reforms', *Indian Journal of Political Studies*, 14, December, pp. 80-103.

——— (1991): 'Report of the Committee Appointed by Sri Jayaprakash Narayan on behalf of Citizens for Democracy for Electoral Reforms', *Indian Journal of Public Administration,* New Delhi, pp. 588-602.

Rishikesh (1998): 'The Crisis of Party System in India', *Politics India, 3(2)*, August, pp. 33-34.

Rokkan, S.(1968): 'Electoral Systems', *International Encyclopedia of Social Sciences,* Vol. V, pp 6-21, ed. D. Shills, Macmillan.

Saeed Amera (2002): 'Assam Assembly Polls (2001) and Proceeding Developments', *Regional Studies*, Vol. 20 (No. 1), Institute of Regional Studies, Islamabad.

Sanderson, John & Michael Maley (1998): 'Elections and Liberal Democracy in Cambodia', *Australian Journal of International Affairs,* Vol. 42 Canberra, p.3.

Sangita, S.N. (1999): 'Political Instability: Need for Reforms', *Young India,* 10(7), 25 September, pp. 10-11

Sartori, G. (1991): 'Comparing and Miscomparing', *Journal of Theoretical Politics* 3(3), pp. 243- 257.

Sato, S. 1997. 'The LDP's Comeback or the Failure of Electoral Reform in Japan', *Cahiers Du Japon* 72: pp. 18-25.

Saxena, Rekha (1998): 'Party System Transition and Electoral Turning Points in India', *Trends in Social Science Research,* 5(1), June, pp. 7- 47.

Schedler, Andreas (1999): *The Path-Dependent Logic of Electoral Reforms in Mexico*, Paper for the American Political Science Association, manuscript, September.

Seshan, T.N. (1996): 'Maintaining an Eagle's Eye', *Elections Today*, Fall, p. 31.

Seshan, T.N.(1996): 'Election in India: The Magnitude of the Task and Challenges Ahead', *Politics India,* New Delhi, June.

Shakdher, S.L. (1984): 'Electoral Reforms', *Journal of Constitutional and Parliamentary Studies, XVIII(1-2),* January-June.

Shastri, Sandeep (1992), 'Indian Constitution: Is a Fresh Look Really Necessary', *Mainstream,* pp. 9-17.

Shastri, Sandeep and M.J. Vinod (1991), 'Dynamics of Electoral Politics: A Case Study of the Karnataka Assembly Elections 1989', *Indian Journal of Social Sciences,* pp. 389-406

Sheth, D.L. (1991): 'Crisis of Representation', *Seminar (385),* September.

Sezhiyan, Era (2001): 'Election Commissions Dangerous Diktat', *Mainstream*, June 16, pp. 7-10.

Singh, Ajay (1992): 'Communalism and Party Politics', *Monthly Public Opinion Surveys, 37 (4-5)*, Jan. - February, pp. 8-11.

Singh, Mahendra Prasad (1992): 'The Dilemma of the New Indian Party System: To govern or not to govern?', *Asian Survey, 32(4)* April, pp. 303-17.

Singh, S. P. (1990): 'Need for Poll Reform', *The Hindustan Times,* 9 May, p. 11.

Singh, V.B. (1991): 'Multiplicity of Candidates in Elections: A Case for Upward Revision in Security Deposits', *Indian Journal of Public Administration, XXXVI (3),* July-September.

Sinha, Anindya (1999): 'The Indian Party System 1989-99', *Seminar*, August, pp. 20-25.

Sinha, Shivendra K. (1998): 'Post Ideology Party System Threat to Democracy', *Politics India,* 3(1), July, pp. 28-31.

Sinha, Shivendra (1998): 'Towards a People Centred Polity: Political Parties, Legislators and Electoral Reforms', *Politics India, 3(4)*, October, pp. 24-28.

Sonstegaard, M. H. (1998): 'A Shortcut Method of Calculating the Distribution of Election Outcome Types Under Approval Voting', *Theory and Decision* 44(3), pp. 211-20.

Stokes, S. C. (1998): 'Constituency Influence and Representation', *Electoral Studies* 17(3), pp. 351-67.

——— (1991): 'Special Issue: Votes without Power', *Asian Journal of Public Administration,* 13(2), December, p. 39.

Sridharan, E., 'Reforming Political Finance', *Seminar,* October 2001, pp. 29-36.

Srivastava Krishna (1994): 'Electoral Financing' *The Hindustan Times.* 23 June, p. 13.

——— (1988): 'State Funding of Poll Opposed', *The Hindustan Times, 18* October, p. 8.

Throup, David (1993): 'Elections and Political Legitimacy in Kenya', *Africa*, Vol. 63. p.3.

Unger, Robert, 'Towards a High Energy Democracy', *Seminar,* October 2001, pp. 70-75.

Vengroff, R., & M. Ndiaye (1998): 'The Impact of Electoral Reform at the Local Level in Africa: The Case of Senegal's 1996 Local Elections', *Electoral Studies* 17(4), pp. 463-82.

Wood, B. D., & A. H. Anderson (1998): 'The Dynamics of Senatorial Representation, 1952-1991' *Journal of Politics* 60(3), pp. 705-36.

Wyatt Andrew (2001) 'Elections in India, 1999-2000: The BJP Makes Slow Progress', *The Round Table*, No. 360, 379-390.

Yadav, Yogendra, 'The Third System', *Seminar*, August 1999, pp. 14-20.

Yadav, Yogendra, 'A Radical Agenda for Political Reforms', *Seminar*, October 2001, pp. 14-23

Yadav, Yogendra (1998), 'Electoral Reforms: Beyond Middle Class Fantasies' in M.P. Singh (ed.), *Ideologies and Institutions in Indian Politics,* New Delhi, Deep and Deep.

Young, Tom (1993): 'Elections and Electoral Politics in Africa', *Africa*, Vol. 63.p.3.

ANNEXURES

ANNEXURE - I

Report of the Committee appointed by Sri Jayaprakash Narayan on behalf of Citizens for Democracy for Electoral Reforms*

THE USE AND MISUSE OF ADMINISTRATIVE MACHINERY

The Election Commission

The position and authority of the Election Commission is integral to a system of fair and free elections. As in the case of the judiciary, the Election Commission must not only be independent in theory but also manifestly appear to be so in the exercise of its powers of organising and conducting elections. In recent years, an impression has gained ground that the Election Commission is becoming less and less independent of the executive than in earlier years of independence, because the choice of the Chief Election Commissioner has not always been based on criteria which would command the confidence of all sections of public opinion. The practice of making it a berth for retiring Government officials has perhaps, been responsible for the feeling that the incumbent so benefited will be beholden to the Government for his office. When this is viewed in the context of the various complaints made during the elections about alleged irregularities in polling and the subsequent counting and declaration results, rumours, not all of them unfounded, are circulated which detract from the prestige and confidence which the Election Commission should enjoy with all sections of the electorate.

---

* *Source*: .... (1991): 'Report of the Committee Appointed by Sri Jayaprakash Narayan on behalf of Citizens for Democracy for Electoral Reforms', quoted in *Indian Journal of Public Administration*, 1991, New Delhi, pp. 588-602.

Larger Body Needed

It is, therefore, necessary to ensure that the Election Commission is so constituted that its integrity and fairness are unimpeachable. Suggestions have been made in recent years that the Election Commission should consist of more than one person and, indeed, Article 324 of the Constitution makes specific provision in sub-clause 2 for the appointment of a Chief Election Commissioner and a "number of other Election Commissioner". But this provision has not so far been implemented. The position of the Election Commission is somewhat analogous to that of the Public Service Commissions at the Centre and in the states which consist of several members. A Commission consisting of a body of three members can arrive at a consensus on major controversial problems or organising elections which is decidedly a superior method of ensuring impartiality to the individual decision of a single Chief Election Commissioner. We would therefore, emphasise the importance of implementing the existing provisions of the Constitution.

Manner of Appointment

Equally important is the manner of appointing the members of the Commission and the choice of the Chief Election Commissioner. The Constitution provides that appointments should be made by the President and this has been interpreted in the usual sense in which all Presidential actions are exercised, namely on the advice of the Council of Ministers. While this may be in keeping with the basic feature of Cabinet responsibility under the Parliamentary system of Government, appointment to this high office by the executive of the day is always open to suspicion and cannot command the prestige and confidence that should be associated with that office. The tendency of the Government is not to look for the qualities of independence and impartiality which would satisfy the public regarding the fairness of the electoral process. Moreover, it is necessary to ensure that the person appointed has no sense of obligation to the Government for his position.

We, therefore, suggest that members of the Election Commission should be appointed by the President on the advice of a committee consisting of the Prime Minister, the leader of the Opposition (for a Member of Parliament selected by the Opposition) in the Lok Sabha and the Chief Justice of India.

State Commissioners

The Constitution further provide that before each general elections to the Lok Sabha and the Legislative Assemblies, the President may also appoint Regional Election Commissioners. This, again, is one of the provisions which have been ignored in practice, with the result that an independent and efficient machinery is not available at the State level for the proper conduct of elections simultaneously of the Lok Sabha and the Assemblies over the far-flung areas of the country comprising an electorate now touching the 300 million mark. The Election Commission has not been able to look promptly into all the complaints of irregularities made between the calling of an election and the polling date. We, accordingly, suggest that Regional or State Commissioners should be appointed either for each State or for two or more contiguous States. At the time of elections, the State Commissioner should have the responsibility of appointing Election Officers, Returning Officers and Polling Officers for various constituencies. The choice of these officers need not be restricted to Government servants. The office of the State Commissioner should be of a permanent nature and it should discharge such duties such as the periodic revision of electoral rolls and maintenance of election records.

Election Rules

According to the present law, rules made by Central Government after consulting the Election Commission are required to be laid before each House of Parliament but they become effective as soon as they are made. It is, therefore, possible to make or amend rules after the dissolution of Parliament, and such rules may seriously affect a general election. This is obviously unsatisfactory. Section 169(3) of the Representation of the People Act, 1951 should be so amended as to provide that the rules become operative only after thev are placed before and approved by Parliament.

Bye-elections

The Committee has noted with regret that the Election Commission has, in many cases where vacancies have arisen, delayed the holding of a bye-election without any satisfactory reason being assigned and, in some cases has left a genuine and widespread feeling that its decisions have not been uninfluenced by considerations of the convenience of the ruling party. The Committee, therefore suggested that a statutory limit of six months be imposed beyond which a bye-election should not be postponed and Representation of the People Act, 1950 amended so as to carry out this recommendation.

Misuse of Government Power and Official Machinery

Almost all the witnesses who gave evidence before us were greatly concerned about the misuse of Government power and Government machinery in furtherance of the election of the party in power and made various suggestions to curb this trend. We make the following recommendations in this behalf:

(i) A convention, backed by legal sanction as mentioned below, should be developed to the effect that the Government of the day should function as a care-taker government from the time of the announcement of the dissolution of Parliament or Legislative Assembly, as the case may be, until the polling day. During this period the care-taker government should not: (a) initiate and announce new policies, (b) promise or start new projects, (c) grant allowances or loans, salary increases, and (d) hold official functions attended by Ministers, Deputy Minister and Parliamentary Secretaries.

(ii) During the aforesaid period, Ministers, Deputy Ministers and Parliamentary Secretaries should not travel except at their own expense and should not use Government aircraft or vehicles. They should not use Government postage for election purposes nor use of Public Works Department for erecting rostrums for their meetings. Generally, the use of Government machinery for election purposes should be stopped.

(iii) During the aforesaid period, no member of the Government should be given time either on radio or television except such time as may be allotted to his party for election propaganda.

(iv) During the aforesaid period, no advertisements of Government achievements should be published at Government cost and no newsreels should be exhibited at Government expense for the propaganda of the Government or the ruling party.

(v) During the aforesaid period, no police officers above the level of head constable and no revenue officer Class I or Class II should be transferred from his post.

(vi) By way of providing legal sanctions for the above proposals, as many of them as possible should be included in the definition of corrupt practices by amending Clause 7 of Section 123 of the Representation of People Act, 1951. In addition, Section 100 (1) of the said Act should be amended so as to enable the Court to declare the election invalid in a constituency if Government machinery or Government power is used in elections to a substantial extent.

(vii) It is necessary to prohibit the use of jeeps and other vehicles belonging to Government and local bodies for election use of any party. For this purpose, it should be provided that during the aforesaid period such vehicles (except public transport) should only be used to the extent and in manner permitted by the Returning Officer in each constituency.

(viii) If at any time prior to the polling day, Government machinery or Government power is misused for election purposes, the Election Commissioner should have the authority publicly to reprimand such misuse. Persons aggrieved by such misuse would have the right to approach the Election Commission for this purpose.

(ix) It should be provided that no candidate and no political party concerned in an election shall give any donation, directly or indirectly, to any public institution during the period from the dissolution of Parliament or the Legislative Assembly, as the case may be, to the polling day.

(x) The above provisions should, as far as possible, apply to by-elections as well. For this purpose the relevant period should be between the date of declaration of the by-election and the polling day.

Corrupt Practices

The Committee recalls the observations of the Supreme Court of India in the famous case of Ghasi Ram *vs.* Dal Singh and others (AIR 1968 SC 1911) in which a large sum of money was placed in the hands of a Minister in Haryana on the eve of elections for disbursement at his discretion, and such disbursement was made by him in his constituency during the 1967 election. The Supreme Court felt that, having regard to the state of the law as it then existed, it did not amount to a corrupt practice within the meaning of Section 123 of the Representation of the People Act, 1951. The Supreme Court nonetheless made these pertinent observations: "Election is something which must be conducted fairly. To arrange to spend money on the eve of election in different constituencies, although for general public good, is when all is said and done, an evil practice, even if it may not be a corrupt practice".

"The dividing line between an evil practice and a corrupt practice is a very thin one. It should be understood that energy to do public good should be used not on the eve of elections but much earlier and that even slight evidence might change this evil practice into a corrupt practice. Payments from discretionary grants on the eve of elections should be avoided.",

But, in Mr. Mohanlal Sukhadia's case which the Court, decided in 1971, it shifted the emphasis to motive. "Ordinarily amelioration of grievances of the public appears to be innocuous. If, however, there is evidence to indicate that any candidate at an election abuses his power and position as a Minister in the Government by utilising public revenues for conferring advantage or benefit on a particular group of people for the purpose of obtaining their votes, different considerations will arise."

The Aiyar Commission censured Bihar's Chief Minister, the late Mr. K.B. Sahay, for laying new water pipelines in his constituency on the eve of elections. "It is difficult to resist the conclusion that the order in question was passed not on its merits but with a view to influencing the voters." The electoral law, however, is inadequate to penalize such practice on the part of Ministers.

The opinion has been unanimously expressed before the Committee by the witnesses who have given evidence on this aspect that such an evil practice should be made corrupt practice within the meaning of the Act, and thus attract the penalties and disqualifications laid down in the statute. The Committee is strongly of the opinion that an amendment on these lines to the Act is imperative.

Radio and Television

In view of the importance of the audio-visual media of communication, the present Government's monopoly over Broadcasting and Television is contrary to the needs of democracy. The Chanda Committee Report has shown the way but, unfortunately, Government has refused to part with its control over radio and television. Even so, in the case of elections certain action can be taken.

First of all, recognised parties should be given time for election broadcasts and while doing so the number of votes cast for them should be taken into consideration. In England, for instance, the BBC allots time in the ratio of 2:2:1 to the Labour, Conservative and Liberal parties on this basis. We suggest that a suitable mechanism be worked out to this end.

In addition, an interesting suggestion has been made that political parties and others should be allowed to buy time on radio and television for the purpose of expressing their points of view during election campaigns. This may also be considered and expenses incurred should be suitably divided between the candidates benefiting therefrom for the purpose of election returns.

Apart from rationing time for election propaganda, the question of preventing tendentious broadcasts and the misuse of programmes and news bulletins by the ruling party also arises. In this connection, a suggestion has been made that an advisory committee should be set up to act as a watchdog and supervisory body to function from the date of notification of an election up to the date of polling. Such a committee may be composed of representatives of recognised parties and some non-party persons of integrity and good repute. Their role should be similar to that of the Press Council of India.

We are of the view that the above recommendations would be of limited value unless radio and television are placed under the control of autonomous statutory corporation. This we regard as of primary importance.

MONEY POWER IN ELECTION

The Growth of Money Power

A major malady in the operation of elections in India has been the reckless use of money. We recognise that many of the obligations imposed on candidates in most keenly contested elections cannot be fulfilled successfully without substantial expenditure. With the rise in prices since 1967 these expenses also cannot be contained within the limits fixed by law either for Lok Sabha or Assembly elections. But we have received ample proof that the current violation of the law by almost all parties is not related primarily to inflation. The steep rise in election expenses, particularly by the Congress Party which has access by reason of its power of patronage to business finance, is the result of a deliberate preference in favour of money power as a major instrument for winning elections. We do not believe, with the current violation both of the law on limits of expenditure as prescribed by the Supreme Court, and the highly unequal access to company finance or black money, that fair elections can be conducted. The blatant exercise of money power has also deeply eroded the faith of the voter in the belief that the people's will has been fairly recorded in recent elections.

'Black' or 'Unaccounted' Money

Evidence led before us by witnesses who had personal knowledge shows that the sums spent in general, by candidates in elections till 1967 did not exceed by far the limits prescribed by law. Even in the 1967 elections, the extent by which those limits were exceeded would, by current standards, be deemed to be marginal. It is believed that in 1971 election the Congress Party alone spent over three times as much as in 1967. There is no doubt that a very large amount was also spent on the Uttar Pradesh and Orissa Elections in February 1974. Since all expenditure in excess of legal limits is contrary to law, it obviously generates, in addition to corrupt practices, moral degradation of the whole electoral process. This makes the limit on election expenditure one of the central conditions of the containment of money power which has been in the last five years so shamelessly abused.

For all these purposes it is necessary to contrive effective measures to prevent the violation of the law and to curtail election expenses.

Without such reduction, the pressure on candidates to seek finance outside the law, whether from company donations or the use of unaccounted money will be irresistible; also to raise the limits on expenditure by the parties as in the recent Ordinance on election expenditure, is merely to encourage and legitimise what is wholly indefensible abuse both of the spirit and the letter of election law. We, therefore, believe that very determined measures for the audit of both party and individual expenditure are essential conditions of restoring faith and a measure of impartiality in the whole electoral process.

Election Expenses

The Supreme Court's judgment in Mr. Manwar Lal Gupta's case held that "When the political party sponsoring a candidate incurs expenditure in connection with the election, as distinguished from expenditure on general party propaganda, and the candidate knowingly takes advantage of it or participates in the programme of activity or fails to disavow the expenditure or consents to it or acquiesces in it, it would be reasonable to infer, save in special circumstances, that he impliedly authorised the political party to incur such expenditure and he cannot escape the rigour of the ceiling by saying that he has not incurred the expenditure, but his political party has done so."

The ruling has been nullified by amending the Representation of the People Act on the plea that it altered the law basically and thus affected unfairly pending election petitions. It was a spacious plea because the Court itself considered its previous judgements and found them in accord with its ruling in the Manwar Lal Gupta case.

Even in regard to the expenditure by political parties on their general party propaganda, as distinct from expenditure to promote a particular candidate's interests, the Supreme Court felt that a "ceiling is eminently desirable, coupled with fling of return of expenses and an independent machinery to investigate and take action." In sum, the accounts of political parties should be made available for scrutiny.

The problem till now has been that the legal right of a party to pour unlimited funds into its general propaganda campaign was being abused to defeat the purpose of the legal ceiling on a candidate's expenditure. In its Third Report, the Election Commission said that exclusion of party expenditure from the candidate's expenditure made the ceiling law unreal. It suggested amendment in the law to include party expenditure. In its Fourth and Fifth Reports it repeated the recommendation. It is a matter of regret that the Joint Parliamentary Committee on Amendments to Election Law did not accept this recommendation.

This means that, if a candidate gives Rs. 5 lakhs to his party, or, for that matter, to any organisation, say a Trade Union or a Chamber of Commerce with which he is connected, and all the expenses incurred on his election are met by the party or the Trade Union or the Chamber of Commerce, he is completely immune from liability under the ceiling law. That law comes into operation only if the payments are made directly by the candidate or his election agent. This position is unacceptable and calls for correction.

The Committee, therefore, makes the following recommendations:

1. All recognised political parties should be required by law to keep full and accurate accounts, including their sources of income and details of expenditure. The accounts should be audited by Chartered Accountants nominated by the Election Commission and should be open to public inspection on moderate charges. Keeping of false accounts should make the office-bearers of the party punishable of a cognizable offence.
2. In every constituency, all the amounts spent for the furtherance, directly, or indirectly, of the prospects of a candidate in an election shall be disbursed through his election agent. These should include amounts spent by the candidate's political party or any organisation or persons supporting him. All contracts whereby election expenses are incurred shall, in every case, be entered into by the candidate himself or by his election agent, and by nobody else. The provisions of Sections 60 to 63 of the (British) Representation of the People Act, 1949 should be referred to in this connection.

A provision to this effect is to be found in Section 171(H) of the Indian Penal Code. But it has been largely over-looked.

Facilities at Public Expense

We considered a proposal made to us that the larger part of the expenditure of contesting elections should be passed on to the public revenues in order to mitigate the force of money power and also to enable a man of modest means to stand for elections. While we sympathize with the purpose of this suggestion, we have gone into it and found it impracticable under conditions prevailing now in this country. We have, however, made a move in this direction by suggesting that certain facilities should be made available in every constituency at Government expense:

(a) Printed cards giving the registered number of a voter and the polling booth where he may cast his/her vote, along with the names and symbols of candidates in the order in which they would appear in the ballot papers, should be made available to all voters. These printed cards should be sent by postal delivery to the satisfaction of the candidates or their election agents.

(b) Each candidate shall be entitled to send to each voter, free of postage, one communication containing matter relating to the election not exceeding two ounces in weight.

(c) School rooms and meeting halls should be available for meetings in furtherance of the candidature of every candidate at reasonable times and at a nominal cost. Reference in this connection may be made to Section 82 of the (British) Representation of the People Act, 1949.

(d) Twelve copies of the relevant electoral roll shall be supplied to each candidate free of charge.

Ceiling on Election Expenses

The present limit of election expenses, Parliamentary and Assembly elections should be doubled. This is necessary in view of our recommendations that party expenses and all other expenses in furtherance of the prospects of a candidate be included in the return of the candidate's expenses. We feel that any further increase in the ceiling is not necessary in view of the facilities at public expenses which we have recommended above.

Deposits

Deposits required from candidates should be increased from Rs. 500 to Rs. 2000 in the case of Parliamentary elections, and from Rs.250 to Rs.1000 in elections to an Assembly or a Council. Proportionate increases should be made in the case of Scheduled Caste and Scheduled Tribe candidates. This increase in deposit is necessary in view of the facilities which we have recommended for being extended to each candidate.

Income Tax Exemptions

Any donation to a political party or for a political purpose up to Rs. 1000 per year per assessee should be eligible for exemption under the Income Tax Act.

Corporate Donations

The Committee has considered various arguments placed before it both in favour of banning donations made by Joint Stock Companies to political parties and against such a ban. We are clear that in principle a Joint Stock Company which if formed by a large number of shareholders holding different political views for the purpose of commercial and industrial activities should not be allowed to contribute collectively to a political party. Even if majority of the shareholders may be inclined to do so it would be doing violence to the feelings of those shareholders who hold different views. We are not satisfied that legalizing company donations will necessarily prevent clandestine payments being extorted from companies. We, therefore, recommend that the present ban on corporate donations should continue. Indeed, we believe that the way in which the ban at present is being evaded by large payments being made for so-called advertisements in the so-called souvenirs of political parties should be prevented by law.

ALTERNATIVE SYSTEMS OF REPRESENTATION

Distortion of Popular Will

On no subject within the terms of reference of the Committee has it heard such conflicting evidence as on the reform of the present electoral system. The Committee was, however, impressed by the near unanimity of opinion on the basic premise that the present system of election of "first past the post" does not lead to a fair reflection of the popular will in the legislatures. On this point opinion is fairly unanimous, and, indeed, the figures cited in the successive reports of the Election Commissioners prove it.

The seat-vote distortion in India has reached grave proportions. The following table relating to General Elections to the Lok Sabha shows the extent of the distortion.

Year	Congress Vote %	Congress Seats %	Congress Multiplier	Vote-seat distortion
1952	45.0	74.4	1.65	+29.4
1957	47.4	75.1	1.57	+27.7
1962	44.7	73.0	1.63	+28.3
1967	40.9	54.4	1.35	+13.5
1971	43.5	67.9	1.56	+24.4

This picture in regard to State Assembly elections is not very different.

The most striking fact is that, in the quarter century of the working of the Constitution, the ruling party at the Centre has won no more than a minority of the votes polled and yet has commanded a predominance of seats in the Lok Sabha such as has enabled it even to amend the Constitution in basic respects. The Committee would like to stress, however, that this factor has occasionally weighed in favour of other parties in certain States such as Tamil Nadu, Kerala and West Bengal.

It is relevant to point out that there is so far no indication of any progressive decline in such distortion with the passage of time. The proportion of distortion ranges normally between 24 per cent and 30 per cent. The long-term operation of this electoral system does not, therefore, hold out any prospect of this distortion being mitigated.

It is noteworthy that even in the home of this system where it has not been challenged, for generations, the inequities of this system have now led to major controversy and demand for electoral reform.

The objections to these distortions are not academic or abstract. They have led to concrete evils and have created a situation where there is danger of people losing faith in democratic institutions and the electoral process. Such a situation is generating large-scale popular alienation and apathy.

Search for a Fair System

These considerations lead to a search for a fair system of election where each vote is equal and the votes of a large number of electors are not wasted or ignored. Systems which provide for these principles are known as systems of Proportional Representation. While this Committee is not interested in any preference for any particular system, it is truly and deeply concerned with the evolution of an alternative system which at the same time would avoid the disadvantages which some of the alternative mooted frequently might entail.

The Committee has heard evidence on this point both from those who support a system of Proportional Representation and others who have expressed the fear that such a system might well lead to political fragmentation and give rise to a large number of parties on the basis of caste, religion, language or parochial interests and increase the power of the party caucus over individual members of the party. On the other hand, others have pointed out that since World War II these fears have been disproved by the stable government enjoyed by certain countries practicing such a system, notably the Federal Republic of Germany.

The Committee has considered the various alternatives to the present system such as the List System, the Single Transferable Vote, the Cumulative Vote and the Second Ballot. It has found difficulties in the way of the adoption of one or many of these systems although some of them have advantages.

Mixed Systems

The Committee would like the adoptions in this country of what might be described as a mixed system which, on the one hand combines the advantage of maintaining the nexus between the member of the legislature and his constituency and does not reduce the importance and independence of individual candidates and which on the other hand, implements the important principle that a legislature should fairly reflect the various trends of public opinion.

The Committee is led by these considerations to recommend the study of certain "mixed" systems. One of these is the West German system which provides for one-half of the members of the Bundestag by single member constituencies on the model prevailing today in India and the election of the remaining half of the members of the

Bundestag from lists of candidates submitted in advance of polling by the various recognised parties in such a way that the Bundestag as a whole fairly represents the voting strength of the various parties and groups.

An objection to this system, which would otherwise be eminently desirable, is that its adoption would lead in a country of India's proportions and population either to increasing the size of the Parliamentary constituency which already is large, or increasing the size of the Lok Sabha which would again not be desirable.

It has been suggested to us that, if two-thirds of the seats in a legislature were elected by single member constituencies and one-third from Lists, the size of the constituencies would have to be increased by not more than 50 per cent.

The Committee has endeavoured to consider some other variants of this system. An alternative system to the German which preserves its mixed character and also deserves study is the following formula:

1. The country would remain divided into single member constituencies, both for Parliament and the State Assemblies, as at present. As at present, candidates of political parties and independent candidates can stand for election. The polling would also take place as at present.
2. Any candidate with more than 50 per cent of the valid votes polled in the constituency would be declared elected.
3. Where no candidate gets an absolute majority of the votes polled, the seat allotted to that constituency will not be filled as a result of this direct election.
4. Before the day of polling, each recognised party will be asked to submit a list of its candidates in order of preferences, state-wise for the Lok Sabha and district-wise for the State Assembly, which would be published in advance of polling.
5. All seats which are not filled by direct election will, after polling, be distributed, state-wise in the case of Parliament, district-wise in the case of a State Assembly, among the various parties in such manner that the total number of seats they get in the Lok Sabha or in the State Assembly, as the case may be, are in proportion to the valid votes polled

> by each of them. This would be done by declaring elected as many members from the top of each party list as will result, as in West Germany, in the total strength of each party, including directly elected members as well as those elected from the lists, being roughly proportionate to the vote polled by each party, including those polled by its successful candidates.

The Committee is not unaware that the system, too, has its disadvantages. One is that, where the pattern of polling is somewhat one-sided, it may not be possible to correct the distortions and the waste of votes that take place. Where, for instance, in a particular State or District, as the case may be about all the candidates or a large number of candidates of a particular party get elected by narrow majorities. There would be little relief for the other parties in this proposed system. This point is proved by a perusal of the figures of voting in Karnataka, Andhra Pradesh and Assam in the Lok Sabha elections in 1971.

Another defect of this system would be that it does not make the prospect of the independent candidate, difficult as it is in the present system, any the easier. On the contrary, for all its merits, this formula would impose on an independent a greater handicap than he is being called upon to bear. The Committee has before it two alternative suggestions for mitigating this hardship.

One is a proposal that independent candidates may also figure on a separate list. This is generally not feasible, because independent candidates have nothing in common and, indeed, many of them may object to being included in a list with other independent candidates whose points of view may be diametrically opposed to their own. At the same time, it is possible that there are worthwhile people who may not be interested in joining any particular political party but who may conceivably group together in an organisation which stresses integrity, character and public record and who, at the same time, would not differ basically amongst themselves. Such organisations may take the form of Voters' Councils which might feel into putting up candidates of integrity. For such a grouping two tests should be required for securing the facility of a list, *viz.*, a certain amount of homogeneity and common values on the one hand and an organisation which sponsors such candidates on the other.

Another alternative suggestion is that the formula should provide that an independent candidate would be declared elected if he secures the highest number of votes as at present despite the fact that he does not poll a majority of the votes polled as is required for a party candidate.

Discussion for Consensus

The Committee is of the view that these various suggestions outlined above would require to be spelt out carefully and in detail, bearing in mind all their implications. The Committee feels that there is considerable merit in them, but is of the view that a matter of this nature should, in the national interest, be the subject of widespread public discussion out of which a consensus may emerge. It is, therefore, placing more than one formula before the public.

VOTING RIGHTS AND ELECTION PROCEDURE

Age of Voting

According to the present law, a person gets the right to vote when he attains the age of 21. There is a strong current of opinion in the country that the voting right should be available on attainment of majority at the age of 18. The Committee is entirely in favour of this change. While there may have been some justification when the Constitution was promulgated for confining the franchise to persons of the age of 21 and above, we do not think that this provision is justified any more. In many families the younger people are better educated and better informed than their elders. In rural areas, while the older people are often illiterate, the younger generation is able to read and write. Moreover in recent years, youth all over the country are becoming the vanguard and catalyst of social transformation. It is desirable that their idealism should be adequately reflected in the legislatures. We are, for these reasons, of the view that the franchise should be extended to all persons attaining the age of 18.

Electoral Rolls

According to the Registration of Election Rules, 1960, Voters' lists are revised once a year. The result is that those persons who attain the voting age after the revision are deprived of their franchise if an election takes place before the next yearly revision.

We propose that any person who attains the voting age should have the right to apply for being registered as a voter as soon as he attains the age. If such application is accompanied by evidence of age, he should be registered as a voter. This should be in addition to the suggestion of the Joint Committee on Amendment to Election Law that there should be as many as four qualifying dates in relation to the preparation of revision of the electoral roll, namely, the first day of January, April, July and October.

Countering Coercion

Evidence was given before the Committee to the effect that the evil of capturing booths and the exercise of coercion in other ways has increased in recent years. In order to curb such malpractices, we suggest that in every constituency the Election Officer should designate a Magistrate who would have the responsibility of dealing with cases of coercion before and during the time of polling. The Magistrate should have the assistance of an adequate police force. He should attend to any complaint of coercion or of capturing of a polling booth that reaches him and should deal with the situation as well as he can and make a report immediately to the Election Officer. Copies of his report should be given at the same time to the agents of all the contesting candidates. This procedure may check the exercise of coercion during elections and would also provide reliable evidence which would be useful in an election petition.

Signature on Counterfoil

In 1972, an innovation was made with regard to voters' signatures. Each ballot paper issued had a counterfoil which is required to be signed or "thumb-impressed" by the voter. This procedure is supposed to help to prevent impersonation. This is an idle supposition. Not a single case of impersonation is known to have been detected because of this device. The only outcome of this innovation has been that the elector's confidence in the inviolable secrecy of his franchise is shaken, so that, in many places, candidates and parties have exploited this innovation to intimidate ignorant voters into voting in their favour. This practice must be abandoned.

Polling Boxes

In order to remove suspicions about irregular practices in handling of polling boxes the Committee suggests that polling boxes should be serially numbered so that, whenever it becomes necessary to use more than one polling box, there should be no room for any mischief.

Transport of Boxes

It is necessary to provide that the Polling Agents of the candidates should have the right to accompany the officers transporting the ballot boxes from the polling booth to the counting centre.

Prompt Counting of Votes

A great deal of suspicion in regard to the fairness of the counting of votes arises from the fact that a considerable interval of time elapses in many cases between the polling and counting of votes. In most democratic countries votes are counted immediately after polling concludes; we see no reason why in India we should not provide for the counting of votes as soon as all the polling boxes from different polling booths are collected at the counting centre. This will no doubt necessitate the holding of election on the same day all over the State, and, preferably all over the country, as it is desirable that the result of elections in one area should not influence the voting in others.

Counting Votes Booth-wise

Before 1971, counting of votes used to take place polling booth-wise. In 1971, this procedure was changed, and instead, ballot papers of all booths in a single assembly constituency were mixed up and then counted.

In its report on the Fifth General Election, the Election Commission has stated:

> The revised procedure, which was made public through the press and radio before the poll was taken in the Fifth General Election to the Lok Sabha in 1971, was generally welcomed by the political parties and the people. (Page 228)

This is contrary to the facts. This report incidentally admits that there was no consultation held on this question, and that parties got the information from the radio or the press.

Before the 1967 elections, some people did suggest to the Election Commission that the polling station-wise procedure of counting be abandoned and ballots be mixed up. The Election Commission rejected the suggestion and in its report on the Fourth General Election had very cogently argued:

> The method of counting now in vogue has certainly the merit of being systematic which would be lost if, as suggested, the ballot papers found in a large number of ballot boxes were first mixed up, put in bundle of 1000 or 2000 and then counted. Even on this pattern, it should not be difficult for the political parties, if they were so minded, to find out broadly how a particular area voted.

The argument that the new system of mixing votes presents intimidation and harassment is not altogether convincing. Most of the intimidation that takes place is pre-election and not post-election. Besides, as the Election Commission has rightly stated, for persons and parties so minded it is not difficult to find how a particular area voted.

Mixing up of ballot papers of various polling booths has given rise to grave misgivings. For one thing it might be difficult to identify offences at a particular booth. For instance, there might be some ballot papers found in bunches or without the signature of the officer concerned. If ballot papers are mixed up, a correlation between them may otherwise not be established. Similarly any complaint at a particular booth may loose its validity if the counting is not done separately. If, on the other hand, counting is done separately and a polling booth overpowered through violence, correlation may be established between the polling of the votes and offence committed. Similarly, counting agents can know by counting at every booth.

The Committee, therefore, comes to the conclusion that the original system of counting votes booth-wise should be established.

Voters, Voluntary Action

It is obvious that free and fair elections cannot be secured merely by rules and regulations. It is necessary that voluntary action of the voters should be organised for this purpose. During the Parliamentary elections of 1971, non-party Voters' Councils were formed in a few constituencies with the two-fold purpose of promoting voters' education and securing free and fair elections. A similar body called Voters Forum was formed in Madras. Although the experiment was tried on a limited scale, it was appreciated by the public and the press.

The Committee recommends that such Voters' Councils should be organised in as many constituencies as possible in both Parliamentary and State election. The Voters' Councils should consist of persons who cherish democratic values but do not owe allegiance to any political party. There should be one Voters' Council in a constituency and also smaller Councils for mohallas and villages in that constituency. The educative function of the Councils should be carried out be explaining to voters the main issue involved in the election and the stand of the contesting parties and candidates in regard to those issues. Unrealistic and deceptive promises given to the electorate should be exposed and the people should be encouraged to cast their votes rationally without being swayed by emotional appeals or narrow sectarian loyalties. As a part of this educative programme, Voters' Councils may arrange question and answer meetings to be addressed by candidates, preferably joint meetings. The other and equally important function of Voters' Councils would be to act as impartial observers in each constituency so as to ensure, as far as possible, that election are not contested on the basis of communal or caste appeals and are free from bribery, coercion and other corrupt practices. The Council should keep a contemporaneous record of any corrupt or undemocratic practice which comes to its notice. Particular vigilance should be exercised on the eve of polling when, according to reports bribery of voters takes place in some constituencies. Voters' Councils should also secure passes from Returning Officer enabling its members to visit particular polling booths at the time of voting and to report on whether the polling was peaceful and free from coercion. Besides this work, Voters' Council would obtain authentic copies of electoral rolls, check improper addition and omissions therein, and also help aggrieved citizens in getting their names included in the rolls.

Election Council

In addition to Voluntary Voters' Councils consisting of persons who do not owe allegiance to any political party, the Committee recommends the formation of an Election Council representing all the recognised national political parties on the lines recommended by the Joint Parliamentary Committee on Amendments to Election Law in Part II, Para 25 of its Report. The Committee observed: "There are several matters in the conduct of elections which can be better regulated by conventions to be evolved by political parties instead of by written law. The Committee feels that if a Political Council comprising the leaders of all recognised parties is set up it will help create the conventions. Two suggestions were made regarding the pattern of the working of the Political Council. One suggestion was that it should be lines on the Press Council; the other was that it should be on the lines of the National Integration Council. The Committee feels that if the idea of setting up a Political Council is accepted it should be difficult to work out the exact form, composition and the scope of function of the Council".

With these observations the Committee concurs. No matter how comprehensive the scope of the law regulating the conduct of elections, there will be matters which convention alone can regulate, and breaches of the spirit of the law without any violation of the letter of the law can be avoided or minimized only by mutual consultation in a recognised forum. We prefer to call it an Election Council to emphasise the nature of its functions which in its view should primarily be to ensure that the properties that ought to govern the conduct of elections are observed by all and to serve as a forum where grievances can be aired in an atmosphere free from recrimination. The Committee would prefer that proceedings of the Committee should be held in camera and that the Election Commission of India should be represented on it.

DISPOSAL OF ELECTION DISPUTES

Finality of Acceptance and Rejection of Nominations

According to the present law, if any nomination paper is wrongly rejected, the whole election is liable to be set aside by the Court which has jurisdiction to hear and dispose of election petitions. It was strongly urged before us that it is necessary to devise some procedure which would enable disputes with regard to wrongful acceptance or rejection of nomination papers to be finally disposed of before the polling takes place. We suggest that the District Court in whose jurisdiction the constituency is situated is the proper forum for the papers of objections to the acceptance or rejection of nomination.

In order to expedite the disposal of such objections the objectors should announce, at the time of scrutiny of nomination papers, that he is going to file his objection in the District Court the next day and the parties should appear in the District Court the next day for having the objection heard and disposed of the same day or, at least, the day thereafter.

The decision of the District Court in such cases should be final and not be open to question in an election petition. In order to facilitate this procedure, the date for the withdrawal of candidatures should be extended by one day.

Disposal of Election Petitions

The present arrangements for the disposal of election petitions involve inordinate delays. The old system of trial by Election Tribunals was replaced in 1996 by provisions making the High Court at the first instance to try election petitions. The object, doubtless, was to ensure that the status of the adjudicating authority was high enough to prevent suspicions of pressure and to create faith in its independence and impartiality. In practice, however, the number of election petitions, following a keenly contested general election to the Lok Sabha or State Assembly, is so large as to cause a congestion of election cases on the files of the High Courts. The provision in Section 86(7) of the Representation of the People Act for expeditious trial of every election petition and its conclusions within six months from the date of its presentation to the High Court not been complied with.

In order to expedite the disposal of election petitions, we make the following two recommendations:

1. After a general election, all the election petitions are filed in the State High Court at about the same time. They should be made ready for hearing as early as possible and, when they are ready, the Chief Justice of the High Court should make available one Judge of his Court for the hearing of each election petition. For this purpose retired judges of

the High Court should be appointed ad hoc in sufficient numbers so that all the election petitions can be simultaneously heard. This will result in a quicker disposal of election petition by the High Courts.

2. There should be no appeal as of right to the Supreme Court from the High Court's order on an election petition. A party wanting to appeal to the Supreme Court may apply for special leave under Article 136 of the Constitution.

ANNEXURE - II

Provisions of the Alternative Bill

(1) A Bill to Amend the Representation of the People Act, 1951*

(New Section 34)

Notwithstanding anything contained in this Act, every recognised political party shall nominate women candidates on behalf of that party, as nearly as may be, in at least one-third of the constituencies in which the party is contesting, in every general election.

Provided that for an election to Lok Sabha, the State shall be the unit for such nomination, and for an election to Legislative Assembly, a cluster of three contiguous Lok Sabha constituencies shall be the unit as nearly as may be.

Provided that for Lok Sabha election, in case of States with less than 3 seats, a cluster of States to be defined by the Election Commission shall be treated as a unit.

(For removal of any doubt, these provisions will apply in all States and Union territories for recognised national parties, and in the respective State or States for recognised State parties).

Provided that in respect of seats reserved for scheduled castes and scheduled tribes, the State shall be the unit for nomination of women for all general elections; and one-third of all candidates nominated for the reserved constituencies shall be women.

Provided that in case of by-elections, the party shall nominate as nearly as may be one-third women candidates for the Lok Sabha and Legislative Assembly, with the nation as unit for Lok Sabha and State as unit for Legislative Assembly. Provided further that, in respect of State parties, this provision will apply for State as unit for Lok Sabha.

---

* Women's Representation in Legislatures: An Alternative to the Government Bill for Women's Reservation, Forum for Democratic Reforms & others, New Delhi.

In the event of a recognised political party not complying with these provisions, for the shortfall of every woman candidate while nominating candidates for elective officer, two male candidates of the party in the State or cluster of 3 Lok Sabha constituencies, as the case may be, as decided by the party shall be deemed to be Independent candidates for all purposes including allotment of symbols.

The Election Commission or the officials authorised by it at the State or Union Territory level shall determine the compliance or otherwise of these provisions after the completion of withdrawal of nominations.

Provided that the candidates so disqualified shall be from reserved vacancies in case the shortfall is in reserved vacancies.

(2) A Bill to Amend Articles 80 and 171 of the Constitution of India

In the Council of States, as nearly as maybe, one-third of all seats, whether elected or nominated, shall be reserved for women.

In the States in which Legislative Councils exist, as nearly as maybe, one-third of all seats filled from each category, whether elected or nominated, shall be reserved for women:

Provided that in case of members elected by members of local authorities, graduates, and teachers, the seats reserved for women shall be rotated, and decided by draw of lots.

Glossary of Main Electoral Systems*

First-Past-the-Post (FPTP)

The system currently used for electing members to the British House of Commons is a plurality system with single member constituencies. Winning candidates simply gain more votes than any other candidate on a single count. This need not be an absolute majority of the votes cast in a constituency.

The Alternative Vote (AV)

The Alternative Vote, which like FPTP is based upon single member constituencies, is a majoritarian system. Winning candidates secure the support of over half the voters in a constituency. The vote is exercised by recording preferences against the candidates on the ballot paper. If no candidate receives more than half of the votes cast on the first count of first preference votes, the candidate who received the fewest first preference votes is eliminated and his/her second preferences are distributed between the other candidates. This process continues until one candidate has achieved an overall majority.

Supplementary Vote (SV)

The Supplementary Vote is similar in method and purpose to the Alternative Vote, the key difference being that, under SV, voters are limited to indicating a first and second preference. Where candidates receive more than a half of first preference votes cast on the first count they are deemed elected. If not, all but the top two candidates are eliminated and their second preferences re-distributed. The candidate with the greatest share of the resultant vote is elected-in the majority of cases, but not necessarily, this will be with more than half of the votes cast.

---

* *Source*: The Report of the Independent Commission on the Voting System, Home Department, UK, October 1998.

Second Ballot

As with the Alternative Vote the main objective of the Second Ballot system is to increase the chances of a candidate being elected on an absolute majority of the vote. Voting takes place on two separate days. If any one candidate fails to achieve an absolute majority after the first ballot, a second ballot takes place. Where more than two candidates are allowed to progress to the second ballot a majority result cannot necessarily be guaranteed but, typically, candidates not performing well in the first ballot will withdraw and throw their support behind a candidate with a better chance on winning.

List Systems

The rationale of list systems is to translate directly a party's share of the vote into an equivalent proportion of seats in Parliament. The precise proportionality of such systems will, however, be influenced by such factors as whether the country is treated as a single constituency for the purpose of voting and the allocation of seats (some systems involve the use of smaller, regional or sub-regional units or two-tier districting), the use of differing electoral formulae for the allocation of seats and the use of thresholds.

Single Transferable Vote (STV)

The Single Transferable Vote system is essentially preferential voting (as in AV) in multi-member constituencies. Voters are to able to rank as many candidates, both within parties and across different parties, as they wish in order of preference. Any of those candidates who reach a certain quota are deemed to have been elected. The surplus votes of candidates elected on the first count and the votes of those with fewest votes after subsequent counts are distributed on the basis of preference to the remaining candidates until sufficient candidates reach the quota and are, as a result, elected.

Mixed System: The Additional Member System (including AV or SV Top-up) and Parallel Systems (AMS)

The title of mixed system describes any system which combines a list system element together with a plurality or majoritarian single constituency system. Under an additional member system, voters cast two distinct votes the first for a constituency M.P. and the second a party vote. The allocation of additional members then serves to correct the disproportionality which arises from the election of single constituency MPs. Under a parallel system, the two votes are independent of each other and the additional members exist to mitigate rather than correct any disproportionality in the return of constituency members.

CONTRIBUTORS

Justice David Annoussamy is a former Judge of Madras High Court, former President of State Commission for Consumer Disputes Redressal, Pondicherry, and currently Chairman of Comparative Law Society, Pondicherry. He has written profusely and extensively on issues of public participation.

Raka Arya is presently working as a lecturer at the National Law School University, Bhopal. She has obtained her M.A./M.Phil and Ph.D. Degree from Jawaharlal Nehru University, New Delhi. She is Bachelor of Laws (LLB) from Aligarh Muslim University, Aligarh. Dr. Arya has taught Political Science for three years (1999-2002) in Vasanta College for Women, Rajghat Fort, Varanasi.

M.P. Dube had his education at the University of Allahabad. Presently he is Professor and Head, Department of Political Science and Public Administration, Kumaon University, Nainital. His field of specialisation has been Indian Political System. He has contributed numerous articles and research papers to journals and edited volumes. Prof. Dube has authored *Role of Supreme Court in Indian Constitution, Dharmanirpekshta Aur Bhartiya Loktantra, Secularism in India.* Besides he has edited *Jawaharlal Nehru: Legacy and Legend, Social Justice and Women in India, Perspectives on Human Rights, Democratic Decentralisation in India.*

Achal Kumar Gaur is Reader in the Department of Economics, Faculty of Social Sciences, Banaras Hindu University, Varanasi. He has been serving this University since 1983. Dr. Gaur did his post-graduation in Economics from Gorakhpur University in 1979. Banaras Hindu University, Varanasi, awarded him the Doctor of Philosophy in Economics in 1984 for his thesis entitled "Federal Transfers with Special Reference to Uttar Pradesh Since Planning in India". Dr. Gaur has written extensively on various aspects of Indian Federal Finance, which have been published in academic journals in India. He has also presented papers in National and International seminars on Fiscal Federalism. Dr. Gaur has authored two books: *Centre-State Financial Relations and Finance Commissions* (1985) and *Federal Finance in India* (1988).

Rajen Harshe is Professor of International Relations at the Department of Political Science, University of Hyderabad, Hyderabad. He is Ph.D. from Jawaharlal Nehru University. He did a part of his doctoral work at the Fondation Nationale Des Sciences Politiques of Paris on a French Government scholarship during 1973-75. He was also a Fulbright Scholar at the Columbia University, New York, during 1985-86. His pioneering work entitled *Twentieth Century Imperialism: Shifting Contours and Changing Conceptions* (New Delhi, Sage, 1997) has already won him international recognition as a scholar on imperialism. He has published extensively in prestigious academic journals and anthologies on the areas related to theories, concepts and processes in international relations as well as political science.

Randhir B. Jain is presently a National Fellow of the Indian Council of Social Science Research at the Indian Institute of Public Administration. He has been a former Dean of the Faculty of Social Sciences; Professor and Head of the Department of Political Science, University of Delhi, Delhi; Professor and Head of the Department of Public Administration at Punjabi University, Patiala and also Professor of Public Administration at the Indian Institute of Public Administration, New Delhi. He has held appointments as Visiting Professor at various Universities in Canada, USA and Germany and has lectured as Guest Professor at a number of Universities and Research Institutions in all the continents. A former editor of *Indian Journal of Political Science*, and a member of the Editorial Board of *The Indian Journal of Public Administration*, he is currently on the editorial board of *Environment and Security* (Canada), a member of Board of Directors of the Centre for Business and Public Sector Ethics at Cambridge, and a Member of the Executive Committee of the Delhi Regional Branch of the Indian Institute of Public Administration. He has authored/edited 25 books and published more than 150 Articles in referred Journals and compendiums all over the world. His latest book is on *Public Administration in India: 21st Century Challenges for Good Governance* (2001 and 2002). He has been a member at large of the Executive Committee of the International Studies Association, a UN expert on Economic Sanctions, and is currently the Chair of the International Political Science Association's Research Committee on Public Bureaucracies in Developing Societies. He was also a member of the Advisory Panel on Electoral Reforms and

Standards in Public Life of the Government of India's National Commission to Review the Working of the Constitution and is on the panel of consultants to various foundations and organisations in India and abroad. He has written extensively on Electoral and Party Reforms.

Madhu Kishwar is a Senior Fellow at the Centre for the Study of Developing Societies, Delhi. She is the founder of Manushi Forum for Democratic Reforms—a platform for informed, research-based interventions for legal, political and policy reforms and editor of *Manushi*, a journal focusing on movements for social justice, economic and political reforms with a special focus on women's concerns and rights.

Sanjay Lodha is an Associate Professor in Mohanlal Sukhadia University, Udaipur, Rajasthan. He has been trained as a Political Scientist with specialisation in International Politics. He obtained his Post-Graduate Degree from the School of International Studies, Jawaharlal Nehru University, New Delhi. Dr. Lodha has completed major Research Projects from various Institutions such as "Indo-China and the Sino-Soviet Confrontation", U.G.C.; "Containment of China", ASRC, Hyderabad; "National election study", CSDS-TV today; "Rajasthan state election study", CSDS-Doordarshan and he is currently working on a Project entitled "Grass-root anti-corruption study, IDS Sussex, UK." Dr. Lodha has published 13 Papers, 3 Books and 4 Book Reviews and has attended numerous seminars, nationally as well as internationally. Of late, Dr. Lodha has been focusing on issues concerning grass-roots corruption.

Bhaskar Majumder did his M.Phil and Ph.D. in Economics from the University of Calcutta. He has published extensively in various referred national and international journals and also articles in popular magazines. Presently, he is working as a Reader in Economics G.B. Pant Social Science Institute, Allahabad.

Clem McCartney is an independent research consultant on conflict and community issues. He has been involved in conflict resolution and political education in Northern Ireland and also in other parts of the world, most recently in South and South-East Asia and in the Caucasus region. His doctoral thesis was entitled "The Politics of Intransigence" and studied the way in which intransigent attitudes are formed and maintained and transmitted in a conflicted society. He has also written a study on the impact of flags and other symbols,

Clashing Symbols and edited *Finding the Balance*, a study of the Northern Ireland peace process with chapters written by politicians directly involved. Most recently *A Comparative Review of Public Policies Towards Improving Inter-community Relations* has been published by INCORE. He is a programme associate of the London based NGO, Conciliation Resources and the Berlin-based Berghof Research Centre for Constructive Conflict Management and Conflict Transformation.

Jayaprakash Narayan is a physician by training, a public servant by choice, and a democrat by conviction. Having served the Indian Administrative Service for 17 years, he resigned in 1980 in the aftermath of Emergency and the failure of the Janata Experiment because of his conviction that India not merely needs a periodic change of players, but a fundamental change in the rules of the game. In order to translate his vision into practical reality, he started working with like-minded colleagues for the formation of Lok Satta and is currently its Campaign Coordinator. During his numerous years of public service, he undertook several projects, initiatives and reforms for public welfare.

Rachana Narayan is presently serving as a Project Fellow at Malaviya Centre for Peace Research, Banaras Hindu University. She is working on a Project entitled "Refugees in South Asia: Conflict Resolution Perspectives" funded by the University Grants Commission. She has done her Bachelor & Masters in Political Science from Banaras Hindu University, Varanasi in 1992 and 1994 respectively. She completed her Doctorate in the year 2000. The topic of her Thesis is "Human Rights Regime and Child-Labour: A Case Study of Varanasi District". She has done a certificate course on "Transforming Civil Conflict" from The European Network University, Amsterdam, The Netherlands.

D.K. Sankaran is an IAS Officer of 1970 batch from the Maharashtra Cadre. Dr. Sankaran has to his credit an M.A. in Economics from the Loyola College, Madras and Ph.D. in Economics and Economic Policy Development from the University of Hawaii (East West Centre), Honolulu, USA. During his long service career of over 32 years, he has held many key positions in the Government of India and the Government of Maharashtra, which include Municipal Commissioner, Thane Municipal Corporation, Divisional

Commissioner, Konkan Division, Chief Electoral Officer and Principal Secretary (Revenue) to the Government of Maharashtra. He is on the Board of NPCIL since 26.7.2002.

D. L. Sheth is Senior Fellow and former Director of the Centre for the Study of Developing Societies, Delhi. He was appointed Member (Social Scientist) to the National Commission for Backward Classes (1993-96). He is associated with Human Rights Movement and served as President of Delhi chapter of People's Union for Civil Liberties (PUCL) (1991-93). Sheth has edited *Citizens and Parties* (1995); with Ashis Nandy, *Multiverse of Democracy* (1996) and with Gurpreet Mahajan, *Minorities Identities and the Nation State* (1998). He is editor of the journal *Alternatives*: Social Transformation and Humane Governance and a founder member of Lokayan: Dialogues of the People. A political sociologist, he has made major contributions to the study of comparative politics, the politics of social issues and grassroots movements.

Sandeep Shastri is presently working as Dean-Research and Social Sciences at the International Academy for Creative Teaching, Bangalore. He is on leave from the Department of Political Science, Bangalore University where he has been teaching since 1985. He completed his M.A. in 1982, M.Phil. in 1984 and Ph.D. in 1993. His areas of research specialisation are Federalism, Electoral and Legislative Studies. He has to his credit 4 Books, 3 Monographs, 15 articles in Edited Books and 50 articles in various National and International Research Journals, besides popular writings. The academic distinctions conferred on Dr. Shastri include Coordinator (Karnataka), National Election Study '96, National Election Study '98, National Election Study '99 and Visiting Fellow to Nigeria from August to November 2001. Dr. Shastri held distinguished positions in various centres of higher learning in USA, UK, Canada, Austria, Japan, and Nigeria and participated in several international and national conferences and seminars in several countries. He has written extensively on electoral reforms.

Priyankar Upadhyaya holds a Ph.D. and Masters Degree from Jawaharlal Nehru University in International Studies and has done post-doctoral research at London University and Uppsala University, Sweden. He has been on the faculty of Banaras Hindu University for the past 23 years. After a long teaching stint at the Department of

Political Science, in March 1997, Dr. Upadhyaya was elevated as the Coordinator of the newly created Malaviya Centre for Peace Research (MCPR) established as an independent and interdisciplinary centre within the Faculty of Social Sciences. The MCPR has over time assumed international reputation for being a hub of intellectual activities on themes relating to a range of peace and conflict issues. Dr. Upadhyaya has brought scholars and activists from across the globe to mobilize community responsibility *viz.* inter-state and intra-state violence. These endeavours include a series of successful town meetings participated by a number of Indian and Pakistani opinion makers and renowned conflict resolution experts from Europe and North America. In recognition of his work, Dr. Upadhyaya has been selected for various national and international awards. Starting with UGC Career Award in 1987 to the prestigious Guest Scholar Award of the Woodrow Wilson Centre at Washington DC, Dr. Upadhyaya has been recognised as Fellow/Visiting Professor at various Universities in Europe and North America.

Yogendra Yadav casts a wide net in his overview of politics in India since independence, paying particular attention to the "Indian model" of democracy and its successes and failures. Yogendra Yadav is a fellow at the Centre for the Study of Developing Societies and he is a Director of the Institute of Comparative Democracy in New Delhi. He holds M.Phil degree in Political Science from Punjab University, Chandigarh (1985) and Masters from Jawaharlal Nehru University, New Delhi (1983). He performs as Election Analyst and Anchor in various TV channels and News channels. He writes on political theory, Indian politics, and has directed the election-related surveys carried out by CSDS.

Index

Abstentions, 193-94
Acceptance and rejection of nominations, 275-76
Accountability, 74, 158
Advani, L.K., 34
Aggregate volatility between Lok Sabha elections 1977-1998, 130
Aiyar Commission, 259
Alliances, 200
All India Muslim League, 183
Alternative Systems of Representation, 265-70
Andhra Pradesh, verification of voter list in, 22-23
Announssany, David, 192
Anti-Colonial Nationalism, 154
Anti- Defection Law, 7, 78
Anti- Sikh Riots, 156
Antulay, A. R., 88
Approval voting system, 83
Arbitrariness, 48
Arya, Raka, 176
Assassination, strategies of, 160
Assistant Electoral Registration Officer (AERO), 12
Association of African Election Authorities, 231
Association of Asian Election Authorities, 232
Australian Electoral Commission, 232
Aya Ram and Gaya Ram, phenomenon of, 78
 syndrome of, 183
Ayyar, Alladi Krishnaswami, 77

Babri Masjid, demolition of, 129, 156
Bahujan Samaj Party, 78
Ban on Defection, 190-91
Bangladesh, 59
Bangladeshi voters, 41
Basic development problems, 158
Better Representation of the People, Reforms for, 192-202
Bhambhari, C.P., 34
Bharatiya Janata Party (BJP), 118, 155, 156
 rathyatra of, 129
BJP- Janata Dal (U) alliance, 72
Bill to Amend the Representation of the People Act, 278-79
Bi-polar alliance system, 71-72
Binary voting system, 70
Black Money in politics, 87, 229
Black or unaccounted money, 261-62
Bofors affairs, 87-88
Booth capturing, 18, 74-75, 80, 95, 178-82
British Raj, 163
Business donations, 91-92
By-elections, 12, 256-57

California voters foundation, 232
Candidates election Expenses—Ceiling and Regulations, 5-6, 92-93
Candidates Instability, multiplicity of, 184-85
Caste-based communalism, 157
Caste card, 7
Caste hatred, 181-82
Casteism, 176
Catholic Emancipation Act, 1829, 180, 265
Ceiling on Electoral expenses, 50-56, 79-80
Challan, 15
Challenges, 8, 32, 50, 114, 158
Chandrashekhar government, 78, 96
Charan Singh, 122
Check on Corrupt Electoral Practices, 191-92
Chief Election Commission, 255, 256
 campaign instructions, 57-58
Child labour, 158
Child marriages, 214
Christianity, 153-54
Clinton's Electoral efforts, 188
Coalition Government, weakness of, 3
Code of Conduct for candidates, 5, 57-58, 85-86, 117
Columbia, 161

Communal allegiances, 160
Communal riots in Mumbai, 1993, 156
Communal roll in India, 162-64
Communalism, 153-54, 157-58, 176
Communist Party of India (CPI), 155, 157
Company donations, 88-90
Comprehensive electoral reforms, implementation of, 64
Conduct of Electoral Rules, 50, 115
Confederation of Indian Industry (CII), 119
Congress Working Committee 1988, adopted resolutions, 81
Consociational democracy, 85, 162
Consumerism, 49
Corporate donations, 265
Corrupt practices, 259-60
Corruption, 3, 65, 74, 79, 176, 204
  sources of, 118-19
Counter political mobilization, 57-59
Counting votes book-wise, 272-73
Criminalisation, 11, 74, 176,
  of politics, 65, 113, 228
Cyprus, 165

Decentralisation of politics, 114
Declining representation of women in State legislatures, 1952-1999, 215-16
Delimitation Commission, 46
Delimitation of constituencies, 46, 95
Democracy, 43-44, 74, 81
  formal institutions of, 30
  standard descriptions of, 203-204
Democratic revolution, 32
Democratisation, 32, 41, 56
Dinesh Goswami Committee, 38, 48, 53, 56, 64, 65, 69, 82, 96-97, 117, 178-80, 182, 184
Disenfranchise voters, 17
Distorted verdicts, 11-28
Djoundurm, S.S., 128
Donations, 105-06, 208-10
Droop Quota, 76
Dube, M.P., 74
Dummy candidates, 46, 124
85 Constitutional Amendment Bill, 218

Ecclesiastical Institutions, 153
Elections, state funding of, 84, 100-101, 119-25
Election advertising, 6-7
Election campaign, 52, 57-58
Election Commission, 1, 12, 13-18, 22, 25, 27, 37-45, 64-65, 113-15, 120-25, 136-37, 149-50, 178-82, 254-80
  addition power, 58-59
  credibility of, 84
  offences recommended by, 58-59
  recommendations, 46-48
  reforms proposed by, 93-94
Election Council, 274-75
Election disputes, disposal of, 275-77
Election expenditure, 5-6, 26-28, 115-17
Election expenses, 262-63
  raising ceilings of, 99-100
Election finance reforms—between a ceiling and a floor, 113-26
  themes of, 115-26
  limits on contributions, 117-19
  monitoring election finance, 125-26
Election funds, 53-54, 89-90
  system of, 105-106
Election of the Leader, 195-96
Election petition, disposal of, 276-77
Election process, problems of, 178-79
Election rules, 256
Electoral campaigning, 26, 50-52, 57-58, 87
Electoral democracy, 163-64
Electoral irregularities, 26
Electoral reforms, 147-50, 188-90
  beyond middle class fantasies, 29-60
  challenges of, 32
  general measures of, 228-30
  issues of, 114-15
  legeslative package for, 56
  moralist perspectives on, 31-32, 74-82
  political consequences of, 32
  principal instrument of, 61-62
  proposals for, 49
Electoral Reform International Services (ERIS), 1, 231
Electoral Registration Officer (ERO) 12, 15-19
Electoral roll, 12-18, 179-80
  computerisation of, 43
Electoral symbols, 201-202
Electoral system, 147-49, 152-58, 177-80
  distortions of, 77-80
  non-participation in, 150
  plurality and majority methods, 82-85
  political consequences of, 173-74
  types of, 75
Electoral information resources, 231-35

Electronic Voting Machines (EVM), 6 27, 28, 81, 85
Encouraging political engagement 207-10
Enhancing minority participation , 161-62
Enhancing women's participation, necessary measures for, 226-27
Enhancing women's representation in legislatures, 212-30
Esman, Milton J., 160, 165
Establishing and electoral trust, 104-05
Ethnic conflict management, electoral strategies of, 159-73
Ethnic minorities, 160
European democracies, 162

Facilities at public expense, 264-65
Fair price shops, 51
Family planning, 46-47
Fate of Secular Nationalism, 152-58
Female literacy, 214
First-past-the post (FPTP) system, 33, 34, 45, 64, 65, 67, 68, 69-70, 71, 159, 164, 171
Foreign Contribution (Regulation) Act, 92, 109
Forms for different purposes, 14
Free and fair polling, 59-60, 160-62
Funds for political activities, 52-53
Funds-raising for campaign, 87

Gadgil Committee on Electoral Reforms, 104
Gaur, Achal Kumar, 128
Gender discrimination, 217, 225-226
Gender equality, 158
Gill, M.S., 99, 182
Gokhale, M.R., 122
Good Governance, 140
Government controlled election fund, proposal for the creations of, 108
Government Bill for women's reservation, 212-30
Great Reform Act, 205
Gujaral, I. K. 99
Gupta, Shaibal, 6

Harshe, Rajan, 152
Hawala scam, 52
Hindu chauvinism, 154
Hindu Raj, 153
Hinduja group, 104
Hinduism, 153
Horowitz, Donald, 160, 169
Human Development Index (HDI), 129, 132-33, 137-39
Hung parliament, 37

Illiteracy, 158
Immigration, 47
Income Tax Act, 80
Income tax exemptions, 265
Inciting communal, 181-82
Independents elected to Lok Sabha in successive general elections, 223
Indrajit Gupta Committee, 65, 91, 101-02, 124, 178, 183
Indian National Congress (INC), 154, 155
Indian Political System, 113
Indian Political scienario—emerging dimensions, 129-32
Indian Polity on MVH, 132-33
Indira Gandhi, 33, 88, 90, 129
assassination, 156
Inter-State Human Development Index, 132-37
International Foundation for Election Systems (IFES), 234
Islam, 153

Jain, R.B., 5, 86
Jainism, 153
Jammu & Kashmir elections, 58-59
Janata Dal, 68-70, 118, 155
Jinnah, 154
Joint Committee of Parliament on Amendments to Electoral Laws, 34, 80, 122
Joint Stock Companies, banning donations made by, 265
Jones, Morris, 31
Jordan, 161
Judicial activism, 113

Karnataka Assembly Election, 66, 68, 70-72
Key issues, 2
Kashmir, violence in, 157
Kashmiri Pandits, 157
Khan, D.G.A., 9
Kothari, Rajni, 77
Krishnakant (late) Governor of Andhra Pradesh, 69-70

Lack of Political Will—The crux of the problem, 185-86
Law Commission, 67-70, 178
  recommendations, 101-102, 228
Lebanese PR System, 164-65
Legal and Constitutional framework, 3-5
Lessons Learnt, 210-11
Liberal regulations, 43
Licence-Permit Raj, 48
Lim Hong Hai, 170
Limits on contribution, 118-19
Limits on expenditure, 115-17
Lodha, Sanjay, 5, 113
Lok Sabha Elections, comparative performance of men and women candidates, 226-27
Lok Sabha Election Results, 1952-1991, 34
Lok Satta, 17, 18, 21

McCartney, Clem, 203
Madhu Dandvate, 186
Madhu Kishwar, 212
Mafia electoral funding, 176-178
Maharashtra, general elections in, 188-89
Mahatma Gandhi, 153
Majumdar, Bhaskar, 145
Making the Electoral system work, 203-10
Maladies, 176
Malaysian system of plurality election, 169-70
Mandal Commission's recommendations, 129-30
Mandal-Masjid controversies, 55
Marketing approach to political development, 206-207
Mathur, Pradeep, 7
Measures to check criminalization of politics, 190-91
Measures to curb polling irregularities, 26
Median voter hypothesis, 128-29, 140-41
Mehta, T.U., 185
Middle-Class Utopia of Sanitised, 115
Minto-Morley Reforms, 163
Mishra, Lalit Narain, 88
Misuse of Government Power and Official Machinery, 257-58
Misuse of Money, 182-83
Mixed system, 81, 267-68
Mohanlal Sukhadia, 259
Mandal Commission Report, 157
Money power in Election, 176, 261-65
  election expenses, 262-63
  facilities at public expenses, 264-65
    ceiling on election expenses, 264
    corporate donation, 265
    deposits, 265-66
    income tax exemption, 265
  growth of, 261-62
Monitoring election finance, 125-27
Muhammad, Noor, 3
Multi-ethnic coalition, 173
Multi-party system, 8, 82-86, 159-60
Muslim separatism, 154
Muslim vote bank in Bihar, 157

Narasimha Rao, P.V., government, 96, 130
Narayan, Jayaprakash, 11, 33, 80, 186, 212, 254, 231
Narayan, Rachana, 231
National Democratic Alliance (NDA), 64
Needed Reform, 82-85
Nehru, J.L., 87, 155
New Economic Policy, 129
New Package of Reforms, 95
New Zealand, 161
Nigerian Constitution of 1978, 166
Northern Ireland, background to political development in, 205-206

Odd-ratio for voting, 131
Opportunistic alliances, 200
Other Backward Castes (OBC), 129

Padia, C., 8
Pai Panandikar, 53, 122-24
Pakistan, 161
Parliament and States, separation of elections for, 198-200
Parliamentary democracy, 176-77
  system of, 148-49
Partition of India, 163-64
Party donation, 79-80
Party financing, sources of, 87-92
Pathak, R.P., 8
Permit Raj, 87
Photo identity cards, issue of, 42-43
Plugging possible loopholes, 224-25
Plural democracy, 171
Plurality and majority electoral reforms, 75-82

Political corruption, 54
Political financing, 86-108
Political leadership, accountability of, 74
Political morality, 184-85
Political parties, categories of, 84-87
contribution of, 90
election expenditure of, 92-100
Political Parties and Candidates, funding/maintenance of accounts by, 189-90
Political socialization, 163
Political will and electoral reforms, 176-85
Poorer States, 133
Post-colonial States, electoral experiments in, 164-70
Post-polling survey of select polling station areas, 18-20
Post-1989 Elections Reforms Proposals, 94-96
Pre-poll verification of Electoral Rolls, 17-18
Proportional Representation (PR) system, 35, 36, 69, 75-76, 267
Proposed Alternative Women's Reservation Bill, 222, 278-79
Provisions of Alternative Bill, 278-79
Public funding, problems and difficulties of, 120-22

Qualification of candidates, 196-97

Radhakrishnan, S., 184
Radio and television compaigning, 260
Rajiv Gandhi, 33, 88, 90, 156
Ram Temple in Ayodhaya, 156
Rashtriya Swayam Sevak Sangh (RSS), 155
Ratan Tata, 105
Readjustment of constituencies, 194-95
Reforms for a better representation, 192-200
Reform of the Electoral Laws, 69, 101, 117, 124
Regional political parties, 138
Registration of political parties, 48
Report of the Committee appointed by Sri Jayaprakash Narayan on behalf of Citizens for Democracy for Electoral Reforms, 254-82
Representation of People (Amendment) Act (RPA), 40, 84, 96, 97, 115, 118, 124-26, 179, 181, 184, 200
Reservation for women, proposals for, 228
Reservation of Seats, 48, 197-98
Rigging process, 18-19
Romer, T., 128
Rosenthal, H., 128
Roy, Ramashray, 53, 122

Sangh Parivar, 154-55, 158
Sangma, P.A., 3, 8, 9
Sankaran, D.K., 188
Santhanam Committee, 118
Savarkar, 154
Search for a fair system, 267
Seat-vote distortions, 256
Secular Nationalism, 154-58
Secularism, 74, 81, 152-58
Selected countries, voter turnout at latest elections in, 148-49
Self-regulation of politics, 60
Sen, A.K., 128
Sen, Sukumar (Election Commissioner), 176
Separation of Elections for Parliament and States, 198-200
Seshan, T.N. (Chief Election Commissioner), 56, 89, 109, 114
Shah Bano case, 156
Shah, K.T., 122
Shakdhar, S.L. (Chief Election Commissioner), 35, 49, 86
Shastri, Sandeep, 4, 64
Sheth, Dhirubhai, 212
Shiv Sena, 155
Sikhism, 153
Single Transferable Vote (STV), 76
Singh, L.P., 35
Singh, Susheela, 8
Slovenia, 161
Social disaster, 150
Social interaction and domination, 146-47
Social and political culture, 7-8
Socialism, 74, 81
Society and Change, 145-46
South Africa, proportional representation system, 170
Sridharan, E., 122, 123
Sri Lanka Two-Round System (TRS) of Presidential Elections, 167-68
Srivastava, Krishan, 108
State Commissioners, 256-57
State Domestic Products (SDPs), 132-33
State funding of Elections, 103-04, 119-25
State-sponsored election fund, 53
Statutory Forms, 24-25

Subramaniam, C., 185
Supreme Court Judgement, 98-99, 116-18

Taiwan, 161
Tarkunde Committee, 38, 64, 68, 122, 186
    Report, 80-82
Tata Electoral Trust, 106-107
Tendered votes, 27-28
Testing Median Voter Hypothesis through Human Development Index, 128-44
Trikha, N.K., 185
Turnbull, G.K., 128

Underworld money, 5
Unemployment, 158
United Kingdom, 205
Universal Declaration of Human Rights, 231
Unrealistic expenditure limits, 123
Upadhaya, Anjoo Sharan, 1
Upadhyaya, Priyankar, 159
US President Election Reform, 234
Use and Misuse of administrative machinery, 254

Vajpayee, Atal Behari, 177
Verma, G.P., 3
Vishwa Hindu Parishad (VHP), 155
Vote catching symbols, 201
Voter identity, 179-80
Voter registration, error in, 21
Voter's Councils, 269, 274-75
Voting Rights and Election Procedure, 270-75
    age of voting, 270
    counting votes booth-wise, 271-72
    polling boxes, 272
    significance on counterfoil, 271-72
    voters, voluntary action, 273-74
Voting and social change, political process of, 145-50
V.P. Singh Government, 95-96
V.R. Krishna Iyer Committee, 185

Women's political participation, 130, 213-17
Women's representation in parliament, 1952-1999, 214
Women's Reservation Bill in Parliament, 212-13, 217, 222
    advantages of, 222-23
    problems with government bill, 218-221

Yadav, Laloo Prasad, 78, 157
Yadav, Mulayam Singh, 156
Yadav, Yogendra, 29, 123, 130, 131, 212

Zimbabwe, 161
Zorastrianism, 153